Gertrude Stein and
the Essence of What Happens

GERTRUDE STEIN

AND

THE ESSENCE OF WHAT HAPPENS

DANA CAIRNS WATSON

VANDERBILT UNIVERSITY PRESS ❧ *Nashville*

This book is printed on acid-free paper.
Manufactured in the United States of America

Design by Gary Gore

Frontispiece courtesy of Department of Special Collections,
Charles E. Young Research Library, UCLA. Collection 2108,
Gilbert Harrison Collection of Material relating
to Gertrude Stein, box 4 folder 16:
Gertrude Stein and Alice B. Toklas having tea.

Library of Congress Cataloging-in-Publication Data

Watson, Dana Cairns, 1966-
Gertrude Stein and the essence of what happens / Dana Cairns Watson.—1st ed.
p. cm.
Includes bibliographical references and index.
ISBN 0-8265-1462-6 (cloth : alk. paper)
ISBN 0-8265-1463-4 (pbk. : alk. paper)
1. Stein, Gertrude, 1874-1946—Criticism and interpretation.
2. Interpersonal communication in literature.
3. Meaning (Philosophy) in literature.
4. Conversation in literature. 5. Speech in literature.
6. Dialogue. I. Title.
PS3537.T323Z96 2004
818.'5209—dc22
2003027602

For Rob, a credit to the species

CONTENTS

ACKNOWLEDGMENTS

Thanks to Stephen Yenser for introducing me to Gertrude Stein and her critics in 1986, for daring me to develop instructions for reading Stein, and for making me pay attention to every word—Stein's, as well as my own. Thanks to Martha Banta for pointing out that my sudden interest in conversation analysis—as inspired by Michael Moerman and Edith Wharton—might be worth pursuing. Thanks to John Heritage for welcoming this novice into the field of conversation analysis, and for being willing to take on Stein at the same time. Thanks to all of them, as well as Jayne Lewis, for encouraging me with praise, challenges, and always more questions and wordplay.

Thanks to Stein's readers and critics for inspiring me to think in ways I never imagined, and to Gilbert Harrison's generous donation to UCLA's Special Collections. Thanks to the warm and helpful people who work there, especially Jeffrey Rankin, for enabling me to read Stein's out-of-print works (many of which are now in print), gaze at photographs, and finger—among other memorabilia—one of her small gloves.

Thanks to the many students who hesitatingly started into a Stein work and were open-minded and creative enough to notice that something wonderfully interesting was happening. These include Allison Raskin, Jake Bern, Aaron Dover, carine risley, Bryan Kocol, Suzanne Karpilovsky, and Tessa Ingersoll. Thanks even to some of the stubborn ones—Mike Hawes and Eugene Pino, for example—who kept asking for more reasons that they should come to appreciate Stein, too.

To Bob Hiller, my eighth-grade American history teacher at Stanley School, thanks for teaching out of discontinued textbooks which showed that imperfect people can accomplish great things, and for truly thinking while he talked to us thirteen-year-olds.

Thanks and love to my parents, Gene and Patty Cairns, for everything.

Thanks and love to Emma Cairns Watson for her patience and her sweet kisses from the doorway of the study. Thanks for singing: "I am Rose my eyes are blue / I am Rose and who are you / I am Rose and when I sing / I am Rose like anything" (from Stein's *The World is Round*). Thanks even more for saying unprompted to a friend, the week before this book was due at the press, "Let's sing it like it's a conversation!"

Thanks and love to Robert N. Watson, who gave unofficial fellowships year after year, was my main reader and copy editor, offered suggestions without expecting me to take them all, arranged a year in Paris for the whole family, and not just accepted but encouraged my natural tendencies to do this (and almost everything else) differently.

Gertrude Stein and
the Essence of What Happens

INTRODUCTION

"Announce what you see"

FOR GERTRUDE STEIN, language is a living but ailing organ of our social body. Modern speech is a symptom of the way bureaucracy threatens to become fascism and conformity damages humanity. Stein's several styles of writing advocate a revision and rearrangement of fundamental orders: the syntax of English sentences, the contained and supposedly individualized selfhood of Americans, interpersonal allegiances, and social and political organization. If there is something wrong with these structures, then language can be studied to diagnose the problem, and language can serve to solve it—or change it, anyway. Stein has been canonized for her eccentricity, but that reputation may be a way of making safe—making cute and quirky—a revolutionary utopian impulse and insight, with a huge force of life behind it.[1] Unlike a strict deconstructionist, who believes (or at least asserts) that *"words speak us,"* Stein builds on the assumption that *people* speak, that we can wield language however we choose (Lehman, 106); she writes on behalf of free will and self-making. Stein does not believe in "an exclusively linguistic universe," as her devotion to her dogs and long walks and especially Alice's cooking—and talk about food—suggests (Lehman, 99). At the very least, "we can say we do like what we have," or that we don't (Stein, "Lifting Belly," 94).[2] And words are not all we have with which to communicate; we have intonations, smiles, glances, kisses, and caresses—as Stein makes clear in three of her titles, we have "Tender Buttons" and a "Lifting Belly," not just "Patriarchal Poetry." Stein is not a nihilist doomsayer but rather a doctor investigating the organic functions of interactive language. How that language works and what it achieves is the essence of what happens.

Stein must have been particularly sensitive to the subtle orders around her. Her writing demonstrates awareness of the unwritten rules of human social interaction manifest in the structures of turn-taking conversation, which were ignored by linguists such as Ferdinand de Saussure and Noam

Chomsky and which have come to the attention of social scientists such as Harvey Sacks only in the last few decades. Stein's biographers attest to her tendency to overstep the silent boundaries of decorum. She was a lesbian, and she was too loud and too cheerful and too fat. She alluded to her own genius too directly. She talked too much, asked questions that were too personal, laughed too hard, and sweated too profusely. This relentless crossing of boundaries that keep people's bodies separate and knowledge separate—keep their interiorities interior—persistently alerted her to the part that social norms play in human subjectivity, and thus in every other human endeavor.[3]

On the other hand, Stein's writing is usually pure pleasure—a game—and serious only in that she's serious about play. She mucks about with words, fools around, teases and tickles and hums. Reviewers call Stein's opera *Four Saints in Three Acts* an "untroubled really very simple pleasure" (Krutch, 75), and my child sings certain phrases with glowing delight. Another reviewer describes *The World Is Round* as "pure delight, simple pleasure" (Becker, 114). In 1913, Mabel Dodge Luhan—then the center of an avant-garde Greenwich Village salon and later a memoirist who worked to alter white and masculine notions of the American West—wrote that "every word lives" in Stein's writing (153). A year later, Carl Van Vechten—a music critic later turned novelist, Harlem booster, and photographer—wrote that there is no "fresher phrase" than those found in Stein's long prose poem *Tender Buttons* (158). French literary and social critic Bernard Faÿ—a friend of Stein who collaborated with her on abridging *The Making of Americans* and then collaborated with the Germans and was appointed director of the Bibliothèque Nationale in Paris in 1940—writes that Mencken, Dreiser, Joyce, Valéry, and Gide "write as you and I take a bus," but that Stein is "sincer[e]" and "courageous" in the "amusing game" of being a writer (59, 58, 60). "Preaching and politics," Faÿ goes on,

> oblige one's mind to take social problems profoundly seriously; they destroy the freedom of the mind, the ability to be interested in the universal and the individual. Science obliges the mind to get used to a rationalistic and systematic method that is no good for the artist. Science trains you to count and avoid understanding; it gives you very good means to measure things, but it insists that you should feel and react as little as possible, while art and literature require a rich and deep ability to react, feel, dream, and act freely.

"So few people," he concludes, "can love and laugh, search and choose, look and live," and "Miss Stein has done it" (60, 63). And in an essay pleasingly titled "Stein Is Nice," Wayne Koestenbaum writes that "we are free to make of her what we wish, and to read her more obscure texts in a state of liberated remoteness from dogma, protocol, and usefulness" (298).

All this points to the problem of treating Stein as a writer with ideas, as interested in solving problems—but these are not the same thing. Ideas include speculation and theory. Ideas can "imagine" and "hypothesize" and "postulat[e]" and "arous[e]" "expectations" even without delivering, and Koestenbaum suggests that Stein thus "insists that we enlarge our capacities—*even if the enterprise turns out to be bankrupt*" (297). Stein's ideas are not especially utilitarian; indeed, she suggested it was a shame that words were put to use (*Geographical History*, 190, 175). She is interested in freedom for freedom's sake, ideas for ideas' sake, being for being's sake. William Carlos Williams (1966, 73–74) wrote in "Asphodel, That Greeny Flower": "It is difficult / to get the news from poems / yet men die miserably every day / for lack / of what is found there" and Malcolm Cowley understands Stein to be working along these lines. Shortly after Stein's death, Cowley wrote that she was "working at some problem that apparently has no connection with man or society"—"something humbl[e]," something less like "atomic fission" than like "the anatomy of junebugs"—and, he predicts, "suddenly it would be found that one or more of [these] discoveries about junebugs could be applied to curing or prolonging human life" (150). I would argue that her playfulness does aid in prolonging our lives: it makes us conscious and makes us strive to express ourselves. But explications of the message sent through her playfulness risk undermining that very playfulness and therefore that very message, and I fear that I too will take her "both too seriously, and not seriously enough" (Canby, 80).[4] While I offer a new and somewhat suspiciously coherent reading of Stein's texts, I agree with Linda S. Watts, who begins *Gertrude Stein: A Study of the Short Fiction*, with "Stein's own instruction for engaging her texts: 'If you enjoy it you understand it'" (Watts, 12, 97). Here Stein echoes another pyramid-shaped and cantankerous writer, Ben Jonson, who was also interested in the details of ordinary human speech: "Pray thee take care, that tak'st my book in hand, / To read it well; that is, to understand" (7).

Stein's writing expresses the meaning between the words—between individual words on the page and between utterances in conversation. She shows us how to read between the lines of our daily—personal but socially circumscribed—lives. Readers often balk at Stein's works, suspicious that they are wasting their time decoding Stein's words, but she was actually decoding theirs, and ours. Stein makes her readers aware of their linguistic processes: reading, writing, speaking, and listening. The poet Robert Haas has explained that Stein "was enormously influential, on some writers who followed her, and on our everyday speech" (Hubly, 69).[5] In *Halfway to Revolution*, Clive Bush rightly argues that Stein's work is politically valuable in its critique of the increasing social control of discourse and knowledge, and that she is at her best when challenging the "unreflected habits of society" in *The Making of Americans* (373), sensing the way the world is changed by mass media (382), and discussing the effects of propaganda in *Wars I Have Seen* (397). In addition to making us aware of our words, and how we speak them, and what they really mean in and out of the contexts in which they are uttered, Stein offers a garbled vision (to use an aptly synesthetic phrase) of a potential new society with a new language and a new idea of personhood.

Stein's education in classes taught by William James is not the only reason to place her writing and its potential social and political ramifications within a strong and long-lived American tradition of thought. Though her work may seem the antithesis of anything practical, she must be understood as a pragmatist. James was the first to put the term "pragmatism" in print, in 1898, although he was already arguing for a somewhat different meaning for the term than Charles Sanders Peirce had implied when he first used it in conversation—and Peirce had lifted the idea from Alexander Bain and the term from Immanuel Kant (Menand, *Metaphysical*, 354n; Simonson, 4). James dedicated his 1906–7 published lectures on pragmatism to John Stuart Mill, "from whom [he] first learned the pragmatic openness of mind" (James, *Pragmatism*, 1). But pragmatism did not just offer Stein an open mind (or correspond to the one she already had). Pragmatism emphasized (and still emphasizes) verbal communication between humans and mutual relationships between other phenomena. For example, James believed that "the knower is an actor" who "registers the truth which he helps to create" (qtd. in Putnam, "Permanence," 17).[6] A colleague of James at Harvard, Nicholas St. John Green, believed that "knowledge is not a passive mirroring of the world, but an active means of making the world into the kind of world we want it to be" (Menand, *Metaphysical*, 225). In *Mind, Self, and Society*, published in 1934, George Herbert Mead posited a theory of intersubjectivity, in which people import (into their behavior, from society) and export (from their behavior, to other members of society) attitudes and gestures which call out for responses from others, ad infinitum (186–89). He goes so far as to say that this "conversation of gestures" is responsible for the rise of language: "Words have arisen out of a social interrelationship" (189). In *Experience and Nature*, published in 1929, John Dewey also emphasized mutuality within communication: "we bring together logical universals in discourse, where they copulate and breed new meanings," and this "dialectic generates new objects" (194). Or, as Timothy Kaufman-Osborn summarizes it, "making sense" is when "knower and known are continuously engaged in creation and re-creation of each other" (ix). These mutualities may have been an important foundation for—or may at least correspond with—Stein's ideas of personal efficacy in a social setting. Interested in the individual, Stein repeatedly asks a question that would haunt the neopragmatist Richard Rorty (*Contingency*, xiii): "How can an inhabitant of . . . a society be more than the enactor of a role in a previously written script?"

The pragmatists may also have encouraged Stein's very confident, even cheerful, potential tentativeness about all things known. Hillary Putnam emphasizes James's "fallibilism," which "does not require us to doubt *everything* [but] only requires us to be prepared to doubt anything." Further, "there are no metaphysical guarantees to be had that even our most firmly-held beliefs will never need revision. That one can be both fallibilistic *and* antiskeptical is perhaps *the* basic insight of American Pragmatism" (Putnam, *Permanence*, 21). In a later essay, Putnam argues for Ludwig Wittgenstein's pragmatism, which can "change our point of view" without advocating alternative theses, and which can challenge the very "language games" in which people speak to determine "better and worse language games" ("Wittgenstein," 27–28, 38). Perhaps desiring to change the "language game" that makes philosophy so authoritative, or just authoritative sounding, Wittgenstein writes: "Philosophy ought really to be written only as a form of poetry."[7] And this is often what Stein does: much of her writing is a form of philosophical inquiry in which she throws assumptions into doubt but does not offer another stable idea on which we can depend instead. Yet her tone of confidence and playfulness prevents readers from confusing her doubt with skepticism or, worse, its common partner cynicism. The fact that Stein is one of very few cheerful writers indicates that she was not plagued by an all-encompassing skepticism. The traditional culture of France and her regulated daily life may have given her a solid platform from which to comfortably ask discomfiting questions.[8]

Language and speech were the main ingredients in Stein's (loose) program for individual development, as well as for societal change, and this too may have been supported by pragmatist thought. Although not addressing conversation directly, James "influenced the study of communication processes" in that he saw communication as the way "to look at and know the world," offer "an exchange of information," and "even offer a negotiation of reality" (Leonhirth, 92).

Pragmatism placed a primary value on communication:

Pragmatism has always been all around communication, near to it, surrounding it, because "as a doctrine" it has always "held that the world is open-ended and in process." The idea of communication was, from the beginning, implicated in James' resistance to the world. James knew that his existence depended on believing that this is an unfinished universe and that each of us can have a hand in making it. That knowledge is knowledge of the possibility of communication. (Shepherd, 247).

In short, communication influences how we see the world and also allows us to manipulate that world. In *Democracy and Education*, Dewey goes so far as to say: "Society not only continues to exist by transmission, by communication, but may fairly be said to exist *in* transmission, *in* communication" (5). More recently, Rorty asserts that "the human self is created by the use of a vocabulary" and that "a talent for speaking differently, rather than for arguing well, is the chief instrument of cultural change" (*Contingency*, 7). In fact, pragmatism has been described as a "resistance movement" that "employ[ed] the hope of communication against the manifest tragedies of complete isolation and total uncertainty" (Shepherd, 253). In writing "differently," Stein resisted her mind's verbal occupation—and then she moved into the outside world, imagining a language that could resist the German occupation of France, as well as make manifest other emancipations.

James's earliest description of pragmatism corresponds to some of the ideas Stein held most dear:

Pragmatism represents a perfectly familiar attitude in philosophy, the empiricist attitude, but it represents it, as it seems to me, both in a more radical and in a less objectionable form than it has ever yet assumed. A pragmatist turns his back resolutely and once for all upon a lot of inveterate habits dear to professional philosophers. He turns away from abstraction and insufficiency, from verbal solutions, from bad *a priori* reasons, from fixed principles, closed systems, and pretended absolutes and origins. He turns towards concreteness and adequacy, towards facts, towards action and towards power. That means the empiricist temper regnant and the rationalist temper sincerely given up. It means the open air and possibilities of nature, as against dogma, artificiality, and the pretence of finality in truth. (*Pragmatism*, 25)

While some readers seem to find Stein's writing full of "artificialities" or at least unidentifiable "abstraction," I believe that Stein's work is in the vein of this type of pragmatism. Stein's descriptions of the careful observations she made in writing *Tender Buttons* and her close attention to conversation patterns demonstrate her observational tendencies. Her incremental repetition reveals, in at least one way, her openness to revision based on further experience, including the experience of having said it and heard it and thought about it one more time. Stein avoids reiterating old habits, tries to escape what had generally been considered closed systems (of syntax, of thought), searches for a way to say and enact what she can envision, and erases whatever intellectual boundaries she comes across with her assertive questions (the ones without question marks). She does not reach "absolutes and origins," but she seems to find a way "towards action and towards power."

It is possible that Stein did not see the urgent need for this action until World War II, but she was playfully proposing and enabling it through her entire life's work. Stein remembers that one of her goals for making *The Making of Americans* was to understand people—"to know what was inside each one which made them that one"—so that she (and they) could "change something" (*Lectures*, 137). In fact, her early works are in some ways more radical than her later writings, perhaps because she is not responding to a particular set of social problems in a politically charged setting. A reviewer of *Tender Buttons* claims that Stein attempts "to express anarchy in art" (R. Rogers, 18). By the end of her life, Gertrude Stein has become a household name, and all American eyes (those who read *Life* and *Time* magazines, anyway) are upon the woman who survived the war incommunicado. Early in her career, though, she is more free to be, free to see, and free to say, since she has love and time and little or no readership. In fact, this very contrast between her earlier lonely freedom and her later experience of public expectation may have pointed Stein toward her recognition of the limitations on the search for meaning and possibility in a society of mass communication and celebrity, too much (apparent) information, and too much (thoughtless) activity.

Ultimately, then, Stein's tapping into the dynamic forms of spoken language contributes to sociopolitical as well as linguistic projects. By listening to everyday conversations, Stein diagnoses the character of individuals and the strengths and weaknesses of society. By writing the ways she does, Stein conditions her readers to understand words differently than they have before. Once we hear differently, we can see differently. We then treat words differently ourselves, altering how others hear. Changing language, by changing us, can change society.[9]

Stein, then, does not propose that we learn to read differently only so that we can appreciate *her* writing. By learning to read anew, which involves changing the order in our minds, we can change order at all levels, personal and social. Seeing differently is difficult; Stein writes: "I like seeing things in each one that are interesting, I even in a way like learning seeing a new way of seeing new, to me, things in them." But she admits: "I like it in a way I say, I find it hard to let myself not resist at all to this thing" (*Making*, 622). By seeing anew, by resisting established orders instead of new ones, and by saying what we see, we can start new conversations with others and within ourselves. These conversations in turn can develop new forms of relationships and ideally can grow a new culture through spontaneous connecting. Put very differently, the world is changing, and words can't mean what they always meant before. This notion is one that Koestenbaum describes as "queer": "Words experience the gravitational pull of nonmeaning, or of fluctuating significance" ("Stein Is Nice," 305). Bush points to Stein's interest in "the adaptation of old form to new content" (*Halfway*, 391). We must learn to notice the differences between what we say, what we mean, and what we see.

Although this is not a book about pedagogy, a classroom discussion of Stein demonstrates her potential influence on a society in crystallized form. My readings of Stein prove her value less directly than does the thinking (and talking) of students in the presence of *Tender Buttons*. Students find themselves freed from trying to guess what their instructor expects them to say (largely because they have no idea). And because the students are grasping at straws, they find new ways of grasping. Stein's work increases semantic sensitivity and intelligence, traits that influence how students read other works and that the great polemical "educationist" Neil Postman argues are crucial for students of any subject. Semantic intelligence should increase students' abilities to insist on and act on their freedoms—freedoms which many of them understand as a given or a formality—so that they can achieve individuality as readers, thinkers, creators, and political animals.[10] Stein teaches us to listen to ourselves as we never have before, as only Stein seems to have heard us, so that we know who we present ourselves to be and can decide and become who we want to be as individuals and as a community.[11] (Stein also made some people think in new ways, or at least made them see that there might be new ways *to* think, during her U.S. lecture tour, the response to which I discuss in chapter 4.) Discussing Stein allows readers to see unforeseen political and social possibilities, and to see how our democracy could be deepened by our own individual semantic changes—and to see, too, why we haven't seen these things. She leaves space into which we must project meaning, partly like a traditional psychotherapist, partly like a deconstructionist, but also like any good conversationalist. Reading Stein is necessarily participatory, not passive, as Harriet Scott Chessman has explored most extensively. In short, mine is a book that makes an argument about a dead author, but it is also a book that hopes to convince each reader that he or she can take great pleasure in, and actually bring about change in, this present world by talking and listening differently.

Stein's understanding of the human mind explains why she writes the way she does. As Postman points out, teachers' understandings of their students' minds determine how they teach:

> There is no test, textbook, syllabus, or lesson plan that any of us creates that does not reflect our preference for some metaphor of the mind, or of knowledge, or of the process of learning. Do you believe a student's mind to be a muscle that must be exercised? Or a garden that must be cultivated? Or a dark cavern that must be illuminated? Or an empty vessel that must be filled to overflowing? Whichever you favor, your metaphor will control—often without your being aware of it—how you will proceed as a teacher. (*Conscientious*, 29)

I think that Stein's metaphors are unique, or at least not the clichés about which Postman warns us. For her, our minds are rusty climbing structures—rusty because they are unmaintained and underutilized, and playground equipment because we are meant to play and exercise on them. Or our minds are dancers that have been repeating the same few steps over and over for so long that we've forgotten—or forgotten to develop—the very capacity for improvisation. To use a more contemporary metaphor, each of our minds is an exciting, one-of-a-kind computer program stuck in the same tiny subroutine in which almost everyone else is stuck, too. We are all using Microsoft when we could be fingering tender buttons.

Stein's writing pulls us out of that infinite loop and makes us notice how much of our thought we take for granted without really thinking. She makes us aware of what has been invisible, directs our attention to the medium (language) in which we usually tread so easily because we step on the stepping-stones, and causes us to ask questions about structures of thought we have always accepted as harmless and inevitable. Long before Marshall McLuhan, Stein seemed to know "the medium was the massage" (and while not stating it in those words, she seemed to explain herself in prose at least as clear as much of McLuhan's writing, which is full of sporadic headlines and strangely shaped word blocks). Stein charts the geography of the mind, a topography shaped by language and just as infinite in its untested permutations. Never one to shy away from the seemingly impossible, Stein imagines how a new mental chorography and choreography could influence a nation's social and political landscape. Stein's early works, including "Q.E.D.," *The Making of Americans*, and *Tender Buttons*, are the perfect documents for reeducating readers in (among other topics) general semantics, alternative thought, and identity.

Not until her later works, written during and after World War II, does she explicitly discuss the need for this reeducation. Her experiences and observations during that time must have motivated her to state directly the need to hone our abilities to resist authority, save our land and our souls from machine-made gadgets, and revive our individual potential. Fascism raised the stakes for epistemology, raised in a political contest questions that were formerly confined to a literary context.

In *The Geographical History of America*, Stein writes:

> I think that if you announce what you see nobody can say no. Everybody does everybody does say no but nobody can nobody can say so, that is no.
> That is the reason that you can say what you see[.]
> And do you see.
> That is what the national hymn says the star spangled banner.
> Oh say can you see. (162–63)

"Say what you see" captures the tense cooperation between sound and sight emphasized throughout this reading of Gertrude Stein's writing. But "oh say *can* you see" also expresses Stein's plea to individuals to notice, contemplate what they perceive, and express their observations and analyses. The epistemological position she takes is that "nobody can say no" because nobody can know what anybody else sees. Solipsism authorizes freedom—and does not preclude dialogue. Stein asks a person to speak up without being afraid of being wrong, and her allusion to the national anthem is also an allusion to her overt suggestion in *Brewsie and Willie* that articulating our thoughts and impressions will save the United States of America from the spiritual and worldly poverty that follows industrialism. Seeking to achieve social reform through language reform, she explicitly tells Americans that they must learn to express complexity. By changing the kind of English people read, Stein intends to change the way Americans articulate their thoughts in speech, making room for thoughts that evade the binary pollster lingo of yes or no, approve or disapprove, guilty or not guilty, Democrat or Republican.

Stein's words request individual readers to say what we see, with the knowledge that, while we cannot be justly corrected, we also cannot count on others' seeing the same things. There is no monologic in Stein's monologues. Stein's writing forces readers to recognize and re-embrace their own unique visions. While encouraging individuality, Stein acknowledges and celebrates the dialogic aspect of self, celebrating our multiplicity and suggesting that the exchanges we carry on with ourselves can provide a model for interaction with others. I hope too that this very monologue—the book in front of you now—is dialogic enough to suggest a variety of ideas about Stein and set the tone for continuing conversations about what we see in Stein, and beyond.[12]

Chapter 1 demonstrates Stein's interest in conversation, as well as in the sights and sounds of words. The chapter documents Stein's early interest in conversation, manifest in the voices that pervade *Three Lives* and several aspects of *The Making of Americans*. This long early novel represents individuals as born into preexisting families and family narratives, writers as born into the world of the already written, and speakers as born into a world of conversations where they can transcend the already said only by first listening. The chapter argues that Stein makes her American readers listen to ourselves, unmakes our mask of Americanisms, and chides us toward building ourselves more legitimately. The new frontier in America has to open within and for the individual, and the new pioneering begins at the lips, where the verb "states" might be prevented from calcifying into the noun "statements" if we were to listen to ourselves and stop copying. The chapter also emphasizes Stein's dispositions and her special training, both of which seem to point to an interest in attention, sensory inputs, and especially the spoken and written word. I begin in this chapter to exemplify some of the richness of the interaction between sight and sound, although much more of that will be demonstrated in chapters 2, 3, and 4.

The second chapter asserts that Stein's reading of the neuroscience in William James's *Principles of Psychology* encouraged her to rearrange her readers' mental associations.[13] James's idea that all thought takes place through habitual associations among thoughts and words, that experience shapes these habits and more experience can change them, suggests that Stein's writing is surprisingly, if still unpredictably, utilitarian—on behalf of anti-utilitarianism (of course). Attending to all sensory aspects of a language leads to a greater associational range, more freedom for words, and an increased flexibility for the mind organized around those words. An extended reading of a long passage from *Tender Buttons* in this chapter demonstrates various ways to read Stein and supports the idea—in content as well as style—that Stein advocates our changing our most standard rhetorical forms. By hypothetically breaking up a portion of this selection into discrete utterances, I also begin to demonstrate the intrasubjective nature of conversation, the way one conversation synthesizes back-and-forth exchanges between different voices and opinions.

Chapter 3 continues my chronological examination of Stein's importation of spoken forms into her writing, in this case in several works in *Geography and Plays*. While chapter 1 demonstrates that Stein's more prosy narratives are constructed from conversations, this chapter shows that Stein turns her attention from the way conversation reveals personality to the way conversation is itself a significant structure worthy of further investigation. My definition of conversation is drawn from the related fields of conversation analysis and ethnomethodology but augmented with enough psychology to take into account internal dialogue (an aspect of conversation treated more thoroughly in chapter 5). Stein explores utterances as multilayered actions that, for example, can simultaneously communicate agreement and heavy disapproval. She attends to the ways interactional conversation—as distinguished from transactional conversation—allows speakers to develop complicated and ever-shifting relationships by negotiating through minutely contextual interpretations of specific utterances. In other words, she points to the realpolitik within politesse. And she engages in a kind of conversation nervously foreshadowed in *The Making of Americans*—with a literary forefather, William Shakespeare. In recalling Macbeth's misunderstanding of the witches, Stein highlights conversational strategies as power plays, not just domestic courtesies.

Chapter 4 discusses Stein's lectures of the 1930s, in terms of both the ideas they express and their effect on audiences during the lecture tour. Stein's *Lectures in America* and *The Geographical History of America*, and her reading as well as her writing, demonstrate her interest in the interplay of spoken and written language. Many of Stein's most important theories—about human nature and the human mind, about geniuses and "masterpieces," about identity, about repetition and insistence—depend on the relationships between sight and sound. The lecture tour itself seems to me an attempt to get people talking and listening, experimenting with their ideas in conversation. Newspaper stories in the cities she visited during her 1934–35 tour suggest that she both succeeded and failed in this endeavor. Her own mysterious popularity may have undermined her project, since people tend not to talk *with* icons.

Chapter 5 explicates Stein's novel of celebrity, *Ida*, and concludes that interpersonal and intrapersonal conversation can serve to erase the boundaries between people at the same time that they enable us to distinguish significant boundaries within the self. This novel and its main character act as sounding boards for various possibilities about the self, and these ideas contribute, with much of Stein's other writing, to a theory of personal subjectivity and social cohesion that depends on conversation.

Having noted the way words work in conversation, and how conversations work to build relationships within the complex self and among others, Stein turns her attention to the influence of larger political structures on conversation. Chapter 6 explicates *Mrs. Reynolds* and *Brewsie and Willie*, both written during World War II and sensitive to the way that war changed habits of speech. In *Mrs. Reynolds*, Stein contemplates how everyday conversation is both influenced by and resists the pressure of the political situation in which that conversation takes place. In both novels, Stein contemplates the characteristic speech patterns of totalitarian leaders, and in *Brewsie and Willie*, Stein explores the proliferation of acquiescent employees who encourage totalitarian speech by accepting it, expecting it, and propagating it in their own talk. I argue that Stein deplored the way these forms of conversation affected original thought, and that she believed improved speech patterns would cure moribund consciousness and even solve economic and political ailments.

My conclusions, "Feminine Endings," make a sudden turn to Stein's shallow but bigoted feminism, only because she seems to have made this turn herself. The first section, "The Woman Who Changed the Mind of a Nation," hears Stein's libretto, *The Mother of Us All*, as expressing her frustration that not enough people are being individuals, truly and honestly conversing, and thus improving the state of their individuality—and, to her mind, the state of the state. Her frustration leads her to some gender stereotypes but also to the realization that an individual can still (kind of) succeed in spite of a group's failure. Her surprising acceptance of common gender distinctions also leads toward the ideas expressed in the second section, "Sublime Amalgamations." Here I suggest that Stein has been advocating a feminine epistemological sublime in the interests of both the individual and the ultimate project of an American sublime, and that she has developed a dialogic language that can best express it.

If William James convinced her the processes of the human mind could be influenced through linguistic experience, and if Stein was struck with an interest in both the sights and sounds of words—words on the page and words in conversation—then she may have seen some potential efficacy in her unusual writing. This critical history treats Stein as a writer with changing, but cumulative, interests: she moves from her interest in the human character and mind to an interest in language and its sights and sounds; then to conversation, and how language mediates the relationship between the individual and herself; and then to the relationship between an individual and his or her social organization. Working with writings from the span of Stein's career, I hope to prove that conversation is at least five important things for Stein: a language form worthy of examination in its own right; the marker by which Stein evaluates American success, on both the individual and political levels; the paradigm for Stein's concept of inter-personal subjectivity that has true agency even while being influenced from without; a telling symptom of any political situation; and a means toward a messy kind of peace and problem solving. While not explaining *how* she wrote—how she managed to put *those* words on the page—this book offers a coherent explanation for *why* Stein might have written as she did, what her words mean, and what can be achieved by reading her.

Most writers try to "build, in sonnets, pretty rooms" or to build novelistic mansions. Modern theorists posit ominously a "prison-house of language."[14] Gertrude Stein builds instead an amusement park fun house of language, full of slides between levels, weirdly convex and concave mirrors, illusory parallels, flashes of color, flickers of tickling. But a writer can be serious without being solemn, and Stein's play has work to do. She shows us the minds we unwittingly have, and the thoughts we could have instead. She shows us the struggle between tyranny and freedom in every moment of ordinary casual conversation. She lets us see what's at stake in language, and she is willing to play, at times, the clown of a verbal circus, so we can become the teachers of our own classrooms and true citizens of a fully human state.

CHAPTER 1

Talking and Listening in
Stein's Early Life and Works

"Interested in the mere workings of the machinery"

USPICIOUS AT AN early age that she was living vicariously and learning only indirectly through reading, Gertrude Stein decided to plunge into the noisy, breathing world around her. As a child, Stein escaped her family into books: "She read anything that was printed that came her way and a great deal came her way" (Stein, *Autobiography*, 74). Wagner-Martin reports that the Stein "children spent as much time as they could away from their family," and in her teens (after her high school burned down) Stein chose to visit libraries in Oakland and San Francisco (19, 24). Linda Simon guesses that Stein's "imagination was stirred by the books she read voraciously. Shakespeare, Trollope, Richardson, Defoe all took her far from the mundane middle-class world of Oakland, and the oppression of her family life" (xi). But when she moved to Baltimore, she immersed herself in a social life again. "There she began to lose her lonesomeness," writes Stein under the guise of Alice B. Toklas, "She has often described to me how strange it was to her coming from the rather desperate inner life that she had been living for the last few years to the cheerful life of all her aunts and uncles" (*Autobiography*, 75). She began listening to people, noting their repeating, and desiring an understanding of their real being—which may explain her interest in psychology in college. Stein writes that she "began very early in life to talk all the time and to listen all the time" (*Lectures*, 136).

Years later, after she left medical school, Stein "had for the moment nothing to do but talk and look and listen," and she "did this tremendously" (*Lectures*, 138). When she decided to become a writer at age twenty-nine, Stein fully appreciated the potential of this type of learning. She listened to and thought about people's words, and she evidently noticed that certain people's words, and certain kinds of words, were ignored or discounted.

When she writes in the 1920s, "I have been forbidden to gain instruction either by narrative or conversation consequently I embroider and literally I count eight," she may point to the way that women who shared information and passed on skills while sewing or knitting together—or who avidly read novels, memoirs, and biographies—were nonetheless considered unknowl-edgeable (*Village*, 12).[1] Stein believes otherwise. In the 1930s, she wrote that "anybody in any village can do" psychology (*Geographical History*, 209)—elevating daily observation and experience and demystifying the uni-versity type of knowledge. In 1940, she claimed that "if you let any plumber anybody talk long enough they will always tell the truth" (*Paris*, 32).[2] Later in the forties, she claimed that it is "quite unnecessary" to study race dif-ferences in an academic setting because any schoolchild who has grown up with children of different "nationalities" knows as much (*Wars*, 8). I am not confident that the lessons learned on playgrounds are always the best kind, but certainly Stein is right that conversations and life experi-ences—gleaned personally or from oral or written narratives—are important means toward knowledge.

Stein's early narrative works—"Q.E.D.," written in 1903 but published posthumously; *The Making of Americans*, started in 1903 and published in 1925; and *Three Lives* (Good Anna's, Melanctha's, and Gentle Lena's), started in 1905 and published in 1909—are pervaded by voices, especially women's voices. While Adele, Stein's persona in "Q.E.D.," suffers at the hands of her beloved Helen, she seems unwilling to extricate herself from the situation because, as she says, "I certainly get very much interested in the mere working of the machinery" (54). This "machinery" includes the subtle wordings and unstated meanings that allow Helen and Adele to agree without either of them yielding (54, 45). In other words, the complexities of social intercourse in this love triangle are the main "compensations" for Adele's pain (54). The wandering conversations in "Melanctha," a story that grew out of "Q.E.D.," reveal that the complexities of social intercourse remained Stein's main concern when most vestiges of interest in the love affair died away. Jeff and Melanctha talk—and talk and talk—in a language that "opened" Richard Wright's ears "for the first time to the magic of the spoken word." In spite of the unrealistic sound of some of the repetitive dialogue, Wright notes:

> I began to hear the speech of my grandmother, who spoke a deep, pure Negro dialect and with whom I had lived for many years.
> All of my life I had been only half hearing, but Miss Stein's strug-gling words made the speech of the people around me vivid. From

that moment on, in my attempts at writing, I was able to tap at will the vast pool of living words that swirled around me. (qtd. in Van Vechten, *Selected*, 338)[3]

In "Melanctha," Stein not only captures something important about the spoken voice, but she also lets Wright hear it and value it, too.

The other stories in *Three Lives* are also filled with voices; Stein emphasized these voices, and readers noticed them. Richard Bridgman (50, 51) notes Anna's "immigrant speech" and Lena's "authentic" voice, and Jane Palatini Bowers (45) asserts that Stein has such a strong "tendency to foreground conversation" that she "allows talk to practically obliterate narrative." Indeed, "Anna's voice"—rather than Anna herself—seems to be the main character: Miss Mathilda's house is full of animals and people "and Anna's voice that scolded, managed, grumbled all day long" (*Three Lives*, 69). In "The Gentle Lena," Mrs. Haydon has "a long talking that she was giving Lena" (252), and hers is just one of the several voices that bully Lena from one situation to the next. Eventually Stein moved out from behind her ungrammatically talkative characters. No longer hiding her interests and writing goals behind fictional spokespersons, she writes in a dissident form of improper but living American English.

Stein's fiction employs and celebrates the words and phrases, originality and banality, of American speakers, and through it Stein points to the renewable vitality of the English language. In 1936, Harvey Eagleson wrote:

> Except for the "portraits" of her friends, Miss Stein's work generally deals with the ordinary matters of life, the ordinary people in life, in the language and words of those people. The first and most essential step in an approach to an understanding of Gertrude Stein's work is to read it aloud. Only in that way can one realize the rhythms and sounds which are an integral part of her work. They are the rhythms of America, of American speech. Only in that way can one understand Miss Stein's peculiar punctuation, for she places marks of punctuation not where they should be placed to indicate syntactical pauses, but where they indicate speech pauses. *Three Lives* and *The Making of Americans* sound like America talking, America talking after supper on summer evenings as it sits in rocking chairs on front porches, America gossiping over back fences. The long, involved repetitive sentences, the characteristic grammatical errors, split infinitives, dangling pronouns, the idiomatic phrases of American speech are all there. (167)

Early on, then, Eagleson points to a method for accessing Stein: read it aloud, and it doesn't sound so strange. Read it aloud, and notice that speech not only helps us understand Stein but that she helps us understand speech. Allegra Stewart writes that Stein was "dissatisfied with the glib and easy use of the mere surfaces of words, the disease that threatens every writer, [and she] began to face the authentic poet's task: the revitalizing of language" (82). Stein detects this revitalization in speakers who are new to the language, and the underclasses, and anyone who speaks in a language every day and chooses, invents, overhears, and perpetuates words and phrases that catch the fancy.

The Potential Remaking of Americans, or Revising America

Even Stein's very early novel *The Making of Americans*, in its 925 pages of longwinded, elongated, and repetitive storytelling, furnishes evidence of her interest in speech. The novel—eventually, on page 728—identifies itself as a history of talking and listening. Based on the history of her own family's immigration to the United States, it seems to be stylistically based on the way family histories get told by elderly relatives, such as the "cheerful . . . aunts and uncles" Stein lived with in Baltimore in 1892 and 1893 (Stein, *Autobiography*, 75). Speakers repeat themselves, starting over to add a few omitted details and, over time, gradually changing or improving their stories. Most people only know what they've heard. The American story is the story of what Americans say, how we boost ourselves (or don't). In 1903, after Mark Twain and Walt Whitman but before Langston Hughes, Ring Lardner, Dorothy Parker, John Dos Passos, and the Lynds of *Middletown* fame—and long before the Ken Burns Civil War documentary narrated by voices in personal communication (usually letters home) and the invention of the Manhattan computer that steals quotations from Internet chat rooms and creates a kind of poetry with it (see Gopnick)—Stein saw that the voice, the stutter, the fake bravado, the lingering words, and the insistent repetition of the human voice is the main story, "the essence of what happens." Long before Thomas Pynchon's Mucho Maas (on LSD) recovers whatever's human in machine-generated Muzak, finds the "power spectra" of spoken words, and says, "The human voice, you know, it's a flipping miracle" (115–17), Stein writes: "Once more I think about conversations," and "Let me tell about the character of the people of the United States of America and what they say" ("Circular Play," 334; *Four in America*, 167).

Conversation plays several roles in *The Making of Americans*. For example, the anxiety of influence that haunts this early book is couched in the idea of conversation. Stein worries about the inevitable conversation in which her own words must participate with every other thing that has been written. In becoming an author, Stein escaped from books and family and chose to develop her own goals and her own art. But completely erasing relationships is impossible.[4] Stein avoided many of the middle-class American traps and trappings when she moved to Paris, loved Toklas, appreciated innovations in art, and wrote a different kind of English, but even her most recent biographers, Linda Wagner-Martin and Brenda Wineapple, put more stock in her family relationships than in anything else when they try to discover Stein's "bottom nature." Just as Stein cannot exactly escape her family, Stein's writing cannot help but keep company with all writing in English. While unique and surprising, Stein's words must stand in some relationship to other words. She can write and write but never erase the books that came before hers, or, as Stein herself writes: "You only add books you never subtract or divide them" ("My Debt," 307)—though that's what Harold Bloom's "strong poets" work to do as they "wrestle with their strong precursors, even to the death" (Bloom, *Anxiety*, 5). As T .S. Eliot posited in "Tradition and the Individual Talent," sometimes the most individual parts of a writer's work come out of their allusions to and contentions with "the whole of the literature of Europe from Homer" (38).

Although literature was not her field of study in school, Stein was a greedy reader of prose narrative and would have been aware of the company her words, if they ever got read, were going to keep. Literary critics often try to understand Stein's writing in relation to her friendships with her fellow modernists, but her oldest friends were books. In "My Debt to Books," Stein describes her wanderings through Paris: "That is the delightful thing about the quays you see books that you never thought it would be possible to see again." She refers to these books by author as often as by title: "Gulliver's Travels, Robinson Crusoe," "Swiss Family Robinson," "Shakespeare, Lavengro and Romany Rye, Trollope and Edgar Wallace," and "Clarissa Harlowe." When she meets up with them, she takes them home and reads them again, often surprised by the differences between her memories of the books and the books' reiteration of themselves.

She claims to have read "at least five or six books a week," a high but not unusual number ("My Debt"). Mildred Aldrich described Stein as "'the greatest reader I had ever known and the most catholic'" (qtd. in Wagner-Martin, 82).[5] Stein's reading, mentioned throughout *The Autobiography of Alice B. Toklas*, included Hawthorne, Henry James, Walter Scott, Wordsworth, *Charles Grandison*, *Pilgrim's Progress*, Burns, the *Congressional Record*, encyclopedias, Fielding, Smollett, Carlyle's *Frederick the Great*, Lecky's *Constitutional History of England*, Lord Robert's *Forty-one Years in India,* Twain, Hemingway, Fitzgerald, the newspapers the *Herald* and the *Daily Mail,* and other letters, biographies, and diaries from Mudie's Library in London. There's more, of course, this time from *Everybody's Autobiography*: Shelley, Thackeray, Jules Verne, Jane Eyre, George Eliot, Tendret (on eating), Prokosch's *Asiatics,* Bravig Imbs's *Professor's Wife,* her friend Sam Steward's *Angels on the Bough,* Louisa May Alcott's *Rose in Bloom,* Darwin's *Descent of Man,* Poe, the children's magazine *St. Nicholas,* Winston Churchill's best-seller *The Crisis,* Dickens, Lloyd Lewis's *Myths after Lincoln,* Leon Wilson's *Merton of the Movies,* Lewis Carroll's and Queen Victoria's letters (not to each other), and Caesar's commentary. Other sources suggest that Stein also read the *Iliad,* the Old Testament, Jane Austen, Sherwood Anderson, Samuel Johnson, William Faulkner, Arthur Young's *Travels in France,* Mary Wilkins's *Pembroke* (which she hated), Shelley's *Cenci,* Walter Pater's *Marius the Epicurean,* George Meredith's *Tragic Comedians,* Norse legends, Longfellow, and Goldsmith.[6]

As the youngest Herslands in Stein's *Making of Americans* say "Wait and see" to their father's implication that they will amount to no good (11), the work itself is also not completely ready to defend its specific differences from these (and other) classic texts. As Stein's written creation refuses to follow a formula, the youngest generation of Herslands intends to live life in a new way. The new generation does not know what it's going to accomplish but feels excited and nervous that it may be something new and important. As Rorty writes, building off Harold Bloom's *Anxiety of Influence,* the "poet" who "makes things new" "is typically unable to make clear exactly what it is that he wants to do before developing the language in which he succeeds in doing it. His new vocabulary makes possible, for the first time, a formulation of its own purpose" (*Contingency,* 12–13). In both the familial and writerly cases, the generations struggle over who has perfected the art of life or who will write the essence of the literary genre. Stein writes: "We, living now, are always to ourselves young men and women. When we, living always in such feeling, think back to them who make for us a beginning, it is always as grown and old men and women or as little children that we feel them, these whose lives we have just been thinking" (*Making,* 4). Bloom posits in *The Anxiety of Influence* (5) that a "strong poet" regards, or at least depicts, previous authors as less evolved ancestors (analogous to Stein's "little children") or as old-fashioned, worn out, and passé (Stein's "grown and old men and women"). If Stein's novel has to participate in a conversation with these other books, then she—like others before her—has purposefully put herself in a position of authority in relation to their posited immaturity or senility.

Most simply, *The Making of Americans* calls itself a "history . . . of talking and listening" (728). Stein waits to get three-quarters of the way through the book to say this, but she may have only at that point discovered what her whole enterprise has been (and, in the interests of an honest representation of a typically messy human thought process, she was not inclined to go back and add it in earlier). Perhaps she discovered that her means to understanding others and her means of communicating that understanding are inseparable. When she thought she was writing about identity, she was writing about talking, writing about writing about talking, and writing about talking about talking.

The Making of Americans is notorious for its failed (or at least bafflingly unclear) classification of people into types. Regardless of their bottom nature, however, and regardless of her ability or inability to classify types of bottom nature, Stein sees the nature of one's talking and listening as an important clue to the development of a real sense of self. The two different tendencies in the novel can be helpfully distinguished by M. M. Bakhtin's terms "analysis" and "prosaics." The "analysis" is the text's attempt to develop, or its appearance of attempting to develop, a system capable of describing everything about human personality. In addition to the autobiographical aspect of *The Making of Americans*, critics have emphasized its painstaking and sometimes pained quest toward ordered knowledge, its "analysis." But Stein's text also contains "prosaics," which are "suspicious of explanatory systems" and suggest "that the most important events in life are not the grand, dramatic, or catastrophic but the apparently small and prosaic ones of everyday life," and which seem to me much more interesting (Morson and Emerson, 64–65). These details of everyday events—including everyday interactions between confused but lecturing parents and their silent but also unsure children—support but also explode the aforementioned systematizing with much more information and nuance than can be accounted for within a system.

In *The Making of Americans* and "A Long Gay Book," Stein develops a taxonomy of human personality, but she gradually becomes more interested in relationship. The charts and categories Stein created while writing the novel are well documented (Stendhal, 50; Wagner-Martin, 84). Wagner-Martin describes "The Book of Diagrams" as "filled with schemata of people [Stein] knew arranged by personality traits" (84). Leon Katz describes Stein's attempt to create "a psychology which defines character by a mosaic of typifying adjectives" ("Weininger," 11). Moving beyond individual character types, Stein writes "A Long Gay Book" in order "to describe . . . every possible kind of pairs of human beings and every possible threes and fours and fives of human beings and every possible kind of crowds of human beings" (*Lectures*, 148). These relationships, constructed through language, may become more important to Stein than the people themselves. She seems to have discovered that conversation is the means by which people present themselves and form these connections.

In listening, however, Stein notices people's tendency to say the same things, or the same kinds of things, over and over. Insincere copying appears to be a weak but prevalent twin of genuine repeating, which comes straight from our own being. More common than repeating, copying is neither genuine nor individualistic. Copiers "know what they want to be and can build it up by little pieces and do again and again. [They] know what they are and see it as a complete thing and make that thing in daily living" (*Making*, 644). These copiers are "always cutting and fitting and fitting and cutting and painting and sometime they come to be that thing . . . inventing themselves in daily living and in dressing" (644). In other words, we can grow a self from the parts of us we like, arranging and discarding pieces of ourselves like clothing, but Stein is sure we cannot be comfortable in these borrowed and cobbled robes. People can copy "the repeating that once came out of them in feeling," copy "others around them," copy "themselves in their way of talking, sometimes in their loving, often in their way of walking, of moving their hands and shoulders, in their ways of smiling, there have been some and always will be some who copy themselves so in all their living, in their eating and drinking, in every moment of their daily living" (195). Thus Stein describes the kind of adamant consistency people claim when they perform themselves.

Stein values repeating, although in the midst of her unmatched repeating and her explicitly stated championship of repeating and her effusive, eternal love poem to repeating, she concedes that "listening to repeating is often irritating" (*Making*, 291). Even sincere repeating can be irritating until the listener's love of repeating turns irritation "into patient completed understanding" (291). When Marianne Moore begins her poem titled "Poetry" with "I, too, dislike it," she suggests that some poetry is annoying, even though there are things that cannot be expressed any other way. Repeating, like poetry, offers "after all, a place for the genuine" (*Complete Poems*, 36). Similarly irritating and important, repeating is the natural way we express our beings. Stein links genuine repetition, a special kind of vision ("seeing"), and an "important feeling" of oneself as an individual, which she sees as the culmination of personal success ("winning"). Stein also values authentic repeating for the information it can reveal about people's "bottom natures." What people do and say, especially what they do and say over and over, lets her see them for who they really are.

For Stein, a person who resists copying is a success because she has obtained an "important feeling of herself to herself inside her" (*Making*, 66) and "an individual kind of thinking that [arises] of itself inside her" (65). Stein explains that "one of the Hissen women came very near to winning, came very near to seeing, came very nearly making of herself to herself a really individual being" (65). When Fanny Hissen and David Hersland marry, they have the potential to "make children who perhaps would come to have in them a really important feeling of themselves inside them" (77).

But Stein hears more copying than repeating, which attests to an American failure. Some people have incomplete senses of themselves because they shrink or expand certain parts of their personalities according to social expectations; Stein's characters represent these possibilities when they feel empty or too full. All three Schilling women feel the emptiness: "the fatter sister" had a "vague fear" because "all that unprotected surface of her makes it easier to see in her that she is just like all the other millions who have been made just like her" (*Making*, 82); "the thinner sister" "had not enough inside her to really fill her" and felt a fear that was caused by "always trying to fill up a hole in her without enough to fill it from the being in her without making some other hole inside her" (82, 83); and Mrs. Schilling was like her daughters in that "something had dropped out of each one of them and they had been indolent or stupid or staring each one of them then and they had not noticed such a dropping out of them" (78). Something important, perhaps an eccentric uniqueness they didn't dare manifest, fell out of these women's lives when they weren't paying attention. What's left is inadequate and conformist.

Confident second-generation David Hersland, who is "all full up inside him, there was not much of any way that anything could enter into him" (*Making*, 85), is incomplete in quite a different way. He is too full of himself, so confident of his idea of himself that he must have bolstered the weak and unsure part of himself with copies from the solid part in him. As a result, he is a bad listener because he does not have room for any other ideas or feelings. Stein makes her readers wish for the freedom—the initiative and independence—to feel and be wholly ourselves. She makes us wish for enough permeability—or unsureness or curiosity or vitality—that we can truly interact with other people.

Stein sympathizes with the difficulty of acting from one's being, particularly in the small things of life. Even people who succeed in making career decisions for themselves can succumb to this copying, because they tend not to give much thought to other, less weighty, decisions and can unknowingly fall into the habit of copying:

> it is a very difficult thing to get the courage to buy the kind of clock or handkerchiefs you are loving, when every one thinks it is a silly thing, when every one thinks you are doing it for the joke of the thing. It is hard then to know whether you are really loving that thing. It takes very much courage to do anything connected with your being that is not a serious thing. It takes courage to be doing a serious thing that is connected with one's being that is certain. (*Making*, 488)

And then we get back to talk. One kind of talking and listening is repeating; the other is copying. For Stein, copying and what I will call "plain old" talking and listening lead to an incomplete sense of self; repeating and what Stein calls "talking and listening at the same time" develop real being. Plain old talking and listening involve hearing yourself as if you were an impressionable somebody else. Plain old talking and listening allow a person to lie to herself, or at least allow her words to contain and finalize her thoughts. But listening and talking *at the same time* is listening to yourself while remembering that you are the one talking: you can make amendments, you can see more complexities than your listener, your words point toward but do not embody your whole thought, and you don't have to expect and create consistency. When Stein says, "I am writing for myself and strangers" (*Making*, 289), she intimates that she is reading and writing *at the same time* and possibly imagining how a multitude of strangers might differently, creatively, and *not* dogmatically understand her words.

But the very motivation behind copying is that we can come to know ourselves in as consistent and limited a way as others know us. Some women strictly enforce their own youthful identities and "make a dance step every now and then in their walking" to project a cheerful innocence or a "lively" pre-"adolescence" (*Making*, 174). Martha Hersland has not only convinced herself that she's tough, she's convinced her husband: "He only heard what she said to him in anything that she had been concerned in and so he never came to any feeling that she was not a strong woman to win out in the things she always loved to be beginning" (75). Men around Mr. Hersland give him a sense of complacent self confidence: "These men . . . were a comfort to him, . . . they made a kind of support around him . . . they made a kind of cushion for him to keep him from knowing when he was through with fighting that he had not been winning." As he gets older, they become "more and more important to him as padding, not to fill him but to keep him from knowing" about himself (146–47). As he feels his multiple failures—aided by his children's telling "him what they thought of him" (149)—the men around him help him sustain his idea of himself. All of these people have a way "of always repeating the whole of them as a serious obligation," or helping others do so (269).

In these several ways, Stein uses what comes out of the mouths of Americans to evaluate their success as individuals. Her characters depict Americans who confine themselves within preconceptions about themselves, each other, and the idea of identity itself. In spite of the American reputation for pioneering, Stein sees too many Americans as weak makers who "accept somebody else's description" of themselves (Rorty, *Contingency*, 28). Rorty describes Nietzsche's criterion for failure as a human being, and Stein's ideas parallel his corollary that a person should strive to "describ[e] himself in his own terms" and "creat[e] the only part of himself that matter[s] by constructing his own mind. To create one's mind is to create one's own language, rather than to let the length of one's mind be set by the language other human beings have left behind" (*Contingency*, 27). Of course, as Stein's opening anecdote in *The Making of Americans* demonstrates—a young man rebels, and his father says, "Stop! I did not drag my father beyond this tree" (3)—sometimes when we think we are being most original, most resistant to the past, we are repeating a revolution that has already occurred. Staging a rebellion is often the most conventional way to repeat the past.

The Making of Americans also mimics and highlights the ways that we learn about nation and family by listening to the people around us. Stein's history of the United States is not only appropriately short and accurate for much of the nation's population—20 percent of the U.S. population had foreign-born parents in 1900—but also realistically impressionistic. While others might have valued the length of their family's habitation in the New World, Stein understands "real" Americans as these newish comers: "The old people in a new world, the new people made out of the old, that is the story that I mean to tell, for that is what really is and what I really know" (*Making*, 3). Truly, "that is what really is." Conventional histories of the United States champion the American Revolutionary War heroes, but there are only so many daughters and sons of the Revolution. In 1900, 6 percent of the U.S. population had parents from Germany, a likely nation of origin for the Dehnings and Herslands: Dehning is a name of German origin, meaning a "bold, free man"; Hersland is either German or Danish. (Even more tangentially, the 1870 census reports a young jeweler named David

Hersland living in San Francisco; might Stein have met him on her wander-ings through the city a couple of decades later?)[7] Furthermore, although the published version of the novel does not identify the Herslands and Dehnings as Jewish, their history corresponds with the histories of many Jewish immigrants: the Jewish population in the United States grew from 15,000 in 1840 to almost 250,000 in 1880, with most of the increase the result of German Jewish immigration (Wittke, 328).[8] Many were peddlers who became merchants and then owners of large stores, and they had a high respect for learning and high ambitions for their children (329). Stein's own family history in America—which begins with an eighteen-year-old male immigrating from Bavaria in 1841 (Wagner-Martin, 3)—corresponds to the historical tendency: "First to come were young, poor immigrant males from the small towns of Bavaria and the Rhineland" (Cordasco, 451), and between 1840 and 1850 approximately five hundred Jewish families from the Old World settled in Baltimore (Wagner-Martin, 3).

Stein's listening to her own family may have inspired a history of the United States that models the narrative structures that children hear on the laps of their grandparents. Standard historical plots are developed through contextualization, summary, analysis, and the needs of the nation, but family history—in nonroyal and otherwise "nonhistorical" families—never quite becomes information.[9] Instead, children develop vague impressions of the past that are pinned on just a few specific events told through the haze of personal memory and the lens of egoistic bias. This history is not arranged chronologically, and events are rarely attached to a date. If personal experi-ence is linked to national events or social movements, this linking is done loosely and inaccurately.[10] Also, because of the role family history plays in the moral education of children, it emphasizes positive and negative char-acter traits or behavior in an attempt to perpetuate the civilized behavior and values that are considered ideal by the family or nation.

Americans are made by continually listening to themselves talking about what an American is supposed to be. Our identities are not only personal and familial but also racial, regional, and national. Perhaps Stein's *Mak-ing of Americans* intends to make Americans by making Americans listen. Americans have not listened to Stein much since 1934, but what is more important is for Americans to listen to themselves—to listen to all the things adamantly copied and carefully omitted, and to start genuinely repeating and hearing what we say when we do. In "Portraits and Repetition" (101), Stein writes that "each civilization insisted in its own way before it went away," and in *The Making of Americans* she makes us notice the narrative propagation of culture through our forced copying of our ideas of ourselves.

If we listened to ourselves, we would probably want to make some changes in our narrative.

In medical school, Stein was taught to diagnose physical illness through listening, and she ended up diagnosing social illness by the same means. The Lynds' *Middletown*, published in 1929, also allowed Americans to hear themselves, and many were surprised to notice the power of peer pressure and social expectation in American life. *Middletown* revealed that not all Americans were innovative, energetic, enterprising, and daring. For example, the Lynds discover that clothes consciousness led to a "decrease in individualism and increase in type-consciousness" (161). Stein urges Americans to *listen* to themselves talk in clichés, just as Jacob Riis, the early photographer, made Americans *look* at American streets, which were not paved with gold. But unlike Riis, who wrote his own autobiography, *The Making of an American* (1901) in the typical vein, Stein creates a new plot of difficult adjustments and innocent, envious imitation. Though most readers look for Stein's legacy in avant-garde writing, such as Harryette Mullen's wonderful poetry, Stein's project has gone on in other forms. For the last several decades, Studs Terkel's interviews have allowed Americans to hear ourselves and our great multiplicity on several big topics, including work, World War II, the Depression, and death. Similarly, Robert Bellah and others' 1996 *Habits of the Heart: Individualism and Commitment in American Life* reveals American ideas about public and private life through the voices of two hundred people. What we learn by reading *The Making of Americans*, what we learn by heeding Stein's advice and listening to ourselves and other Americans speaking, is that there is a difference between the official national characteristics and the characteristics of the real people.

For example, Americans tend to be characterized as steadfast pioneers who start impossibly ambitious projects and see them through to the end. Americans are reputed to be like Theodore Dreiser's ruthless and relentlessly goal-oriented Frank Cowperwood. But David Hersland, a second-generation American, likes so much to begin that he rarely finishes anything. He has theories about how to eat, how his children should be educated, how to make a fortune, and how to care for the health of his children, and he acts on each new theory before his last beginning has progressed very far at all.[11] Stein describes his "kind of being" as like those who "have arabian nights inside them": they begin their story again and again and never end it, "always changing and beginning" (*Making*, 121, 124). Stein's modernism already saw, in reality, the indeterminacy that postmodernism would demand of fictional narrative. The model of Scheherazade's stories in *The Arabian Nights* is appropriate for this long American novel, because almost-great American fortune hunters begin again and again in their efforts to succeed. Those who succeed entirely don't have to try again.[12]

Myth and reality are also at odds in the area of individuality. According to Stein, new nations such as the United States value conformity, not individuality, to the extent that they do not allow people to be unique. Even before World War I, the Depression, and World War II—events which made national conversations of critique and reform common and even patriotic (if carefully expressed as anticommunist)—Stein was worried about the effect of industrialism on the American character. In *The Making of Americans*, she laments the "adolescent metallic world" that expresses itself in a penchant for producing ticky-tacky products with machinery (48). Stein connects this method of production with every other activity of American life, activities with which we define and project who each one of us is as an individual: our habits of thinking, writing, talking, dressing, decorating, and supporting ourselves. She asserts that

> vital singularity is as yet an unknown product with us, we who in our habits, dress-suit cases, clothes and hats and ways of thinking, walking, making money, talking, having simple lines in decorating, in ways of reforming, all with a metallic clicking like the type-writing which is our only way of thinking, our way of educating, our way of learning, all always the same way of doing, all the way down as far as there is any way down inside to us. (47)

The renowned American "type" makes it difficult for us to believe that Americans are conformists, and yet Stein seems to have felt enough conventional pressure to notice a discrepancy between myth and reality.

Stein attributes American conformity to American youth—what a more censorious Van Wyck Brooks in *America's Coming-of-Age* calls "the incurable boyishness, the superannuated boyishness of the Emersonian tradition" (87). That youth leads to conformity is an idea antithetical to the American myth that promised freedom in the new, young world, although writers such as Sinclair Lewis also pointed this out to their readers.[13] Stein supports the belief that open spaces breed freedom and eccentricity with her description of the Hersland children growing up on ten acres in Gossols. In the West, where the "young man" David Hersland went "to make his fortune," Gossols is still a kind of frontier: "This was the new world in a new world and it took this newest part of this new world to content him," because he was "restless" (*Making*, 35, 43). But Bridgepoint, an older part of this new world, from which David moved and where the Dehnings live, is the new world in its unpolished conformist adolescence.[14] With the imminent (or already consummate) adolescence of even the western frontier, the new frontier in America has to open within and for the individual.

In a world with no frontiers to establish, the real pioneering seems to lie in unbuilding. "Attacking" and "resisting" are the defining characteristics of Stein's two types of humans, and Stein describes herself as a resisting being. An attacker jumps enthusiastically from one idea to another, building up and moving forward. But a resister strives toward wisdom through questions, unmaking in order to understand. For this type of person, "a puzzled feeling"—a doubt that has not been formed into words—is the first step toward wisdom (*Making*, 310). Later, Stein explains that her progression of understanding is from "a puzzle" to "a conscious puzzle" to confusion to bafflement to "a clear whole one, and then at last a completer whole one" (357). Her senses allow Stein to progress through these levels of understanding: "Always I was hearing, feeling, seeing every one else feeling, listening to, seeing this one. Slowly then this one came to be a complete one to me" (310). If she's right about herself, then this method corresponds to the type of resistance I see Stein generating toward the common language of our society. Her doubts and questions undress us, unmake our mask of Americanisms, and force us to try building ourselves again more legitimately.

Much of this discussion has had little to do with conversation but much to do with change, with sensing something wrong in the United States, and with Stein's eventually prescribing a change in our behaviors. *The Making of Americans*, then, is a history of the making of the nation itself, not its origins as much as its ongoing creation, its self-production in the eyes, by the hands, and as told by the voices of Americans themselves. Unlike later authors such as Dos Passos and the Lynds, Stein doesn't cite a great number of different voices. She sees essences, the structural "tender girders" of language (to use a phrase from Mullen's poem about Stein; see p. 217n22). Here in *The Making of Americans*, Stein mainly grouses, expressing her anxiety of influence and struggling to make good on her decision to become a writer, but later she finds a possibility for change through the adoption of different structures: by remaking conversation, we might remake America. In fact, a *Boston Post* reporter, Grace Davidson, mistakenly referred to Stein's novel as *The Remaking of Americans*.

Stein's love of the human voice is not blind (or deaf), and, from her earliest work, Stein emphasizes the parts of the American nature she would have different. She emphasizes American blindness and American monologuing, both of which come from feelings of inadequacy or overconfidence—emptiness or fullness, in her terminology. Americans are made by listening to themselves and believing. But Stein implies that attention to the makings of conversation—its structures and complexities—could enable Americans to make themselves differently, to be more adaptive, freer.

In the most scrutinizing piece of criticism on *The Making of Americans,* Priscilla Wald in *Constituting Americans* emphasizes Stein's interest in the relationship between language, the self, and society:

> Stein examined how external stimuli—language, physical sensations, even directives—influence the experience and understanding of "self." Her discoveries laid the groundwork both for theories, explored in *The Making of Americans,* of how cultural assumptions shape the experience of self and for the stylistic experimentation of that work through which she analyzed and represented that process. (261)

Stein writes to explicate the complex interaction between who we are and what we say in order to determine where one can begin a revolution of self, art, and society.

Sound Writing

Stein is interested not only in conversation, but also in sound itself. Her contemporary reviewers repeatedly encouraged Stein's readers to read out loud (Winter, 82; Dodge, 153). One reviewer writes that "it is a relief to read something that doesn't intend to make sense in the ordinary sense and so sets you free to use some of your unused senses to make sense" (Winter, 82). Another reports that some readers "could see with their ears and smell with their eyes and taste with their whole selves" (Lerman, 145). In her lecture "Plays," Stein worries over the question, "Could I see and hear and feel at the same time and did I" (*Lectures,* 115). She forces her readers to try.

In *The Gutenberg Galaxy* Marshall McLuhan posits the effect of print on the mind: print encourages us to see more and hear less. He writes (in boldface type): "The interiorization of the technology of the phonetic alphabet translates man from the magical world of the ear to the neutral visual world." McLuhan links this change in sensory emphasis to a change in thought and interpersonal states. He asks (again in boldface): "Does the interiorization of media such as letters alter the ratio among our senses and change mental processes?" And he asserts (this time in regular type): "No other kind of writing save the phonetic has ever translated man out of the possessive world of total interdependence and interrelation that is the auditory network" (18, 24 22). Stein seems to have thought about these same issues less pseudoscientifically, but no less boldly and intricately. Her interest in sound may arise from her personal dispositions, but she may also recover the aural nature of language in order to improve our interactive networks and goad our minds into working differently.

Stein claims that her primary interest is sight, but this may be explained by her complaint that the French read out loud to her instead of letting her read the words herself. She writes that she likes "to read inside and not outside," and that she sometimes overcame this problem by reading over their shoulders (*Everybody's*, 163, 17). Instead, then, of understanding Stein's statement to mean that she was interested only in the sight of words, I take it to mean that she liked reading to be a private matter. She liked to see the words and turn them into sounds on her own. In fact, it is difficult for written words to mean by sight alone, which is one reason it is sometimes difficult to teach deaf children to read. According to Walter Ong, in *Orality and Literacy*, "the world of sound" is "the natural habitat of language." He continues, "'Reading' a text means converting it to sound, aloud or in the imagination" (8).

Stein's interest in the creative friction between these two language media points to her interest in sound as well as sight. In "An American and France," Stein explains that a creator must live between two civilizations or two languages, because creativity comes from the opposition between them, and she even worries that the world's shrinkage will hobble creation—an anticipation of twenty-first-century anxieties about globalization. When the world was so big that people rarely knew of other civilizations, creation could occur, because people had two languages: they had "a special language to write which was not the language that was spoken" (65). The language of talking must be related to the language of writing if their difference is a necessary condition for creativity. In his history of the Frankfurt Institute, *The Dialectical Imagination*, Martin Jay holds: "The distance between Hebrew, the sacred language, and the profane speech of the Diaspora made its impact on Jews who were distrustful of the current universe of discourse" (34). Jay proposes a possible connection between this dual language system and the development of the Frankfurt Institute's dialectical theory—a theory that becomes relevant in this volume at the end of chapter 6.

Stein's attention tended to be voice activated, which is one reason Stein may have had to re-sound others' conversation—and disliked people reading aloud to her. The tone of a voice was likely to distract her from the very words it was saying. In *The Autobiography of Alice B. Toklas*, Stein writes (that Alice reports that Stein said): "I don't hear a language, I hear tones of voice and rhythms, but with my eyes I see words and sentences" (70). Leon Mendez Solomons, a graduate student and Stein's colleague in Harvard's Psychology Laboratory, noted that "Miss Stein has a strong auditory consciousness, and sounds usually determine the direction of her attention" (Stein and Solomons, 15). Stein's auditory consciousness also interested her in rhythm. Reiterating that she was distracted by sound, she writes that "hearing tires me very quickly. Lots of voices make too much sound, any one voice sounds too much like that voice." But she soon adds: "On the other hand as I write the movement of the words spoken by some one whom lately I have been hearing sound like my writing feels to me as I am writing" (*Everybody's*, 88). Stein transforms the conversations she has heard into written words and rhythms and then can reconstitute them in her own voice and better feel their movement. Her method might signify an imperialist domination of those whose words she revises (or replays). As I argue in chapter 3, however, her interest in talk reveals her developing interest in the deep structures of interaction.

Stein plays with the sounds of words throughout her writings, as the next two chapters will demonstrate. For clear instances of Stein's playing with sounds, see *Bee Time Vine* (36), where she writes in the poem "Miguel (Collusion). Guimpe. Candle": "Collection of eggs white, white as know excellent. / Are the holds extra skinned." "Eggs white" sounds like "egg whites"; "white as know" sounds like "white as snow"; "excellent" and "extra" (and even "collection") have the sound of "eggs" in them. About another piece in *Bee Time Vine*, "In," Virgil Thomson cites Alice B. Toklas as saying that what is important is "definitely 'sound.'" He adds that "G.S. would have denied this, since she regularly denied that sounds and their play were a major consideration in her writing" (*Bee Time Vine*, 44). Thomson also reads the title "Yet Dish" as "Yiddish" (52). In the poem "Early and Late," near "Teas and teas," Stein writes "Tease and tease" (245). In "Decorations," she writes: "I do not wish to write down what I hear" (186); but ten pages later, in "What Is This," she writes: "I love conversation. / Do you like it printed. / I like it descriptive. / Not very descriptive. / Not very descriptive. / I like it to come easily / Naturally" (196–97).

Perhaps Stein's "auditory consciousness" led her to wonder about the difference between the sight and the sound of words (independent of a particular voice or even other limiting contexts). She may or may not have had to make sounds as she wrote, but, for example, she did write: "She likes the poet to mutter. He does. The olive" ("Advertisements," in *Geography and Plays*, 343). If we mutter while we read, "the olive" becomes (more profitably within the context) "they all live." Her and our muttering brings (more) meaning to life. If we don't notice Stein's "Loud Letters" (*Geography and Plays*, 345), we are missing something fun, as well as killing meaning—or, less criminally, not bringing as much meaning to life as we could.

A Sensible Education

While the writings themselves are the best evidence of Stein's interest in sound, her extensive undergraduate studies with William James, her experiments in Harvard's Psychology Laboratory, and her medical school training also indicate serious interest in sensory impressions, particularly the senses by which most of us experience language. During her years at Harvard Annex, Stein took seven courses with James, including five graduate courses in experimental psychology, and, even before meeting him, she was assigned his *Principles of Psychology* in her course with Hugo Münsterberg (Bowers, 13; Wagner-Martin, 35, 31). In medical school, Stein devoted much of her time to investigating the sections of the brain and spinal cord that accept and process sensation.

James emphasizes personal sensation—an individual's experience as that individual attends to it—and many readers have noted Stein's own interest in attention and sensation. In the second paragraph of the preface to *The Principles of Psychology*, William James defines the data of psychology as "*thoughts and feelings*," "a *physical world* in time and space with which they coexist," and the knowledge we come to have about this physical world through those thoughts and feelings (6; his italics). Throughout his works, James advocates our trusting our own perceptions and impressions, and he also points out that we develop perceptions and impressions only if we are paying attention.[15] Lloyd Frankenberg suggests that "Gertrude Stein's work as a whole might be called a study in attention, including inattention" (vi), and Rosalind S. Miller also describes Stein's and Solomons's experiments as studies in attention.[16] The subjects of these experiments—and for the first one, the only subjects were Stein and Solomons themselves—were to do one language task while being distracted with another. They were to write down words they heard at the same time that they attempted to read a book; they also tried to write their own stories or anecdotes while being distracted by someone speaking to them. Miller concludes that Stein and Solomons were interested in determining how much of human attention is triggered by sight, and how much by auditory signals (Miller, 51; Stein and Solomons 13–15). Decades later, Stein asks: "Is the thing seen or the thing heard the thing that makes most of its impression upon you at the theatre?" and "Does the thing seen or does the thing heard effect [*sic?*] you and effect [*sic?*] you at the same time or in the same degree or does it not?" and "Of course in reading one sees but one also hears and when the story is at its most exciting does one hear more than one sees or does one not do so?" (*Lectures*,101–2). Stein's writing allows readers to continue a personally administered attention experiment. Stein hands us a looking glass with which to examine our own consciousnesses.

The pedagogical methods used in the Johns Hopkins Medical School curriculum, as well as Stein's particular knowledge of brain physiology, further support my insistence on her interest in the sensory perceptions of written and spoken language. The misconception that Stein dropped out of medical school and preconceptions about early medical school education mix to create an impression that Stein was escaping a stuffy rigidity in preference for airy Paris. But in the 1880s, U.S. medical schools began to emulate European ones by foregoing lectures and instead teaching through experience (Rothstein, 108).[17] William Osler, a prominent gynecologist from whom Stein took a course her fourth year (Wagner-Martin, 50), admitted to giving "a talk" once a week, but he was more satisfied with holding "a regular weekly amphitheater clinic. Of these he explains, 'I like the clinical clerk and the patient to do the teaching, adding comments here and there, or asking the former questions'" (Rothstein, 109). Already Stein was learning from conversation, and she was learning from the people who feel the symptoms instead of the experts who diagnose them.

This modern medical school education taught future doctors to trust their own senses and instincts. Professor William Thayer called their method of teaching "self-education under guidance" and writes: "The method of authority has given way to the method of observation and inquiry" (qtd. in Ludmerer, 64, 66).[18] Professor Franklin Paine Mall preferred the clinical approach to book learning: "When anatomy is studied in this way [through dissection rather than through lectures], the student must indeed be stupid not to discover the many defects as well as errors in some of our favorite English text-books" (qtd. in Ludmerer, 66).[19] In short, medical school training taught students that sensory impressions and experiences are more reliable than summaries (generalizations of sensory impressions) by authorities. If I am right about her, Stein would have embraced this form of education; her appreciation of it is one of the few facts that might explain her staying in medical school for the duration.[20] Teaching Stein to trust her senses and ignore authority must have been like teaching a lion to roar.

After deciding not to take the summer course which would have allowed her to obtain her medical degree, Stein remained at Johns Hopkins for a fifth year, and she continued her work on the brain (Wagner-Martin, 51).[21]

Professor Lewellys Barker maneuvered (without success) to get Stein's original work published in two prominent journals of anatomy (Wagner-Martin, 51–52). In his 1899 textbook *The Nervous System and Its Constituent Neurones*, Barker refers to Stein's investigating "bundle[s] of fibres" in the brain and trying to discover where they lead (725–26). Titled "Centripetal Fibres in the Fasciculus Longitudinalis Medialis," this section of Barker's book shows that Stein's object of attention is a bundle of centripetal fibers, which, as Antoine Keyser succinctly explains, "project the various streams of stimuli from the sense organ receptors towards the posterior lobes of the brain" (Keyser, 64).[22] In his autobiography, *Time and the Physician*, Barker parenthetically comments: "Among these students [at Johns Hopkins] was Miss Gertrude Stein, and I have often wondered whether my attempts to teach her the intricacies of the medulla oblongata had anything to do with the development of the strange literary forms with which she was later to perplex the world" (60). Stein's work on the brain may have been motivated by the same interests that led to her unusual writing. A doctor would cite her interest in the neural networks activated by our habits of attention to sensory input; a literary critic might tend to call this same motivating interest an experiment in reader response or a challenge to our habits of language use. Either way, Stein's words—even as early as *The Making of Americans*—challenge readers' attention, disallow our habitual responses, and inspire something new in the way of reading and writing, speaking and listening.

CHAPTER 2

Modifying the Mind:
William James and *Tender Buttons*

RICHARD RORTY (*PHILOSOPHY*, 24) characterizes the early pragmatists (William James and John Dewey) as talking about experience and the neopragmatists (William Quine and Donald David-
son) as talking about language, but William James's *Principles of Psychology*
had already suggested that language is one form of experience.[1] From the
outset, James contends with the problem that phenomena cannot really
be experienced; we attentively let them be "*undergone*" and then fix them
in our memories: "The dance of the ideas is a copy, somewhat mutilated
and altered, of the order of phenomena" (*Principles*, 17)—and this dance
of ideas necessarily takes place in words. James implies that language is a
significant experience when, treating the topic of aphasia, he discusses *how*
various injured and healthy people imbue language: by sight, by sound, by
the feeling in [their] fingers as they hold a pen, and so on. Thus language
is both the means to noting experiences of other types and an experience
in itself.

The experience of language helps instill the network of associations
within the mind, which is what produces—or simply *is*—the structure
of that mind, though James points out weaknesses in this theory, too
(*Principles*, 1218). Assuming that the theory is even partly true, Stein could
change her readers' habits of mental association by changing the arrangements of words on the page. In this way, the choices she makes—the very
ways she arranges those words—are an artistic adaptation of James's scientific work. Every mind is a black box, a function machine of countless
inscrutabilities, and we can never know how one person's words might strike
another person's fancy, but Stein's works, from *Tender Buttons* to *Brewsie and
Willie*, seem inspired by James's speculations about the workings of human

cognition. While Stein is often understood to write differently because of her homosexuality or her womanhood—as lacking a heterocentrist world-view or writing *l'ecriture feminine*—James's discussion of the means by which *human* minds think would have let her see her project as more uni-versal. Stein calls attention to our necessary habits of human thought, not just heterosexual or masculine thought, and makes us question assumptions that so many of us hold so deeply we haven't noticed them.

In *The Principles of Psychology*, James states that all thought occurs through association and that memory is only a matter of paths (620). He speculates that our minds are networks of associations that have developed through experience:

> *The highest centres* [of the human mind] *do probably contain nothing but arrangements for representing impressions and movements, and other arrangements for coupling the activity of these arrangements together.* (73; his italics)

James's idea that the mind consists of arrangements, and of arrangements of arrangements, coupled with his assertion that linguistic experience can form these arrangements, suggests that Stein's weird series of words might have the capacity to rearrange those arrangements in our minds. Stein redesigns her readers' neural pathways, developing in us a greater number of associational paths leading out from each stimulus. Her words elicit expectant attention; they mildly prime the reader to interpret other words in certain ways (or productively uncertain ways). For example, in *Tender Buttons*, when Stein writes, "A seal and matches and a swan and ivy and a suit" (11), the reader might think of an animal (a seal), then a wax seal (to go with matches), then an animal again (a seal to match with a swan, and now "match" has transformed from a noun to a verb or an adjective), then possibly a coat of arms (animals surrounded by ivy), and then coupling in general (matches, suit, a pair of animals). These few words prime us to no-tice a variety of meanings for each one. An Ivy League suit? A swimsuit to accompany the water animals? ("I vie" could even prime us for a different kind of "suit.")

Stein began learning about the brain in college, because James's text-book reviews contemporary works on cognitive science. As Louis Menand reports, in those days "psychology was just what philosophers did when they talked about minds," and in Germany James had studied "what was then the hottest area in science: physiological psychology, sometimes called psy-chophysics," which based its work on the assumption that "every conscious event has a physical basis" (259). In James's text—as well as in most works on cognitive science today—localization is introduced through the study of aphasia, a "language deficit caused by damage to the brain" (O'Grady, 348).[2] As one modern text asserts: "The study of aphasia is by far the most important tool in the investigation of language in the brain" (ibid.). Before the technology that could detect hot spots—the active parts—of the brain, (though not before the 1867 discovery that "*brain-activity seems accompanied by a local disengagement of heat*" [James, *Principles*, 105; his italics]), specialized brain areas were located by studying the brains of aphasics post mortem. Different kinds of aphasia led to hypotheses about the possible chain of events that must occur between hearing or reading verbal stimuli and responding in kind. The study of the brain is likely to have let Stein see strong and complex relationships between the senses, language, and knowing.

Stein's writing often reads as if she has Wernicke's aphasia, the "most important type of fluent aphasia."[3] A person with Wernicke's aphasia is "generally unaware of [his] deficit," speaks without hesitation, correctly uses "function words" and normal syntax, but "rarely makes any sense" (O'Grady, 351). But Stein is more interested in the normal than the abnormal workings of the human mind: "the normal is so much more simply complicated and interesting" (*Autobiography*, 83). She also recognizes the skill of the normal brain to make sense of *whatever* inputs it receives. She may even be aware that Carl Wernicke in 1874 asserted that "speech acquisition coincides so closely with the development of consciousness that it may be considered as a gauge thereof" (69). Her writing rearranges the arrangements, and the arrangements of arrangements, in the highest centers of her readers' minds, affecting our very consciousness. The sensations of Stein's words in our brains enables Stein to enable us to cut shortcuts through and build extensions to the more common neural pathways of association. Her word placement forces us to expand the number of places in the brain to which we send information about any particular word; we send out all-points bulletins to discern possible meaning.

William James's *Principles of Psychology* might even have suggested Stein's sense of the efficacy of language in changing people and societies. In his first chapter, "The Scope of Psychology," James speculates on how memory works. Describing "the associationists'" ideas, James writes:

> This multitude of ideas, existing absolutely, yet clinging together, and weaving an endless carpet of themselves, like dominoes in ceaseless change, or the bits of glass in a kaleidoscope,—whence do they get

their fantastic laws of clinging, and why do they cling in just the shapes they do?

For this the associationist must introduce the order of experience in the outer world. The dance of the ideas is a copy, somewhat mutilated and altered, of the order of phenomena. But the slightest reflection shows that phenomena have absolutely no power to influence our ideas until they have first impressed our senses and our brain; . . . a very small amount of reflection on facts shows that one part of the body, namely, the brain, is the part whose experiences are directly concerned. . . .

. . . it will be safe to lay down the general law that *no mental modification ever occurs which is not accompanied or followed by a bodily change.* The ideas and feelings, e.g., which these present printed characters excite in the reader's mind not only occasion movements of his eyes and nascent movements of articulation in him, but will some day make him speak, or take sides in a discussion, or give advice, or choose a book to read, differently from what would have been the case had they never impressed his retina. (17–19)

This description of the complex way our minds associate ideas with each other corresponds with descriptions of the way the words associate in a Stein work such as *Tender Buttons*. But even more importantly, James's assertion that our future actions will be affected by each mental experience suggests that Stein's strange and strongly sensory writing could have consequences (and might have even been intended to have consequences) beyond the field of literature. Stein encourages us to develop new ways of understanding and forming our own language, new ways of talking, new orders in our neurons, and even a new social order—but all that comes later.

James asserts that the brain undergoes constant remodification (*Principles*, 227). The brain is "an organ whose internal equilibrium is always in a state of change," like a "kaleidoscope" in which "the figures are always rearranging themselves" (239). He goes so far as to say (in an echo of Heraclitus) that the mind's incessant fluxion means that no state of thought can ever be repeated: "*no state* [of thought] *once gone can recur and be identical with what it was before*" (224). He asks, "How is a fresh path ever formed?" (1183) and then offers examples of "how often experience undoes her own work, and for an earlier order substitutes a new one" (1217). His examples of how our eyes and minds adjust to our wearing unusual glasses, looking through prisms, or moving on ice instead of land demonstrate how quickly we form new associations, and "the habits of a lifetime [are] violated" (820)—an afternoon of ice skating can make one forget habits of walking for an hour. "When we have been exposed to an unusual stimulus for many minutes or hours, a nervous process is set up which results in the haunting of consciousness by the impression for a long time afterwards. . . . [P]rofound rearrangements and slow settlings into a new equilibrium are going on in the neural substance," and they gradually develop into memory (609). In other words, also James's: "Excitement of peculiar tracts, or peculiar modes of general excitement in the brain, leave a sort of tenderness or exalted sensibility behind them which takes days to die away" (542).

In contrast to the excitation of "peculiar tracts," habits are associations that have dug deep paths in our minds through repetition. James defines habits in terms of well-worn, highly eroded waterways (*Principles*, 113, 427). In reaction to certain stimuli, we become automata, and he is not talking only about habitually putting on socks or buttoning buttons, although he mentions both of these (118). Even reading has become instinctual: "the art of reading (after a certain stage in one's education) is the art of skipping" (992). We quickly pass over signs, ignoring them in order to get to what is signified (872). We do not fully revisit information that we assume to be familiar.

What makes us conscious is hesitation, deliberation, and choice. James writes:

> Consciousness . . . is only intense when nerve-processes are hesitant. In rapid, automatic, habitual action it sinks to a minimum. . . . In hesitant action, there seem many alternative possibilities of final nervous discharge. The feeling awakened by the nascent excitement of each alternative nerve-tract seems by its attractive or repulsive quality to determine whether the excitement shall abort or shall become complete. Where indecision is great, . . . consciousness is agonizingly intense. Feeling, from this point of view, may be likened to a cross-section of the chain of nervous discharge, ascertaining the links already laid down, and groping among the fresh ends presented to it for the one which seems best to fit the case. (*Principles*, 145)

A collection of subtle stimuli can point in a variety of directions, and so a person must act consciously, mentally stepping in to decide which way to go. James calls this widely drawn arc of association "submaximal excitement of wide-spreading associational brain-tracts" (244), and "*suffusion*" and "*fringe*" (249; his italics).[4] The more "wide-spreading" the associations, the more necessarily conscious the thinker must become. In a more beautiful phrase, he states that the mind "is at every stage a theatre of simultaneous possibilities" (277). James defines genius in terms of this living, active consciousness (400). But genius is hard to sustain in the ordinary business of life. Daily experiences form habits of sight and thought that are almost impossible to change. James asserts that learning something altogether new is easier than seeing the mundane in new ways.

But he may have inspired Stein to try. No matter how weirdly it reads, Stein's *Tender Buttons* represents a domestic space, with its sections titled "Objects," "Food," and "Rooms." Buttons are an example James uses to describe thoughtless, habitual actions, and "tenderness" is the very word he uses to describe the effect of new and different stimuli on the mind. In *Tender Buttons*, we certainly are looking at the mundane from an unusual perspective, or through a prism, one that forces our thoughts down different paths than they would usually tend to take. Stein does not use words as if they were buttons to be pushed, and she actively prevents readers from jumping to any single reaction or firm conclusions. For example, "A Box" reads:

> Out of kindness comes redness and out of rudeness comes rapid same question, out of an eye comes research, out of selection comes painful cattle. So then the order is that a white way of being round is something suggesting a pin and is it disappointing, it is not, it is so rudimentary to be analysed and see a fine substance strangely, it is so earnest to have a green point not to red but to point again. (*Tender Buttons*, 11)

Her first two "out of" phrases suggest the manifestations and consequences of certain behaviors ("kindness" and "rudeness"), but the next two "out of" phrases undermine that assumption. The four phrases in this first sentence make a reader think about the relationship between the components of each pair, and we tend to assume that the relationship we find should be similar; James says the mind makes great use of "the *notion* of sameness" (an ability measured on most standardized tests), which accounts for its very structure (*Principles*, 435; his italics). The desire to find sameness leads readers to consider all possible meanings of each of the eight components of the four expressions, and readers probably feel hopeful of success until they get to "painful cattle." The wish to collate that phrase with the others compels the reader to become much more creative in reconsidering the possible meaning of all the other components. The reader has to determine what "comes out of" means, such that "kindness" is to "redness" as "rudeness" is to "rapid same question" as "eye" is to "research" as "selection" is to "painful cattle." In forcing us into thinking about these words or terms, Stein forces us to notice our less habitual associations. We notice similarities of sound ("-ness" is repeated three times; "rudeness" and "redness" sound alike), and we notice semantic relationships (research and eye, for example). We notice what we are habitually trying to do (find this parallel set of relationships), and then we think of alternate activities (Is this a linear plot? Is she talking about what we are doing, as in boxing ourselves in, instead of anything exterior to our reader response?), in addition to alternative denotations of the words.

The next sentence alludes to "order," but "a white way of being round" forces us to disorder our nice little mutually exclusive boxes of color and shape concepts. "Something suggesting a pin" encourages us to acknowledge the vagueness of similarity instead of letting us continue to pretend that the notion of sameness on which our thoughts are founded is firm bedrock. Later in this sentence, Stein seems to state her goal more directly than usual: she wants us to "see a fine substance strangely" and "to have green point not to red [its opposite, and a likely spontaneous next thought] but to point again" (and again) instead of losing its power once it has fired off the beginning of a chain of habitual associations and reactions.[5]

Have I undermined Stein's goal by coming to this conclusion? "Is it disappointing, it is not"—because I have only a tentative grasp on these words. They have not fired and emptied. They are still firing (along with previously unacquainted synapses), and they will continue to point and point again because "rudimentary" is related to "rudeness," "earnest" points ahead to a sincere pledge of something to come, and there are so many other loose ends that the stanza cannot be neatly sewn together, wrapped up, or boxed. Stein's words, here and elsewhere, do not let us rely on habit. She relies on our habits only enough to use them against other habits, to encourage us to encourage her words to mean as much as they can, and to let our minds do more than we usually demand from them.[6]

James cites Josiah Royce's precept that "consciousness constantly tends to the minimum of complexity and to the maximum of definiteness" (*Principles*, 943), but Stein won't let it. If the times we hesitate and decide are the times we are most conscious, then Stein heightens our consciousness by producing strings of words that cause our instincts to contradict each other. When that happens, according to James, we lose those instincts and "lead a life of hesitation and choice, an intellectual life" (1013).[7] A review of *Tender Buttons* cites an anonymous "friend" of Stein as saying, "She is impelling language to induce new states of consciousness" (R. Rogers, 19). In his review of the same work, H. L. Mencken says that Stein's writing requires "a resilient cerebrum" (15). Instead of running our minds through the regular channels, Stein makes our thoughts spread out of the main river, streaming between stimuli and less common reactions. These tributaries form deltas where our minds can consciously wander and wade, playing and testing the waters. As in scientific abbreviation, these deltas mean "change."

James shows that when people practice looking through prisms, their minds start to violate the habits of a lifetime. Perhaps then it is no accident that Stein chose to begin *Tender Buttons* with the prose poem "A Carafe, That Is a Blind Glass," which reminds many readers of refracted light.

A CARAFE, THAT IS A BLIND GLASS

A kind in glass and a cousin, a spectacle and nothing strange a single hurt color and an arrangement in a system to pointing. All this and not ordinary, not unordered in not resembling. The difference is spreading.

Chessman posits that this "word-painting may be 'a cousin' to the actual 'carafe,'" since it holds, but doesn't quite hold, meaning (92). Comparing Stein's project to Emerson's, Chessman writes that both believe that "to see the world newly requires, not a new world, but new perception" (93). Ruddick understands this passage to be self-reflexive: the poem's "gesturing toward . . . connections" that "fall short of shaping the poem into a single, monologic (or systematic) meaning" (*Reading*, 195). While first writing that the issue of sight is an unrelated one, Ruddick then hazards: "Maybe the poem, or *Tender Buttons* as a whole, is meant to initiate us in a new kind of *seeing* that exposes *connections* among things without authorizing a single system of classification" (196; her italics).[8] Stewart calls this passage "a meditation" and follows the etymology of "carafe" back to Arabic *gharrfa* (to draw water) and then notes the similar Indo-European root *ghar-* (shine, glare, glow) which is the root of "glass" (87–89). Also seeing "religious ritual" in *Tender Buttons* (133), Stewart concludes that "for Gertrude Stein the activity of writing is the ritual of deracinating one's own consciousness" (138). Digging up human consciousness is a way of airing the roots and encouraging new growth, as well as planting something wholly new.

Perhaps then I am only putting in neurological terms what these others have said in spiritual (and botanical) ones. Together, "blind," "glass," and "spectacle" suggest that Stein is discussing vision (and its distortions), although in each case Stein's other words seem to prime the reader to notice other possible denotations of those three words. "A carafe" may be blind because it contains, but it can also refract light through itself (or even through the liquid it contains), such that the light points and spreads. Stein's words "kind," "cousin," and "resembling" also point toward the less distinct associations she would have us recall. Toklas seems to have called puns (double entendres) "double tenders" (Steward, *Murder*, 113), but eventually a choice must be made, a preference admitted, for the juggling mind must let go of some ideas while grasping others.[9] I think that Stein is beginning a treatise on epistemology and language, and that here she describes the many ways she sees a carafe as a metaphor for a word, which is the container of our perceptions. A word can contain meaning, but it can also do more, point to more, and that array of possible meanings is the very difference Stein advocates we notice. This stanza of Stein's prose poem is like James's prism, in that it can change forever our mental associations. Her diction and word arrangements, her emphasis on sight and sound, encourage us to travel our less developed paths of association. Instead of firing from "carafe," say, to cheap sangria, Stein's readers' thoughts will spread out over a delta of more.

Tender Buttons Disturb a Center: Questioning Our Rhetorical Religion

This whole first passage in *Tender Buttons*, "A Carafe, That Is A Blind Glass," is explicated quite often, but elsewhere critics have tended to address their attention to short bits and extracted phrases, developing their interpretations of Stein's work from these pieces. Stein's words, however, should be contemplated not just in pieces but in the order she put them on the page, and in longer sections. Reconsidering her 1983 book thirteen years later, Marianne DeKoven notes: "I would now read the whole paragraph rather than just the first sentence" of "A Portrait of Mabel Dodge at the Villa Curonia" ("Introduction," 476). Marjorie Perloff writes: "To assume that Stein chooses her words more or less randomly, that she is merely being 'playful,' is to ignore the careful contextualization that makes such play possible" (105). Agreeing wholeheartedly, I choose to discuss the longest paragraph from *Tender Buttons*, all of it, and to see and hear what can be seen and heard there. I will also be demonstrating the mental calisthenics involved in reading Stein. If you agree with Stephen Booth that there is pleasure to be gotten in the "understanding of something that remains something we do not understand," then read on (*Precious*, 6).[10] To start with my conclusions, the following long sentence from the section, "Rooms" suggests that Stein is suspicious of the standard structures of conventional English, the easy routines that these structures afford thought, and the predictability of everyday rhetoric which allows people to get away with not thinking.

She suggests that people have fallen asleep, become unconscious of the world and themselves by becoming habituated to and relaxing upon "congealed . . . phrases" (Loy, 94)—prefabricated, retold untruths:

> A religion, almost a religion, any religion, a quintal in religion, a relying and a surface and a service in indecision and a creature and a question and a syllable in answer and more counting and no quarrel and a single scientific statement and no darkness and no question and an earned administration and a single set of sisters and an outline and no blisters and the section seeing yellow and the centre having spelling and no solitude and no quaintness and yet solid quite so solid and the single surface centred and the question in the placard and the singularity, is there a singularity, and the singularity, why is there a question and the singularity why is the surface outrageous, why is it beautiful why is it not when there is no doubt, why is anything vacant, why is not disturbing a centre no virtue, why is it when it is and why is it when it is and there is no doubt, there is no doubt that the singularity shows. (*Tender Buttons*, 73)

Stein would probably agree that these words cannot be "understood," since, for her, "understanding" implies passively following a leader or author rather than coming to know through experience. But there is still meaning to be gleaned here. As James says, a collection of stimuli, each one *"ineffectual"* in itself, can eventually add up and can "at last overcome a resistance" (*Principles*, 89; his italics). If we are forced to look at the words, we start to see what's there. We note "syllables that we perceive one by one as we read or listen, syllables whose relations to one another flicker and change as we and they progress to the end" (Booth, *Precious*, 20).[11] Experiencing this stanza in "Rooms," searching it for sights, sounds, relationships, subsequent meanings, and anything else accessible to an attentive reader, evokes a variety of meanings which all seem to add up to a comprehensive declaration of mental independence from the commonplaces that express the normal order of things. One can arrange that range of meaning (a process Stein encourages by means of the repeated presence of "range," "arrange," "arrangement," and even "orange" throughout *Tender Buttons*) into a "single set"—one and yet multiple, *e pluribus unum*. Playing, paying attention to Stein's unusually tendered, quite tender, suggestions toward meaning, rearranges one's mental arrangements, which should remind readers of the messy ways *unum* arises out of *pluribus*, and maybe even reintroduce pluralism into our minds.

Instead of telling us what she's talking about, Stein obliges us to figure it out. Without a right or wrong in view, the exercise forces readers into a more complete experience of single words—their sounds, their spelling, their various denotations and connotations, their relatives. Ferdinand de Saussure, W.V.O. Quine, and Jacques Derrida (among others) may be wrong when they argue that isolated words have no meaning. But maybe they are right, because although lonely words lose some meaning, they take on more or other—they are never alone in our minds. According to James:

> If we look at an isolated printed word and repeat it long enough, it ends by assuming an entirely unnatural aspect. Let the reader try this with any word on this page. He will soon begin to wonder if it can possibly be the word he has been using all his life with that meaning. It stares at him from the paper like a glass eye, with no speculation in it. Its body is indeed there, but its soul is fled. It is reduced, by this new way of attending to it, to its sensational nudity. We never before attended to it in this way, but habitually got it clad with its meaning the moment we caught sight of it, and rapidly passed from it to the other words of the phrase. We apprehended it, in short, with a cloud of associates, and thus perceiving it, we felt it quite otherwise than as we feel it now divested and alone. (*Principles*, 726–27)

Stein says she discovered this feature of words on New Year's Day 1927, when she was getting her hair cut short and reading with her glasses out in front of her, but she had studied James in the fall of 1893. Even one word, or a set of words, can give rise to an array of associations, considerations, and imaginings. Stein's focus on the word is a love affair—but also a political campaign. Developing semantic consciousness should prevent knee-jerk reactions to language; readers pleasingly educated by Stein's *Tender Buttons* might become less easily manipulated by words.

Instead of helping us understand this "religion" she mentions, Stein makes us come to know it personally. Stein often wrote about the artistic endeavor in terms of religion (see Watts, *Rapture*, 25; S. Watson, *Prepare*), and this Jewish writer teaches us to protest our traditional catholic reading habits. Words were her artistic medium, and she's a reformist. In this passage, the words that seems adjectival because of their syntactic positions ("almost a," "any," and "a quintal in") only make Stein's meaning more vague. The noun "religion" is complicated rather than clarified by the words that seem as if they should act as modifiers. "Almost any religion" or "any almost-religion" would have been comparatively easy to understand, but those are not (therefore) what Stein offers. By refusing to let her readers' thoughts lean on the shoulders of adjectival ensigns, Stein makes us look directly at the noun "religion." I see "re" and "lig," which reminds me of ligaments.[12] Something that is done again? Something that binds one thing to another? I also see "re" and "ligion," which reminds me of "legion." Something that a whole legion of people do over and over? ("Legion" means "to gather," as I am gathering all this information together.) "[A] quintal in religion" sounds like "a Quintilian religion," which suggests this religion might refer to ancient, common, and powerful rhetorical conventions. In fact, Quintilian valorized conventions, as here: "Custom . . . is the surest preceptor in speaking: we must use phraseology, like money, which has the public stamp" (49). All Stein's stored-up meanings rub together, and they add up to something about conventional (reused, repeated) rhetorical habits of binding together words—or ideas, people, communities, and political bodies. If one were writing in this unusual style, one might choose to write the reasons for it. *Tender Buttons* may be a treatise against the habitual use of language and also a primer for a new kind of attention. Stein risks having her ideas misunderstood because she does not write in familiar forms, but standard prose could neither change habits nor awaken consciousness.

With so many more words left to read in the sentence, and such unusually tendered suggestions, a reader must feel in great doubt about meaning. The sounds of the words and the anataxis encourage a reader to rush through "a relying and a service in indecision and a creature and," but Stein's practice so far has taught the reader to slow down and look around. But where to look? "And" is the perfect word to express associations without suggesting hierarchies, making the sentences "[a]dditive rather than subordinative," a phrase Ong (36–37) uses to describe one of the "characteristics of orally based thought and expression." "And" does not allow us to guess where the central idea in this phrase will be found, so we look at everything. The unusual situation of "relying" in the sentence makes interpretation less than automatic. The article "a" immediately before "relying" primes us for a noun rather than what sounds like a verb (and subsides into a gerund). Through this false priming, Stein forces us to look carefully at words we thought we already knew. Unable to skip over "relying" (as we can when it is in its customary setting), we are forced to look at the word and consciously enumerate all it might mean. One might note the visual—and socially functional—similarities between "religion" and "relying" or recognize the etymological parallels. "Relying" is "re-" + "lie" and means "to fasten together," just like "religion." "Relying" suggests reclining back, or lying down again, or even telling another untruth. Collecting all that stored meaning, I get an image of a person or a whole group of people mentally reclining, relaxing on the retold untruths that have already been fastened together for them.

Stein's anataxis pulls readers further, on toward rediscovering the associational "fringes" and related entanglements of more and more words. Our reading habits, our expectations of coherence and similarity, compel us to take what meaning we find in "a relying and a surface and a service in indecision and" and try to contrast it with that already blossoming in this complicated tree of associations. "Surface" makes me skim forward, surf ahead on its soft sounds and slippery connotations. It pushes me on to the next word and the recognition that "surface" and "service" sound quite a bit alike. The "surface" could describe the character of the reading process when I read normal sentences in which I feel fluent and which lead me to take words for granted. Surface-y sentences might be "a service in indecision" because they allow us to avoid making decisions: our habits keep us from noticing that there are any decisions to make. The surface offers a service on which readers rely, but Stein's writing offers no stable surface on which readers can stand together, or even alone (and her phrase could mean something very different from my paraphrase). "In" and "in-" call out to one another and trade places, suggesting that surfaces may offer services that lead not toward decision but toward not-decision—and these are not exactly the same place. On either hand, Stein's sentence leads us toward ambiguity, keeps us thinking, guessing, adding, and noting a network of complexity.

In the phrases that follow "a creature," Stein's discussion of knowledge—how we use language to think, and to avoid thinking—seems more direct than usual: "and a creature and a question and a syllable in answer and more counting and no quarrel and a single scientific statement and not darkness and no question." A question, like a living thing, can grow into a variety of answers and even more questions. But "a syllable in answer" responds to "a question" with a yes or a no, clipping off further potential discussion or discovery.[13]

"More counting" contrasts with this clipping off; counting can go on and on (and "more" is one of the words used most in *Tender Buttons*). "Count" is also from a root from which grew two different French words: *compter* (to count) and *conter* (to narrate), which may connect adding numbers with adding more words, or just more meanings. The bullying exclusivity of "a single scientific statement" may allow for "no quarrel" and "no question" and admit of "no darkness"—but may indeed be a means toward obscuring truth, or at least obstructing *more* ideas or information.

"A question" becomes "no question" by the end of Stein's list, but probably more would be gained if that question developed into many questions.

In "an earned administration," words tend to have an "urned" servitude to meaning, and an urn is a much more oppressive type of carafe—opaque from within because of the blindness of the dead. In "an earned administration," words are dead, cremated, and locked in stasis. They become mere gofers in a bureaucracy. The etymological roots of both "earned" and "administration" mean "to serve," the first in Old English and the second in Italian. But if we try to free them from that servitude and look at their glorious pasts, their family relationships, and even their quirky associations in our own minds—their fringe—we see that "earned" is also related to harvesting, and the *ministrare* in "administration" is also in "minestrone." Stein—her mind never far from her belly—seems to offer a cornucopia of vegetative words to chew on. Instead of being served as the rich and varied fresh vegetables they could be, words have been overprocessed and made less nutritious. They have come to serve a bureaucracy instead of the individual speaker. Elsewhere, Stein writes: "A language tires. / A language tries to be. / A language tries to be free" (*Last Operas*, 153).

The words in the next phrase demonstrate the potential energy of words. They are given lives of their own—as we have lives of our own, entangled with others' lives—and not subordinated to our simplest needs. The rhymed couplet, as well as the perfect iambic tetrameter, marks "a single set of sisters and an outline and no blisters" as a "single set" itself, but it hardly wants to be crammed into my schemes for meaning. Maybe a protofeminist insight couched in feminine rhyme, "a single set of sisters" may be a strong enough group to escape the proposed "outline" of acceptable words or thoughts. Perhaps they color out of the lines or speak off their scripts and as a result are healthier and happier—not so tightly confined that they get blisters in the iambic march of feet. "A single set of sisters" may be both strongly united and multiply diverse.

Stein offers a critique of our (usually necessary) habits of thought, making us aware of our dependence on these habits by making it useless for us to lean on them blindly. Thus far, Stein's long sentence concerns itself with the predictability of everyday rhetoric, which allows people to get away with not thinking. Her lack of punctuation, and the fact that she takes words out of their common contexts (syntactically as well as semantically), means that a resourceful reader notices much more semantic ambiguity, a wider penumbra, than usual. The visual and auditory associations that Stein imbeds in her word streams provide another fringe of association. In addition to the multiple connotations and the sight and sound reminders, other associations work through the proximity of experience: Stein's words are in an order that allows one word to prime another for one denotation, and yet another nearby word primes us for another denotation (or detonation). On top of this, the pairing of two or more words in close proximity eventually allows one of those words to call up the other, such that Stein programs our associations and then calls up that programming—and hacks it before it becomes a routine—as we move through her work. Association is further complicated by the fact that if two things are associated, the words and things associated with them will also be associated with each other (James, *Principles*, 252). Stein makes us notice this fringe, and the fringe's fringe . . . and then we notice that it's all fringe. Accretive complexity forces us to recognize the arbitrary character of the single, simple meanings we may derive. Instead of just privileging the previously marginal, Stein makes us doubt the central itself, and the principle of centrality. By making it all fringe, Stein highlights a concern about our ignoring some things and taking others into account, especially when we do so unthinkingly. The actively engaged reader is not only made conscious of reading and thinking processes but also must make conscious decisions (or remain purposefully undecided) while reading. Words have potential energy, a potential individuality given additional meaning by their community (and vice versa), a potential complicating equivocation, and they offer resistance even when they are "used"—if the reader notices.

The rest of the sentence seems to be a conversation between two not completely opposing positions. Instead of emphasizing a binary distinction between "section[s]" and "centre[s]," or "questions" and certainties ("no doubts"), Stein's two sides waver between (a synonym for and etymological relative of "doubt"), and wave toward, each other. A resistance to binarisms also shows itself in the way Stein builds similarity between the usually very different meanings of "surface" and "centre." While the "surface" and the "centre" of a three-dimensional object are very different places, Stein's "surface" and "centre" refer to approximately the same concept. The "centre" is the mean value, an average that does not correspond to any of the real values it is supposed to represent, and the "surface" is a superficial summary that skips the details. The "single surface centred" puts a single but inaccurate representation in a primary position so that it looks conclusive and stops all further investigation, but it only pretends to represent the truth about something.

Following out some looser speculations, if we personify "section" ("And the section seeing yellow"), then "section" seems envious, perhaps of the "centre" about to be mentioned (yellow is also near the center of the continuous spectrum). "The section seeing yellow" sounds like "the sex (or sects) un-seeing, yell, 'Oh.'" This homophonical allusion to "sex" recalls the female "sisters," connecting that sex with sects or schismatic religious groups. Since rhetorical convention has already been established (always tentatively) as a religion, then this sect may have broken away—or may be trying to break away—from common rhetorical conventions. Perhaps this sect values speech over writing (because it is unseeing? or even unseen?) and speaks out (with a seemingly inarticulate "Oh!") instead. Perhaps the sects *shun* seeing, making the choice to hear and speak more deliberate.

In opposition to this set, this envious section, this yelling sex, is "the centre having spelling." The "centre" is written, spelt out instead of alluded to through sound play, which suggests the orthodoxy of orthography. If spelling had not been standardized, more potential meanings would always be present. This "centre" is also the generality that overcomes the importance of outlying sections (thus the jealousy or "seeing yellow"). It is the norm to which "sects" are (or a sex is) contrasted and away from which they break. "The centre" is also described by "and no solitude and no quaintness and yet solid quite so solid and the single surface centred and the question in the placard." "The centre" is not secluded (it has "no solitude"), and it is not agreeably peculiar (it has "no quaintness"). These descriptions sound like criticism of the center. But the reassuring voice seems to come back: "and yet solid, quite, so solid!" (my punctuation). The center has substance; it is forceful and hearty, sound and reliable, tangible and unanimous. On the other hand, "no solitude," since it holds a sound that approximates "no solid," works to undermine this reassurance. How solid can the center be if it is just the midpoint between everything else? It may be an average, but it has no singular substance of its own, just as there never has been an American family with 2.5 children.

The description of the "centre," which continues in "the single surface centred," is reminiscent of the reliable and serviceable surface earlier in the sentence, one that allowed us to understand quickly, without paying careful attention or taking time for much thought. If surfaces are cursory readings and centers are generalizations inferred from that type of reading, then the two words which seem to mean points on a sphere that are radially (half-diametrically) opposed become surprisingly alike. The promising, positive space Stein envisions is somewhere between the surface and the center.

Stein's reform of English is also a reform of science, since both depend on our mental tendencies to simplify, generalize, categorize—to delimit fields of inquiry and look for the core of any issue. Stein criticizes what science sometimes becomes, how thought is prone to becoming less thoughtful and more automatic. "The question in the placard" may refer to the political slogans of the time, which may question but which always do so from a stance of self-certainty. "The question in the placard" might be a nineteenth-century version (if there were one) of questions posted near exhibitions at museums or zoos: "How does the kangaroo rat feed its young?" One lifts up a flap, and the answer is immediately available underneath. There is always an answer. In one of his early lectures, Harvey Sacks explains that questions "arise out of something you're trying to deal with" instead of beginning as the type of things students see on exams. As I now blame the ill health of education on "teaching to the test," Sacks believes "it was the death of academic psychology that it grew up in a university. That implies that they did experiments for which it could be seen from the start how the result of those experiments would look as answers to quiz questions" (29). Along the same lines, a question in a placard already knows what the center of the issue is, while (what I will call) a living question has not yet discovered its center (nor, probably, has it discovered the surfaces that distinguish it from other questions or fields of inquiry). We might be better thinkers if we expected a question to lead to "more counting" and more questions instead of "a syllable in answer" or "a single scientific statement." Neil Postman reminds us that, in U.S. schools, science is taught with as much unexplained authority and required memorization as every other topic—a very unscientific way of teaching science (*Technopoly*, 192–93). While Sacks situates the blame in the words "academic" and "university," Stein uses the word "science" to highlight the failings of people who take (or ask others to take) scientific conclusions (or anything else) on faith. One can easily slip from valid scientific method to an antithetical authoritative position.

If all the words from "the section" to "the placard" are voiced by one speaker, that speaker is one who can doubt the value of a center but also reassure herself of its overall importance. It is also possible to break this passage down into a dialogue between speaker A and speaker B. Note that the bracketed commas are intended to be read two ways—as being there, and as not being there—and that this difference changes the meaning quite a bit.

A: and the section seeing yellow and the centre . . .
B: . . . having spelling and no solitude and no quaintness . . .
A: And yet solid, quite, so solid, and the single surface centred and the question in the placard.
B: And the singularity?
A: Is there a singularity?

B: And the singularity?
A: Why[,] is there a question?
B: And the singularity?
A: Why[,] is the surface outrageous?
B: Why[,] is it beautiful?
A: Why[,] is it not when there is no doubt?
B: Why is anything vacant?
A: Why is not disturbing a centre no virtue? Why is it, when it is? And, why is it, when it is? And . . .
B: There is no doubt, there is no doubt that the singularity shows! (73; my punctuation)

Converting this monologue into dialogue may certainly seem arbitrary, but I suspect Stein wants to blur the exaggerated boundary between those modes of speech. Speaker A prefers the solidity of the center to the jealousy of the section, while B points to the drawbacks at the center, particularly the way an emphasis on the middle cannot take singularity, individuality, or specificity into account. The singularity may be a section of, or even an exception to, the centered surface of a thesis or generalization. Speaker A's response to B's question "And the singularity?" (i.e., How does your generality account for that?) is either "Why is there a question?" or the more breathless "Why[,] is there a question?" In other words, how can there be any question about the importance or validity of this center or, even, *is* there any question about its validity. But Speaker B is insistent and asks again, and again. Speaker A's response may be to change the direction of the conversation and go on the attack by asking why B thinks this surfacey center is so terrible ("Why is the surface outrageous?"). But the repeated question may finally throw A into doubt: "Why[,] *is* the surface outrageous?" or "Is this surfacey center really a gross offense that I just hadn't noticed before?" B's response, "Why[,] is it beautiful?" can be understood as similarly ambiguous: either B asks why A thinks a center is so beautiful, or B might be consenting to look at the issue from A's perspective and ask herself, "*Is* it beautiful?" A reader can continue to explore the differences between reading "why" as the beginning of a question and reading "why" as an interjection. "Why" as a question assumes the condition; "why" as an interjection doubts the condition. Stein's phrases, read in these different ways, express the ambiguity of each speaker's point of view rather than emphasizing the polarity of their positions.

This is madness—but I hope it shows the method by which Stein's carafe (like Keats's urn) "teases us out of thought." When B asks, "Why is anything vacant?" she may wonder why some things go unused, why some words are ignored because they are assumed to be empty of significance. Stein encourages paying attention to everything possible. While James would not advocate this kind of unfocused attention (see Ruddick, "William James," 52, 56), he *does* complain of the tendency of some scientists to consider certain data irrelevant (and so not to consider them at all) when developing a theory. In "The Hidden Self," James laments that the "ideal of every science" is "a closed and completed system of truth," because this leads scientists to ignore "phenomena unclassifiable within the system" and to consider them "paradoxical absurdities" which "must be held untrue" (90). James condemns "the extreme slowness with which the ordinary academic and critical mind acknowledges facts to exist which present themselves as *wild* facts with no stall or pigeon-hole" (91; his italics). While James refers to pigeonholes in scientific theory—his example is that there is no room for spiritual healing in contemporary ideas about psychotherapy—Stein carries this one step further: if we accept ready-made words and phrases, we may never develop the words to hold new ideas that might compose a more successful system. Ong writes that "perception of objects is in part conditioned by the store of words into which perceptions are nested. Nature states no 'facts': these come only within statements devised by human beings to refer to the seamless web of actuality around them" (68). Stein is working with an old language, but she thinks that new forms might allow new thoughts, or at least new relationships between old ones.

In the last part of the exchange, A asks, "Why is not disturbing a centre no virtue?" Here, A still wonders why disordering things isn't bad and seems to begin to convince himself (again?) that it *is* bad. At the end, B, the speaker more resistant to the center, uses the language of certainty that belongs, not rightfully but at least characteristically, to A. "There is no doubt," says the doubter, "there is no doubt that the singularity shows." Like Stein, B is a bully on behalf of open-mindedness—B's problem, like that of Rorty's "ironist theorist," is "how to overcome authority without claiming authority" (Rorty, *Contingency*, 105).[14] And thus B asserts that details, exceptions, will be seen, no matter how much resurfacing, synthesis, summary, or gathering into a center is done. Stein makes us notice, but after reading her we notice for ourselves, these unsilenced singularities (and perhaps we become one of them).

Here, then, conversation occurs between two strains of thought that are not direct opposites. Since they seem somewhat sympathetic to each other, the voices are willing to listen to one another and to collaborate on an idea. Stein does not just capture and summarize two polar positions.

The collaborative presentation of thought corresponds to the analytic way of thinking that Ong describes as occurring in primarily oral cultures, where people learn through listening, repeating, recombining, and "participating in a kind of corporate retrospection" (9). Stein writes with all of these methods. She highlights our binary process of thought, adding enough qualifiers and resistance to be thought-provoking and puzzling to our orderly thought processes, but she does not suggest that there is any radically other place from which to start thinking. These two voices, as suggested here and represented more clearly in her later work, are as close as Stein gets to an alternative: opposites who do not hold too strongly to their positions, who listen, who speak openly and try to work toward an idea together instead of trying to win. As Stein says later, "the winner loses," and as Deborah Tannen points out, an "argument culture" shouldn't be our ideal: "When a problem is posed in a way that polarizes, the solution is often obscured before the search is under way" (*Argument*, 21).[15] Or as Rorty advocates, redescription and communication should replace argument as a form of conversion (*Philosophy*, 62–64).

Where do I see the "centre" of the sentiment of Stein's intricate sentence? She seems to warn that people use language not originally but terminally, making it work in bureaucratic service. We therefore don't think originally but tend to believe what we are told and ignore the details we know. Centers have their uses and are beautiful in their ways, but no word or observation is vacant. Context and association are of great importance, but each word (or idea or person) is important enough to warrant scrutiny within that context. And finally, meaning can develop in the spaces between words or voices.

Our habits have led us to the state of affairs in which Stein finds us. They take us down the easy paths of preconceptions, prevent us from noticing the new or different, and keep us from using our minds' potential for complexity. James describes a condition of "*psychic* blindness" with which one can physically see, but one cannot quite notice, or assign meaning, to what is seen (*Principles*, 52; his italics). Stein points out her readers' psychic blindness as she simultaneously offers a reading experience that acts as a therapeutic cure. In the interest of undermining our habits, Stein produces a literature that makes her readers notice their psychic blindness—but they blame her for it, accuse her of making *no* sense when she will not make the *usual* sense. Our habits have become so ingrained, our main neural pathways so nearly mechanized by "normal" language, that we find ourselves (I hope only at first) at a loss when reading Stein. But then we notice that any word has a fringe or suffusion of associations, and that we can choose among them instead of depending on habit to get us to meaning. According to James, we become more conscious: "New conceptions come from new sensations, new movements, new emotions, new associations, new acts of attention, and new comparisons of old conceptions, and not in other ways" (442). Consciousness is a goal in itself, and probably one of Stein's early ones, but later she seems to worry that this mental or psychic blindness might keep us from seeing and knowing new things. As she says, the world stays largely the same, but our composition of it—the ways we see it—changes. If these ways of seeing become too rigid and unchanging, we cannot progress. We can only repress.

CHAPTER 3

Conversational Relations in
Geography and Plays

Recognizing the Real in a Collage of Words and Phrases

RAGMATISM MAY HAVE provoked Stein's interest in the content of the supposedly empty in-between, not the borderland so much as the fenestra or fontanel—something related to hearing or mind, apparently closed off, but still open for the entrance of meaning. David Kadlec points out that William James advocated in *The Principles of Psychology* that "empiricists should account for not only terms but also the relations . . . [and] that grammar itself had served to empty experience of the conjunctions that marked the points of transition between the 'larger objects of our thought.'" In other words, the rules of grammar allowed "particle words, or syntactic markers," power *only* within a sentence. These small words can make "hierarchies of the clauses within sentences, [and form] pyramids of meaning and value out of the phrases and words held therein," but they have been emptied of meaning in relation to the outside world. James, however, "appealed to the expressive value of syntactic markers, or connecting words," writing that we have "a feeling of *and*, a feeling of *if*, a feeling of *but*, and a feeling of *by*" (Kadlec, 30).[1] Kadlec goes on to show the way Stein's *Tender Buttons* is "an anti-imperialist's assault on the distinction between expressive and functional parts of speech" (30–31), and he also suggests that Stein's "aesthetics" is founded in her "understandings of the conceptual affinities between cubism (and also the collage arts that eventually sprang from Picasso's and Braque's cubist portraits) and pragmatism and Darwin's writings" (252n55). In sympathy with this reading, I believe that Stein started seeing the meaning in the spaces between one speaker's phrases and another's. She heard the interpersonal meanings, as well as the logistical ones, between subsequent phrases, such as these from *Mexico* (*Geography and Plays*, 321):

A great many people were blamed.
A great many people were blamed.
Robert Nestor. I have heard of him.
Of course you have.
Be careful.
Be very careful.
There is no danger.
There is no danger.
Not to me.
Not for me.

Or these from *Counting Her Dresses* (*Geography and Plays*, 279):

 Act I
Can you spell quickly.
 Act II
I can spell very quickly.
 Act III
So can my sister-in-law.
 Act IV.
Can she.

Readers of *Mexico* are induced to wonder what Robert Nestor has to do with people getting blamed, if the speaker is to be careful because of some kind of censorship or threat, if repetition means agreement or mockery (or something else), and if "to" is so different from "for." Readers of *Counting Her Dresses* might ponder the relationship between the speakers, when the second seems naively to brag about her spelling skills and then may be somewhat arch about the first speaker's sister-in-law's similar ability. In neither case, however, and in spite of the simple—even common—words and phrases, do we know exactly what's happening.

Stein's plays represent people's verbal actions, their conversation, and she calls attention to the organic structures of human interaction by giving us nothing else which would distract us, such as the basic elements of plot and character. Taken out of their restrictive contexts, the utterances with which Stein fills her plays are freely valenced. While in a real conversation they would be tied down, here in Stein's texts they float free. The reader's mind is forced to associate, to guess, to hazard, and to hesitate, all the time noticing the many ambiguities of common statements. Stein includes phrases we've constantly met, but to which we rarely give even a full second's thought.

This more intimate meeting encourages us to realize just how complicated we all are, and just how much we let context and expectation (and other norms) limit our ideas and influence our behavior. Collage takes pieces of the world and cuts, shapes, and recontextualizes them for greater analysis—a new view, a longer look, a serious critique, a surprise, a laugh—and that is what Stein does in her plays with pieces of conversation.

For my purposes—and, I think, generally—conversation is the back-and-forth exchange of utterances, usually by different people taking turns talking and listening (but including the interaction of differently motivated voices within a single person). These utterances are not just words and sentences, and they are not just messy imitations of written structures; utterances are actions. Expressed another way, conversation is an activity, not just a word game. Conversation enables the exchange of information, ideas, and feelings through interactive performances, which involves the exchange of words in inflected utterances, body language, and the minutely contextual interpretation of those specific utterances. This transaction between (or among) psychological entities is refereed by rules that offer boundaries to steer through peaceably or with which to collide conspicuously. In other words, conversation can be the soul's expression, but that intimacy is almost always regulated by rules; even when expressing our deepest feelings, we are usually still locked inside the strict but almost unnoticeable confines of conversational rules. These rules, as well as inflectional choices and some improvisational problem solving along the way, enable us to send and receive messages, because we not only interpret what others say to us; we also evaluate their words in relation to what they could have or should have said.[2]

Stein seems to see her art as more real than the real, to believe that her plays—such as the first one, *What Happened*—can show *what really happens*. Daniel-Henry Kahnweiler describes Stein's work as cubist, since she and the cubists worked with "the most stripped forms" and the "commonplace" in their "reaction against affectation." He suggests that "it is important to understand that in Gertrude's work as in that of the Cubists we are dealing, in spite of appearances, with a realistic art, an art full of naturalness, of simplicity" (xii–xiii). In spite of what his biographer argues, Picasso and Stein probably both "rejected abstractionism and liked to think that [their] work was if anything more, certainly not less, real than the real thing" (Richardson, 406). When Stein arrived in New York after thirty-one years abroad, she told reporters, "I am essentially a realist" ("Fancy Writing"). Perhaps, then, Stein's writing is alien to us only because our sense of reality has become so conventionalized.

Gertrude Stein and Alice B. Toklas probably left more than one calling card at Picasso's door, and in his 1914 collage *Still Life with Calling Card*, Picasso included one of these visiting cards from "Miss Stein" and "Miss Toklas." In turn, Picasso left this artwork as a *carte de visite* at 27 rue de Fleurus.[3] Picasso's *Calling Card*, however, is an apt symbol for the ways Stein's work does and does not correspond to the cubist enterprise. Many of the pieces Stein situates in her writing seem to have been plucked from conversations that would have occurred during the polite visits for which these calling cards were substitutes. While both Stein and Picasso produced collages, language and objects are quite different things. This very fact has been cited to Stein's detriment: an early review of *Tender Buttons* compares Stein's writing to Picasso's "compositions produced by combinations of actual materials . . . nailed and glued together to form patterns" but asserts that Stein's attempts in this vein must fail, since words are "in themselves symbols" (R. Rogers, 19–20). In short, Stein's project seems to fail because one can't exactly do cubism with words. Stein, however, is not treating words as objects. Instead she works with pieces of conversation, phrases such as "how do you do," and she offers a creative analysis of the mysterious ways conversations can work. One can make collages of words and phrases, as well as of objects, and the found objects in Stein's plays are pieces of conversation.

While conversation in Stein's writing has been noted early and often (sometimes as an indication of Stein's laziness as a stylist), it has not been meaningfully explored. In 1923, Edith Sitwell reviewed *Geography and Plays* and wrote that the book had "an irritating ceaseless rattle like that of American sightseers talking in a boarding-house (this being, I imagine, a deliberate effect)" (26). Sitwell and others have not sufficiently wondered why Stein would deliberately produce this effect. Edmund Wilson describes "Have they Attacked Mary He Giggled," published in *Vanity Fair* in June 1917, as "a sort of splintered stenographic commentary made up of scraps of conversation as they reverberate in the mind and awaken unspoken responses" (61). Wilson and others did not audibly wonder why these responses are so automatically "awakened" in us—why certain bits of language lead automatically to certain other bits. Interactional spoken language, in particular, is predictable because of its informal but stubborn rules. If it weren't, listeners would not be so quick to know what someone should have said. James R. Mellow asserts that Stein and the poet Guillaume Apollinaire each "had a highly developed aural sense of language." They both "creat[ed] poems—collage-like—out of snippets of conversation overheard in a bistro on the rue Christine," and, in many of their poems, "the structure of the lines was carried by repetitions, percussive phrases, natural pauses, the sense of sound" (124). Alison Rieke observes that Stein's

> writing [has] the appearance of being more assembled than written, and assembled out of close deliberation over particular words. . . .
>   Stein was always an arranger of words, concerned about their junctures, the stoppings and startings of phrases, the role of the artist in piecing these pieces to give them places. (63)

But why does she do this?

Stein's writing expresses the deep structures of conversation, the processes and motivations and emotions behind it. The trivial statements of which conversation is so often formed appear in her work, but with a different purpose than they do in Ionesco's later plays, which seem to emphasize the trivialities and to critique the empty clichés that fill human minds in the middle of the twentieth century. Instead of bringing cynicism to her tea table, Stein sought out the powerful purposes and organizing principles hidden within the give-and-take of polite stock phrases. And to continue her task of making her readers attend to the associational relationships among individual words we've always taken for granted—making us know *about* instead of just know *of* those words, to use William James's distinction— Stein highlights the complex thoughts expressed within, and the complex relationships developed by, simple conversational phrases. Stein's collages of spoken phrases create an educational game for her readers that teaches us about the way we talk, the way we speak effortlessly every day.

Discussing Stein's plays in relation to conventional theater, Jane Palatini Bowers asserts that the dialogue in Stein's drama expresses well the differences between real dialogue and what we think of as real dialogue because we are used to hearing it on the stage. (Similarly, Pynchon's Mucho Maas introduces Oedipa Maas as Edna Mosh because of "the distortion on these [radio station] rigs, and then when they put it on tape" [114]). In her wonderful introduction to Stein's work, Bowers reminds us that

> plays are not natural but fictive utterances. Dramatic dialogue is . . . not a natural phenomenon but an artificial one. However, the pretense of naturalness is at the heart of dramatic mimesis; Stein's conversation plays at once engage in and expose this pretense. They sound much like real conversations and not at all like conventional dramatic dialogue, thereby revealing the ways in which dramatic dialogue is not like ordinary discourse. (111–12)

Bowers, though, does not end up arguing that Stein's "conversation plays" mimic real conversation better than does conventional drama. Bowers decides that the words in Stein's plays "are not windows onto a non-linguistic world. They are themselves the world—a world of conversations without stories" (112)—and this is not how we usually talk.[4] Bowers reasonably concludes from this analysis that Stein's plays are "closed systems of discourse" (115), that they "subvert the conventional form of dramatic dialogue," and that "when conversation is about language and language-making activities, language becomes an object of interest in its own right and is, itself, the object of discourse" (117). By representing "conversations without stories," Stein creates an alternative realism, but I think it is not so much an alternative purely linguistic reality as much as a written form that exposes unperceived aspects of real chat.

Stein is multiply oral. She demonstrates a particular interest in the complex patterns found in friendly conversation over food: the motivating forces behind the things people say in those settings, the ways our utterances can mean more than what we meant (and how we might creatively build on this knowledge), and the ways politeness can contain and yet express conflict. Along the way, Stein discovers long-overlooked structures of spoken language, which conversation analysis began to theorize several decades after Stein's death. At the end of this chapter, my reading of "Susie Asado" links this well-known piece from *Geography and Plays* with the functions of conversation as a means toward apparent cooperation—as a way of seeing eye-to-eye or dancing to the same drummer, to return to the issues of sight and sound—if not substantial agreement.

Food and Talk

Although I respect and tend to concur with Bowers's analysis of *Can You See the Name*, I think it is worth noting that this short play—which Bowers calls "typical in all other ways of the longer conversation plays" (113)—diverges from the typical early Stein play in at least one way: there is no mention of food (or dishes or a table) in it.[5] Of the sixteen brief plays published in *Geography and Plays*, only one of them, *I Like It to Be a Play*, does not contain any of the ingredients for a social gathering founded on food and talk (although it does contain the line "The rest of the day was spent in visiting" [288]). Stein's plays contain a "desert spoon," "turkey," "cut[s]," and "slice[s]" (*What Happened*); "meats," "mints," "candles," a "table," and "cloth" (*Not Sightly*); "cauliflower and green peas" (*Please Do Not Suffer*); and "table . . . linen," "excellent eating," and "coffee" (*Mexico*)—to list just a few examples. In *He Said It*, "sugared prunes" and "pressed figs" lead toward a "fruitful evening." Two of her titles refer to food: *White Wines* and *Turkey Bones and Eating and We Liked It*. (And remember: the central section of *Tender Buttons* is called "Food" and is stuffed with savory dishes.) Sometimes, Stein writes formally complete sentences to describe food: "This is the last time we will use seasoning" (*For the Country Entirely*, 237), and "We eat our breakfast and smoke a cigar" (*Bonne Annee*).[6] If these plays are partly representative of real or at least realistic conversation, Toklas must be reporting accurately when she writes: "Conversation even in a literary or political *salon* can turn to the subject of menus, food or wine" (*Cookbook*, 3).[7]

Stein's words reassemble (and encourage readers to revise their thinking about) one of life's most common recreations: the chat. Without any stage directions, Stein's plays manage to suggest noisy settings, such as afternoon tea on the veranda with a polite group of visitors (as in "Susie Asado") or sitting at a cafe (at the end of *Do Let Us Go Away*). Although in *Do Let Us Go Away* (215), Stein writes (or has Theodore say), "My principle [*sic?*] idea is to eat my meals in peace," Stein's meals—and snacks—seem to be accompanied by talk. Bowers finds that these plays "suggest that there is no non-linguistic world, that the only 'event' taking place in the world of the play is speech" (110), but it seems to me that somewhere nearby people are eating.

I suspect that Stein is interested in interactional conversation. The basic difference between transactional and interactional conversation is that the first is for business and the second for pleasure. Transactional conversations take place between people of fixed status working to accomplish a goal within the framework of their institutionally established roles. People participating in a transactional conversation must obediently and consistently perform their fixed roles throughout the conversation. The latitude in an interactional conversation is much greater, because the relationship is personally instead of institutionally defined. The goal of the interaction is itself to define the relationship, which means there is much more experimentation with levels of intimacy and ratios of power (see Cheepen, 118–21).

Not completely unlike literature, interactional conversations occur in nonfocused situations. Before the wide use of technological means to "reach out and touch someone," extensive interactional conversation would have taken place most often over food. Interactional conversation is the kind late nineteenth-century sociologist Gabriel Tarde describes: "By conversation I mean any dialogue without direct and immediate utility, in which one talks primarily to talk, for pleasure, as a game, out of politeness" ("Opinion," 308). Bronislaw Malinowski—whose term for this kind of conversation, "phatic communion," has taken on such different connotations that it is useless here—described interactional conversation as "'the language used in free, aimless social intercourse' which occurs when people are relaxing, or when they are accompanying 'some mere manual work by gossip quite unconnected with what they are doing'" (qtd. in Cheepen, 16).[8] While transactional conversations occur in focused situations "in which 'there are strong limitations on negotiations between participants,'" interactional conversations occur in nonfocused situations in which "'the highest value is on mutual sense making among the participants'" (Tannen, "Oral/Literate," 3).[9]

Stein probably hated transactional conversations. She did not easily assume a predetermined status or role. At Johns Hopkins, Stein disapproved of the condescending teaching styles and sexism of two medical school professors, communicated her dissatisfaction to them, was told to attend their classes or withdraw from them, and withdrew (Wagner-Martin, 48–49). Her break with her brother Leo seems to have been the result of his increasingly persistent assumption of his own superior status as a speaker (and her implied inferior status as a silently agreeing listener).[10] Even more to the point, when Stein drove a medical supply car during World War I, "she was officially the driver" and Toklas "was officially the delegate," because Stein "flatly refused to go inside of any office and interview any official" (*Autobiography*, 177). Furthermore, "Mademoiselle Stein has no patience she will not go into offices and wait and interview people and explain," and "Gertrude Stein hates to answer questions from officials" (178, 233). In her cookbook, Alice later commented that "Gertrude Stein did not like going into offices—she said they, army or civilian, were obnoxious" (60). As a grown woman, Stein did not let age or gender tell her how to behave and thought of herself as both a baby and a husband.[11] And during World War II, she did not let her nationality, her ethnicity, or her sexuality determine her behavior: instead of fleeing to the United States to get away from likely persecution as a Jew and a lesbian, she remained, staunch but vulnerable, in rural Vichy France.[12]

But Stein did love to talk and listen, and interactional conversation seems to have been her chosen forum. She seems to have been well appreciated by friends throughout her life, friends who liked to sit and sew and talk, who liked to wander the roads around Harvard at night and talk, who liked to ride on streetcars and talk, who liked to eat and talk (Wagner-Martin, 31, 46, 106). Reportedly, she enjoyed conversation more than needlework, she usually wasn't headed any particular place when she walked, and she liked to strike up conversations with strangers. From behind the wheel of her car, which she called Auntie Pauline, Stein started conversations with pedestrians throughout Paris (Wagner-Martin, 148). Toklas reports that one of their cooks' stipulations was access to their reading library and conversation with Stein—a request Toklas attributes to the woman's immediately noticing "Gertrude Stein's easy democratic approachableness" (*Cookbook*, 194). According to Wagner-Martin: "For those who found warmth in the rue de Fleurus afternoons, admiring Stein's ability to lead and respond to conversation, any description of those interchanges pales beside memories of immense energy, golden language, and unfeigned sympathy" (161).

Talk is the common thread (as indeed it wanders through each of our lives), but not everyone has written, as Stein did: "Generally speaking anybody is more interesting doing nothing than doing something" (*Everybody's*, 109). Stein did not approve of people bustling around just trying to fill time, but "generally speaking" may also be understood as "generally *when* speaking."[13] Perhaps people are more interesting when they are just chatting ("doing nothing") than when they are trying to accomplish some important transfer of information ("doing something"). In a lecture, Stein said: "There was more sense of movement to us in Paris when a few doughboys loafed about the streets. They impressed the French as something vital, active; you felt the essence of what was happening. But when they were doing anything, you forgot the essence" (Evans).[14] Conversations dictated by institutional roles and rules—"conversations as prearranged"—are less interesting to Stein than conversations that evolve naturally and immediately while loafing—"conversations as arranged" (Stein, *Novel of Thank You*, 10) As Stein's labels suggest, and as her writings demonstrate, even these spontaneous conversations have a kind of order.

The Motivations behind *What Happened*

In her lecture "Plays," Stein explains that *What Happened* was the first play she ever wrote. She describes the situation of its creation and her intentions:

> I had just come home from a pleasant dinner party and I realized then as anybody can know that something is always happening.
> Something is always happening, anybody knows a quantity of stories of people's lives that are always happening, there are always plenty for the newspapers and there are always plenty in private life. Everybody knows so many stories and what is the use of telling another story. What is the use of telling a story since there are so many and everybody knows so many and tells so many. In the country it is perfectly extraordinary

how many complicated dramas go on all the time. And everybody knows them, so why tell another one. There is always a story going on.

So naturally *what I wanted to do in my play was what everybody did not always know nor always tell*. By everybody I do of course include myself by always I do of course include myself.

And so I wrote, What Happened, A Play.

Then I wrote Ladies Voices and then I wrote a Curtain Raiser. I did this last because *I wanted still more to tell what could be told if one did not tell anything*. . . .

I came to think that since each one is that one and that there are a number of them each one being that one, the only way to express this thing each one being that one and there being a number of them knowing each other was in a play. And so I began to write these plays. And the idea in What Happened, A Play was to express this without telling what happened, in short to make a play *the essence of what happened*. I tried to do this with the first series of plays that I wrote. (*Lectures*, 118–20; my italics)

Stein came home from a dinner party—a social gathering over food—and was struck by the fact that all during dinner everyone was able to talk about all sorts of things that had happened. Never one to attempt what she knows has already been done, or even what she knows can be done—"if it can be done why do it" (*Lectures*, 157)—Stein decides not to tell the kind of stories that people know. Nevertheless, she still intends to tell "what happened," and perhaps at this dinner party she noticed that one of the things happening was that people were expressing themselves ("each one being that one") through the rhythms of their speech and creating relationships ("there being a number of them knowing each other") out of their utterances. One of the answers to her repeated question "what is the use of telling another story" might be that stories are the building blocks of social relationships. This self-presentation and casual confederation is something that happens all the time, and yet it goes largely unnoticed, probably because it seems so natural and effortless. In relation to her artistic project, at least, Stein is less interested in the stories people tell than in the deeper social and linguistic structures in which that storytelling takes place.[15]

When Stein says that she wants to "make a play the essence of what happened," she is not only talking about the deep structures of what happens within a conversation about something else, she is also emphasizing action. Although "essence" might suggest the inherent nature of something's being, "what happens" suggests activity. In French, *essence* means "fuel" or "gasoline," which may be significant in light of a metaphor Stein repeatedly employs: "As I say a motor goes inside and the car goes on, but my business my ultimate business as an artist was not with where the car goes as it goes but with the movement inside that is of the essence of its going" (*Lectures*, 194–95). I take "inside" to refer to the pistons and belts, but Stein's exploration of "the essence of what happened" looks even farther under the hood. It studies the fuel, the *essence*, which we never see move, but which is constantly undergoing a change (we *burn* gasoline, after all) and enables the car's motion. If the motor's movement is the wording that expresses relation and narrative, then the fuel may be the very structure of language and the motivations and mindsets of speakers. The best definition of the whole phrase, I think, is DeKoven's understanding that it means "an abstract rendering of an event," because "event" is a noun, but one that is not in stasis (*Different Language*, 85).

On the other hand, "essence" is derived from "to be," which—in spite of all my arguments otherwise—suggests that Stein wants to represent the existence, even the permanent nature, of something rather than its activity. Ryan (68) supports this possibility (although she actually believes something else about the phrase) when she says that "Gertrude Stein found that life was indeed a quality and not an action" and contrasts Stein's idea with Aristotle's assertion that "life consists in action." Kenneth Burke takes this same position: "The essence of a thing would not be revealed in something that it does. It would be something that a thing is" ("Impartial Essence," 187).

In spite of these opinions, I keep hearing "what happens" as action, which reflects back on "essence" and changes it into something more dynamic than an inherent truth about something. Ryan believes that Stein's plays "present the essence, and only the essence, of the moment" (69). I agree, in that I think that Stein's kind of essence—in contrast to the typical kind, of course—is fleeting, changing, in flux. Think of the way attitudes and goals tend to shift during the course of an informal conversation, especially with new acquaintances, of whom you are getting a new sense with each phrase they speak. You want to be congenial, you want to impress them, you want to agree with them, you are surprised by them, you want to know more about them, you are disappointed in them, you want to mollify them, you want to disagree with them, you want to convince them to change, you decide it's not worth it, you want to keep your mouth shut, you want to get out of there, and so on. In short, Stein seems to muddy another binary choice between "essences" and the "flux of continually changing relations" (Rorty's phrase in *Philosophy*, 47). She uses the first word to describe the other, since she seems to see the "flux of continually changing relations" as the very essence of what happens, and she represents this essential flux in her artistic investigation of conversation.

What Can Happen When People Talk and Read

What Happened, probably written in 1913, around the same time as *Tender Buttons*, is similar to *Tender Buttons* in style, but its subtitle is *A Five Act Play*. In her lectures, Stein asserts that an exciting scene (in a play and in real life) is one in which the characters with whom you have become acquainted (throughout the play or over a lifetime) say things that surprise you, things you would not have expected them to say. She writes: "Generally speaking it is the contradiction between the way you know the people you know including yourself act and the way they are acting or feeling or talking that makes of any scene that is an exciting scene an exciting scene" (*Lectures*, 106). Stein meets this requirement and doesn't. Her characters are strangers. It is not clear even whether each is a single person who has a number for a name or whether each "speaker" is a chorus of the designated number of people. The chorus seems likely, because in act 3, "Three" and "The same three" speak; act 4 is spoken by "Four and four more." Another possibility is that these numbers refer to how many people are on stage and taking turns speaking. But even though these characters are strangers about whom we know nothing, we discover that we hold some expectations for them, because we are likely to be very surprised when we read what they say.[16] In this way, Stein demonstrates that most of the expectations we have about what a person might say at any given time depend not only on insight we might have into the speaker's individual character but also on very generally understood contexts.

For example, "Act I" of *What Happened: A Play in Five Acts* begins:

(One.)
Loud and no cataract. Not any nuisance is depressing.
  (*Geography and Plays*, 205)

The reader probably does not expect anyone, let alone someone called One, to declare—perhaps self-reflexively?—"Loud and no cataract. Not any nuisance is depressing." Here, again, is a crossover between sound and sight: a "cataract" can be a loud waterfall or opaqueness in the eye. "Loud and no cataract" could mean that water is loud, but that it is not a large, single cataract of rushing water falling in one direction. Perhaps instead of cohering into singularity or agreement with others, One's opinion divides into different channels of meaning—interesting also because someone called One might be expected to have a single opinion or a unified sense of self.[17] The phrase might not only describe bodies of water as a metaphor for speech, knowledge, and group identity; it could also be a command to hear and see—to pay attention to these different senses—without the cataract of partial blindness or the blinding assumption that meaning flows together in a single, rushing stream. Stein herself seems to have avoided speaking in one voice; remembering their first meeting, Toklas recalled Stein's voice as "unlike anyone else's voice—deep, full, velvety like a great contralto's, like two voices" (Toklas, *What Is Remembered*, 23). Elsewhere in *Geography and Plays*, Stein writes: "Loud voices are attractive. When two people talk together they have to talk louder" (*Turkey Bones and Eating*, 246), and I read this as approximately synonymous with "loud and no cataract." Stein likes loud assertion but not a single unified channel of communication. In yet another play in the same volume, she announces: "There is no blindness where the talk is cheap" (*Scenes. Actions and Disposition of Relations and Positions*, 114). Turning something usually thought of as negative into something positive, Stein (in my favorite of her aphorisms) approves pure talk, talk without consequences and commitments, because it allows a freedom to dilate—to see more widely. Let me repeat: "There is no blindness where the talk is cheap."

At first, "not any nuisance is depressing" sounds wrong. We all know some nuisances can be depressing as well as annoying. But "not any new sense (or new scents) is depressing" sounds like further encouragement to hear and see (and even smell). We are being encouraged to use our senses to gain new meanings, or new senses. "Not any *new sense* is depressing" may mean that new senses are never depressing, but it also implies that just having and knowing old senses *is* depressing. Stein's differentiation between knowing and understanding, her valuation of knowing over understanding, and the link she saw between understanding and following mean that it makes sense to hear "knew sense" here also—that these new senses would lead us to knowledge. People who want us only to understand and follow, however, might esteem cataracts that can pull people along with them.[18]

The second "character" to speak is Five—which could be another silly name for a single speaker or may make a reader think of the five senses. Five might also include One, since four people could walk onto the stage after One's initial lines, and since the numbers "four," "five," and "one" all appear in Five's first spoken line. Five responds with paragraphs of new senses and dialogue about meaning:

(Five.)
A single sum four and five together and one, not any sun a clear signal and an exchange. (*What Happened*, in *Geography and Plays*, 205)

That this is a play, suggesting that One and Five are probably talking to each other, already somewhat limits the context of Five's statements. The "single sum" might refer to the single focused sense or meaning that we understand from most sentences, the cataract of which One spoke. We usually add four or five meanings (of words, or larger semantic units) together and get one meaning. Rather than a "sun" with rays shooting out in all directions—a word with many divergent implications, a sound prior to cognition—we pretend that we send and receive "a clear signal" and have a coherent "exchange." The limitations that we automatically put on our understanding bury potential meaning. This destruction of meaning is comparable (whether Stein would have known so or not) to burning books at Fahrenheit "four and five together and one." On the other hand, Stein's suggestion that we understand words in new ways both destroys and revitalizes the books themselves.

Stein's writing will not let us avoid the metaphysics of presence; she insists that we remember that the moment or the line of writing always contains more than we can say about it. Unlike a deconstructionist, Stein refuses to see multiple meanings as merely each other's cancellation. The likelihood that Stein is advocating a messy, compositely meaningful kind of reading and listening, and highlighting some of the tendencies and drawbacks to restricted interpretations of linear texts, can be further clarified by ideas from Alan Kennedy's *Psychology of Reading*. Kennedy asserts that visual and auditory perceptions are categorical, that we see something one way or the other but not both at the same time (34). Kennedy writes that "a large number of different patterns of stimulus information (the input) serve to evoke a single conceptual decision (the output)," and that it is in "instances where the perceptual decisions taken prove to be wrong . . . [that we] catch a glimpse of the system in action" (35, 40). In the process of normal reading, we channel dozens or hundreds or thousands of signs that point in multiple directions into a single cataract of meaning, according to Kennedy:

When we read a single word its many potential meanings become available as a conscious experience. But when we read a series of words we are scarcely aware of these individual elements at all. . . . For the fluent reader the particular words, and their particular order, that produce this train of thought can be rapidly dismissed. (86)

There is no doubt that Stein upsets our reading fluency. Kennedy continues: "Only that sense of a word that can be adapted to the train of thought in progress will survive" (89). In the case of *What Happened*, Stein states the context is "a play." By doing so, she creates a very broad context but one still not broad enough to hold the words she writes underneath that subtitle. This single clue to reading her words only makes it more difficult to contextualize what she writes. Stein thus lets the various meanings of her words "endure"; they "survive," and we have to "become conscious" of them as multiply meaningful entities instead of one-dimensional pointers to something else. This terminology does not apply just to the words; it applies to us. The multiplicity disallows uniform reactions in Stein's readers; we are prevented from becoming reading machines and are thus kept alive and conscious.

Stein's knowledge of neurology again proves relevant. In the same textbook that refers to her research on the "centripetal" or "sensory neurons" which bring information into the brain, Barker describes these neurons in the following way:

A single neurone of one system is often, by virtue of a number of end-ramifications, able to enter into conduction relations with a number of neurones in a neurone system of the next higher order . . . ; in other instances, on the contrary, the terminals of a large number of axones of one neurone system may be so arranged that they can influence only a smaller number of neurones of a neurone system of the next order. . . . In the one case there is a "multiplication of elements" in the direction of the conducting path, in the other a "reduction of elements." (*Nervous System*, 320)

Context usually deletes all but one of the possible signals a word can send to us. But Stein's words keep their many possible signals, mutiplying instead of reducing the "end-ramifications" of her words. Stein's writing shuffles the brain's mailing lists.

Looking at the letters, as well as at the words, hearing the whole string of words together—an amalgamation encouraged by the words "a single sum"—reveals the damage that results from our tendency to "use" and understand words in too limited a way. A fluent reader moves directly from the written word to its relevant meaning, but a less fluent reader goes from the written form to the sounds of the letters and then to meaning. Children sound out words when they read; many adults do not even hear the words in their mind's ear. By encouraging our sounding out of her words and phrases, Stein works to make us less fluent readers—and less likely to expect flowing cataracts of meaning.

Attending carefully to Five's words, then, one might also see and hear (hyperattentively): "A sin gal sum four and five to get her and won not any son a clear signal and an exchange." This sentence seems to describe some kind of rape or purchased sin: a prostitute or "sin gal" is bought, won, or otherwise gotten by "four and five together" and purposefully produces no son. Choosing to read allegorically (which can be another means toward numerous meanings), we may glean that the prostitution of language, its *use*, keeps it from living, or giving life to offspring meanings.[19] The goal of Stein's writing is not to use a set of words to mean conclusively one thing or the other; complexity arises in the reader's getting shunted away from one meaning after another, and—according to Booth—this grasping is what gives the most pleasure. But in most writing, words become just clear(-ish) signals which are exchanged like money.[20] Since "single" and "signal" are so much alike, it is natural to switch their places in the sentence, resulting in "a signal sum" and "a clear single," which both reiterate the power of a clear sum's signaling a single meaning. "An exchange" also sounds like "annex change"—perhaps encouraging us to exchange our single signals by adding (annexing) a change (leading to "some four and five" rather than "a single sum"). As easily as "single" and "signal" can be transposed, so can "some" and "sum." "Some four and five together" becomes "sum four and five together," which reminds us of the addition of pluralities (the expression "4 + 5") required for unity (the sum). A "single some" also combines unity with multiplicity. Stein's subtly repeated theme suggests that many are still many, even when they add up to something, a sum. Moving from letters and words to whole conversations, this theme suggests that many voices can combine into one community, and that the community may indeed be stronger if those voices are individual and multiple rather than repeating echoes of one voice.

Five goes on to argue for growing, thriving, multiplying words:

> Silence is in blessing and chasing and coincidences being ripe. A simple melancholy clearly precious and on the surface and surrounded and mixed strangely. A vegetable window and clearly most clearly an

exchange in parts and complete. (*What Happened*, in *Geography and Plays*, 205)

Stein's poem is a "vegetable window," which sounds like "veritable window" or "venerable window" and acts like both, allowing readers to watch words growing from their roots to their fruits. One reason Stein's words seem particularly vegetative is that her arrangements of words prime us for fringe meanings and associations; they sprout like potatoes, like neurons. These ripe words help us notice and appreciate the beauty of the whole plant, but Stein doesn't encourage us to pick them and eat them. We cannot glean only a single message from her text and then discard it or consider it digested. If a writer is tending a garden of words, a reader should be reaping instead of hunting.[21]

The tiger in the next paragraph of *What Happened* hunts very differently, although it would not be the first time that hunting and overaggressive courtship were linked. Stein cites this paragraph in her lecture "Plays" as an example of expressing "the essence of what happened" "without telling what happened" (*Lectures*, 119):

A tiger a rapt and surrounded overcoat securely arranged with spots old enough to be thought useful and witty quite witty in a secret and in a blinding flurry. (205)

This cutting collection of words is filled with sharpnesses—tigers, spotted leopards, raptors, and wit—and suggests an image of a sharp-witted person surrounded by listeners. Perhaps a quick, quiet, sharp woman in a fur coat is "surrounded" by a "rapt" audience. Perhaps men "sir round" her, and think of something akin to rape. Although men circle her, she has somehow "arranged" to range (among them? away from them?) safely. She is seen (showing herself off with her furs and her wit) in order not to be seen (in secret liaisons?); she wears a kind of showy camouflage. Perhaps she has age spots ("spots old") and a fur coat: she could be wrapped ("rapt") in the skin of a "tiger," or, more likely, she is the tiger or raptor wearing a (leopard?) spotted "overcoat." If she were an animal, her skins would camouflage her; since she is an old woman, her aging skin and quick wit protect her from certain kinds of suspicions. She is "securely arranged," and dangerous in a "secret" way.[22]

The lives of the words themselves are endangered, but they act as their own camouflage, threatening this surrounded person (with rape), as well as representing something about her (she's wrapped, and perhaps "ripe") and protecting her (by keeping her audience, or her possible attackers, "rapt"). Wit is the essence of her personal self, as well as the weapon and shield which protect that self. Stein suggests that a good wielder of words can purposefully create blinds with them. In this instance, the words are not just the vegetables or the hunted, but also the hunters. The power of words to protect themselves and the speakers who are conscious of those multiple meanings is in the camouflage afforded by double (or more multiple) meanings.

This tiger paragraph is unusual in its story of what happened, because it can be read in an almost standard way and seems to describe people in a particular configuration communicating in certain ways with one another and continuing their established relationships. While the narrative is entertaining, and a bit of a relief to come across when reading Stein's usually much more opaque paragraphs, its vividness may mislead us into stopping there. But if we go on looking at and listening, we see that Stein writes about words by analogy when she is writing about tiger women.[23]

This same paragraph links to previous ones through the repetition of the word "surrounded" and the reiteration, through synonyms, of a few concepts. "Rapt" seems to follow from "chasing"; "arranged" is related to "mixed strangely" and may have to do with "parts" and "complete"; "old enough" might be related to "ripe" old age; "blinding" is related to "cataracts"; and the other kind of "cataracts," in their watery, noisy sense, relates to "flurry." The blinding fury in "blinding flurry" is another emotion to go with "depressing" and "melancholy." Is Stein saying something about sight, emotion, patterns, surroundings, hurriedness, and attack? If I mix strangely these notions, then I arrive at the possibility that our hurriedness and focused sight makes us attack meaning and arrange it into certain limited patterns, and that this is depressing.

Expatiating on the rest of *What Happened* could take more pages than my readers can be expected to tolerate, but let me offer a few observations on the play as a whole. The repeated references to things that expand ("a cake is powder" [205], "a very wide cake" [206]) and grow ("a wide oak" [206]) and to other fruits and vegetables and flowers suggest the yeastiness, the organic growth, of words. Further growth is suggested by references to eggs and stigma. The "little sac that shines" could be an egg sac or a cocoon, but the black eye of "shines" might remind us of the violence done to growing things. The "exchanged box" and "the chance of swelling" are simultaneously sexual, pregnant, and violent. Three says, "a special sense a very special sense is ludicrous." "Ludicrous" may have come to mean absurd or ridiculous, but "ludic" means "playful." "Special" is related to "species"—a word often associated with plants and animals and a taxonomy that does not constrain individual variation. In these senses, then, Stein's "special" kind of writing is "ludicrous." Finally, if we are to treat words as living, growing things and not do violence to them by limiting them, it makes some sense when Four and four more say, "a birthday is a speech" (208). Each time we speak we are giving birth to living, flourishing words.

Conversation Patterning as the Essence of What Happens

That section of *What Happened* is quite different from many of Stein's plays, but her emphasis on the workings of interpersonal relations remains strong through all of them. As her first play, *What Happened* seems to explore quite poetically the more general topic of human relations—for example, this sexy old woman's vulnerabilities and simultaneous powers of manipulation—but soon Stein's plays consist of short utterances, the very building blocks of persona, the letters of the alphabet of relationship. The goals and findings of academics in the field of conversation analysis—discourse analysis "with a sociological turn," which takes a close look at "the organization of conversation" (de Beaugrande, 207)—parallel and illuminate Stein's exploration of this topic.

Harvey Sacks is usually credited as the developer of the methods and goals of conversation analysis. A sociologist, Sacks wanted to work with the most fundamental data possible; the best he could locate were tapes of telephone conversations on a suicide help-line. Instead of statistics and summaries already shaped and tainted by other people's assumptions (which are usually unknown to the next person who works with them), Sacks looked at the details of real human experience—albeit in this limited context, but that was necessary and helpful too, the way limited variables tend to be—and found patterns. Developing out of the data with which Sacks began, conversation analysis attends to the minute, the way small things add up to big ones. As one critic (and participant) puts it, conversation analysts regard "macro-level concepts such as social structure and culture . . . [as] abstractions," and they "argue that the causal effects of macrosocial forces are not analytically distinct, but can only be understood by analyzing participants' orientations toward them as revealed in the talk itself (Sawyer, 47, 49). Sacks also saw potential social change within language change. As David Silverman explains: "For Sacks, one way we could identify social change would be by noticing shifts in the properties of categories used in everyday language and in how these categories were actually applied" (17).

Like Sacks's pioneering work in conversation analysis, Stein's plays "simply focus on what people *do*" (Silverman, 48). And parallel to Stein's interest in the action-enabling *essence* and her metaphor of the car's movement, Sacks uses a mechanical metaphor to describe his project, for instance when "he describes interactions 'as being spewed out by machinery, the machinery being what we're trying to find; where, in order to find it we've got to get a whole bunch of its products'" (65–66).[24] Silverman points out that "Sacks is [also] consistently interested in how members *use* the machinery" (66).

Tape recordings of conversations allow conversation analysts to listen repeatedly to the same conversation and to note myriad details. Although tape recordings are their preferred subject of study, conversation analysts also transcribe overheard conversations, using special symbols and noting overlapping speech, pauses, and other sounds and nonsounds. Transcribed English conversations are hardly recognizable as real conversation, or even as English.

Writing is a "technology" that only approximates one's "natural" use of language, which is spoken aloud within a specific temporal position. Walter Ong argues that writing reduces "dynamic sound to quiescent space, [and separates] the word from the living present, where alone spoken words can exist" (82). Writers can represent word choice, word order, and even a hint of pronunciation through creative spelling, but even the most thorough and creative use of punctuation does not allow us fully to represent the pauses, emphases, and risings and fallings of our voices. The very fact that writing can travel physically through space and time decontextualizes (or recontextualizes) it. Nor does our writing represent the short incompletion, the lone cutoff word, the almost meaningless phrase. Even when we attempt to write in our (metaphorically-) speaking "voice" we tend to modify it for proper grammar and more appropriate word choice. The quiet, private moments in which we write let us make slow or late decisions and erasable revisions untraceable in time.

But Stein's plays do not look like transcription, nor does her other writing. She does not develop special symbols to suggest pauses or overlappings, and she primarily uses regularly spelled English words. She disdained neologisms—this was one of her declared reasons for disliking James Joyce's work—and never resorted to using any of the special symbols for phonetics, accents, or emphasis. A 1923 review of *Geography and Plays* reads:

> It would seem that Miss Stein's chief difficulty . . . is the lack of speech notation for written words, to correspond with the conventional and standardized signposts to the interpretation of written music. Perhaps

the day of the oral word artist is coming back in an idiom more closely attuned to our modern consciousness. Perhaps Gertrude Stein will be found, if not among the forefront of those new singers, at least in the ranks of the pioneers that made their song possible. (Crawford, 27)

Stein is an "oral word artist" who found a different way: not tapes, not transcriptions, but an emphasis on structures and patterns, motives, the thing itself. After all, what is left of conversation when we take out its purported meaning? In at least one obvious way, Stein's plays seem *less* like conversation than other writers': without any given dramatic context, without coherent exchanges that include clues to what's going on, Stein's writing in her plays makes no sense to most readers. Since we understand sense from the conversations in which we participate and the dialogue of most of the plays we see, Stein's writing is like nothing we've ever heard—or *noticed* that we've heard—before.

But the *assumptions* and *methods* of conversation analysts, in addition to the data, reveal a clear relationship between Stein's work and theirs. That there is an order to be found in spoken language is a shared primary assumption. Earlier linguists such as Noam Chomsky chose not to analyze actual speech because they believed it was not orderly enough to "permit formal description" (Heritage, 235). Conversation analysts assume that informal conversation has an order to it and that "no order of detail can be dismissed, *a priori*, as disorderly, accidental or irrelevant" (241). Stein, like Sacks, was able to see order in conversation where others could not. And, like conversation, Stein's writing itself should be assumed to have an order—however unfamiliar or complex—and to suggest alternative orders.

Another shared assumption is that there is value in looking *at* the very things—words—with which we usually see and describe other things. Emanuel A. Schegloff describes the work of conversation analysis as based on "the distinctive and utterly critical recognition . . . that talk can be examined as an object in its own right, and not merely as a screen on which are projected other processes." Further, "commonsense knowledge cannot properly be invoked as itself providing an account, rather than providing the elements of something to be accounted for" (xviii, xlii). Schegloff describes Sacks as having noticed something worth studying in the very tools with which we usually study everything else. William James also directed his attention to *how* we know things, as well as to *what* we know: he didn't let our objects of thought distract him from noticing thinking itself, and thinkers themselves. Similarly, Stein is not interested in happenings so much as in how and why they get talked about.

The prattling data of conversation analysis requires practitioners to notice what most people ignore in the daily sounds around them. Their methods, then, beyond tape recording and transcription, most basically involve paying close attention to detail and trying not to ignore anything. Schegloff reminds us that it was difficult for him and his colleagues "to penetrate through the blinders of the implacable familiarity of the mundane materials with which we worked" (lix). To notice informal conversation, Sacks had to see anew. Stein certainly works with the "mundane materials" of gossip and domestic middle-class life; it has long been debated whether her art transforms this material into something noticeable and valuable or whether it remains as ordinary and flat as ever.

Conversation analysts have found that "participants [in a conversation] analyze and understand, from moment to moment, the contexted character of their lives, their current and prospective circumstances, the present moment," and that "the very terms of that understanding can be transformed by a next bit of conduct by one of the participants (for example, a next action can recast what has preceded as 'having been leading up to this')" (Schegloff, xxviii). In other words, all utterances are *context-shaped* and *context-renewing* (Heritage, 242; his italics). A reader of Stein's *Tender Buttons* experiences this growing and changing context more finely, on the level of the word instead of the utterance: each word renews the context; each word is "recast" as the words following it reflect back upon it. This renewing and recasting can also be seen in her plays, as I will demonstrate in the next section. Subsequent phrases tell us how previous phrases might have been meant, and how listeners interpreted them.

Conversation analysts, then, assume that there is a describable order to the way spoken language is used, and they intend to describe it in the pieces they can find: How does turn-taking work? When do topic loops appear? How do people most politely avoid saying what they are asked to say? How do they know what they are expected to say? How are conflicts rhetorically, though not substantially, resolved? Conversation analysts want to find out our "rules" of conversation, the ones we pick up, use, and follow—or, if we don't, the ones we know we are breaking (sometimes only in hindsight). These rules—descriptive in that they try to describe what happens, and prescriptive in that we sometimes are aware we are following them and sometimes let them prevent us from saying what we imagine we'd really like to say—may be a miniaturized pattern of the ways humans work. Utterances formed of words are important building blocks in human relationships, and the structures underneath the stories people tell may teach us something about society's organization. In her writing, Stein constantly negotiates between generic expectations and eccentricity, and we do the same in our daily lives. That's a lot of what happens.

Some Discoveries: Subtle Antagonism, or Free Play in Language

Stein's plays tend to be weird, but clear voices often can be heard, interrupting the audience's general confusion—though tending to leave one still baffled afterward. Reading her plays is like walking by a group of strangers and hearing part of their conversation: "Let us wait and see"; "Follow me"; "Yes I have a brother"; "I will do it tomorrow"; "Jenny give me the keys. Oh yes. I am waiting" (*Do Let Us Go Away*, in *Geography and Plays*, 226). You know what they said, what you heard, and what that means, but *why* did they say it and what were they really talking about? Often, however, just from a short exchange, we can tell quite a bit about the speakers' relationship—and thereby can tell *how* we can often tell more than we are told. A couple of words can capture annoyance, long-term enmity, general frustration, embarrassment, hero worship, enthusiasm, and so on. "Good-bye" is one thing, but "good-bye good-bye good-bye" is another (215).[25]

I imagine that Stein's afternoons were full of polite and interesting conversations with visitors—as she said herself, "someone always comes for tea" ("Gertrude Stein Arrives")—and her play *Every Afternoon: A Dialogue* is full of short pieces of conversations. Through decontextualized utterances, Stein draws a reader's attention to the complexity within what looks like simplicity. It is the lack of context that enables the great latitude or "play" in interpretation; contextualized speech can usually be interpreted pretty easily. Many of the following lines from *Every Afternoon* seem to represent polite accord, but they can also suggest misunderstanding or at least annoyed disagreement.

1— Is there any change.
   Naturally.
   I know what you mean.
2— Of course we did.
   Yes indeed we did. (254)
3a— What did you do with your dog.
   We sent him into the country.
   Was he a trouble.
   Not at all but we thought he would be better off there.

Yes it isn't right to keep a large dog in the city.
Yes I agree with you.
Yes.
3b— Coming.
Yes certainly.
Do be quick. (256)
4— Who cares for daisies.
Do you hear me.
Yes I can hear you.
Very well then explain.
That I care for daisies.
That we care for daisies. (in *Geography and Plays*, 257)[26]

The exactitude of pronunciation suggested by these polite little statements (which include no contractions) implies a stiffness in the conversation and evokes the image of people sitting straight in their chairs. Although examples 1, 2, and 3a suggest easy agreement, the others hint at discord. "Coming. / Yes certainly. / Do be quick" suggests that even though the second speaker says, "Yes certainly," his or her idea of "coming" is not as immediate as that of the first (and third) speakers. "Do you hear me. / Yes I can hear you" suggests that the first speaker has doubts about the listener's ability to understand. "*Can* you hear me" would indicate that the speakers are discussing whether one can physically hear the other, but "*do* you hear me" suggests that the first speaker doubts that the listener (if not just stubborn) is intellectually or emotionally capable of understanding that speaker's logic or feelings. In this case, the first speaker can politely use the word "hear" to his obliging listener while inaffably accusing him of incompatible sensibilities.

Other pairs of statements in this play also simultaneously signal agreement and reproof. In this group, the paired statements are almost repetitions, and yet they still manage to suggest disagreement:

5a— Don't tempt him.
Do not tempt him.
This evening there was no question of temptation he was not the least interested.
5b— Neither was she.
Of course she wasn't. (255)
6— Why do the days pass so quickly.
Because we are so very happy.

Yes that's so.
That's it.
That is it. (257)
7a— You mean you are taught early.
That is exactly what I mean.
7b— And I feel the same.
You feel it to be the same. (255)
8— Not now.
You mean not now. (259)[27]

In examples 5a, 6, 7b, and 8, the second speaker uses almost the same words as the first but still manages to undermine the first speaker's authority. In 5a and the last two lines of 6, the second speaker might only be correcting the first speaker's grammar, but small differences can mean wide divergence of opinion. In these examples, the first speaker does not seem to understand the seriousness of the situation; the first speaker is not emphasizing certain words—"not" and "is"—to the second speaker's liking. In these examples, the second speaker may be asserting autonomy by stating the same sentiment emphatically. Conversely, in examples 7b and 8, the second speaker undermines the first speaker's autonomy by speaking *for* him or her, since saying "you mean" and "you feel" is presumptuous and degrading. In 7b—"And I feel the same. / You feel it to be the same."—a simple infinitive changes the meaning significantly. In effect, the first speaker is coerced into agreeing with what was said—an analysis perhaps, instead of just the general emotion with which it was said. Or the first speaker is indirectly told not to *feel* but instead to be more objective in forming and stating opinions. It isn't surprising that contractions have different emphases than whole words—"it's" differing slightly from "it is"—but in example 8, even though the second speaker pretends to repeat what the first speaker says with the use of "you mean," "now" seems to mean a different time than "now." Stein repeats words, writing the same words even in the same order, but they mean something different each time, often because we know how conversations work. These passages make us recognize that we do.

In polite conversations, we try to be agreeable, and we camouflage our differences with dictional amiability. Example 5 demonstrates a series of agreements that serve only to undermine each speaker's authority and to distance the speakers. When the second speaker says, "Do not tempt him," seeming to assert that he or she came to that conclusion autonomously, the first speaker undermines any authority that might be associated with that autonomy by pointing out how obvious that sentiment is: "there was no question of temptation he was not in the least interested." The second speaker then undermines everything she has just said by saying that "she" wasn't at all interested either (I'll hazard to assume that this means that she had no intention of tempting him in the first place). And the first (and last) speaker agrees completely ("of course"), in order to again say something like, "*Anybody* would know *that*." This five-line conversation develops a tense relationship between these two speakers, but it makes no sense at all as an explicit transmission of information. Everything they've said has been unsaid, and nothing they communicate about their quite testy relationship is said directly.

If we can use language to agree with each other even when we are disagreeing, then it's possible to conclude that there is a limit to how well words can help us understand each other. K. J. Phillips writes that Stein "tinges the great majority of lines in 'Every Afternoon' with skepticism about language" and that, paradoxically, because of the promiscuous way words will support more than one meaning, a 'difference' can 'make no difference'" (Phillips, 36).[28] I disagree with Phillips enough to say that *no difference* can *make* a difference. Phillips claims that Stein was frustrated with a language that had so much slack in it, a looseness that made communication unsatisfyingly partial. My point is that Stein loved and fooled with those wide margins for greater semantic latitude.

John Dryden has described the effects of the slack in words: "As long as words a diff'rent sense will bear / And each may be his own interpreter, / Our airy faith will no foundation find; / The Word's a weathercock for ev'ry wind" (*The Hind and the Panther*, part 1, ll. 462–65). Dryden is writing about the frustratingly indeterminate nature of the authoritative word of the Bible—a paradox in itself. "The devil is in the details" is weirdly applicable. While so many writers begin with the Bible as their foundation of rock, only to discover that Dryden has accurately represented that foundation's airiness, Stein draws from the airy words of casual conversation and discovers that these interactions, especially in context, express human interrelations with great substance, consequence, and clarity. But words, especially in informal chat, may not have to be authoritatively informative. Words have another capacity: the unquestionable and important power to form relationships between us. (And perhaps if they did not have so much play in them, our contrariness would not allow us to form friendships at all.) As Stein writes: "To come into the relation means that if there is a response something has been said. This is not too exact" (*Scenes*, in *Geography and Plays*, 99).

In *Geography and Plays*, Stein demonstrates that the alternating utterances spoken during casual conversation by individuals in groups form an important corpus of knowledge that is both eccentrically wise and worthy of further regard—in all senses of that word. Her plays suggest that one should read (and listen) for multiplicity rather than linearity, for both the sake of the word—compared in *What Happened* to both an endangered animal and a growing vegetable—and our own living sakes. If we keep understanding *more* in what is said or written, and if we keep talking, then we will not be blind to other orders and new understandings. The indefinite significations of words do not just confuse; they also enable social relationships by allowing polite discord. As Kenneth Burke writes in a positive review of Stein's opera *Four Saints in Three Acts*: "Even as nonsense it sings well: indeed, its very ambiguity may have prodded the composer to express its *quality* as utterance; if what was said was vague, *en revanche* [in return] it was said with extreme mobility of emphasis" ("Two Brands," 73). As readers, we are the composers of Stein's plays. Her words encourage us to express—and then to notice—the quality and mobility of our own utterance.

Repairing Friendship in "Susie Asado"

While not made up of fragments of conversation, "Susie Asado"—written in 1913 along with *What Happened* (and they were published together in December 1922 in *Geography and Plays*)—is interspersed with suggestions of interactional conversation, as well as speech in action, two of the essential elements of friendly chat.[29] Speech in action allows people to cooperate (pass the salt, hold the tray, bring the pot), and again the main purpose of interactional conversation is to rebuild or continue to build the bond between friends (see Cheepen, 14). Both functions are specific to spoken language (although perhaps they could be reproduced in letter writing, the converse of the pen). "Susie Asado" reads:

> Sweet sweet sweet sweet sweet tea.
>> Susie Asado.
> Sweet sweet sweet sweet sweet tea.
>> Susie Asado.
> Susie Asado which is a told tray sure.
> A lean on the shoe this means slips slips hers.
> When the ancient light grey is clean it is yellow, it is a silver seller.
>> This is a please this is a please there are the saids to jelly. These are
> the wets these say the sets to leave a crown to Incy.

Incy is short for incubus.

A pot. A pot is a beginning of a rare bit of trees. Trees tremble, the old vats are in bobbles, bobbles which shade and shove and render clean, render clean must.

Drink pups.

Drink pups drink pups lease a sash hold, see it shine and a bobolink has pins. It shows a nail.

What a nail. A nail is unison.

Sweet sweet sweet sweet sweet tea. (*Geography and Plays*, 13)[30]

"Susie Asado," with different levels of blatancy and subtlety, suggests sweets and sweet tea; salt in an old silver saltcellar; jelly; and rare bit (aka welsh rabbit, a version of cheese on toast). We also can note the vats (in which fat might be rendered) and pots (in which the rare bit is begun), and we seem to be heartily and repeatedly encouraged to drink up ("drink pups"). Food seems to be passed around ("this is a . . .") and accepted ("please") with some of the same words and with a rhythm reminiscent of the nursery rhyme "The House That Jack Built."[31]

The "aimless social intercourse" not so much *in* but *evoked by* "Susie Asado" might also remind us that sight and sound are common components in metaphors of relationships: we see eye to eye, enter into another's view, chime or strike in, echo, harmonize, and are on the same wavelength with other people. "Sweet tea" might be given to a sweetie or may lead people to become sweeties. (Alice and Gertrude stopped for cake and praline ices on their first walk together; then Alice was invited to Saturday dinner [Wagner-Martin, 88]). The repetition of a name—either the name of the person addressed or of a third person about which the speaker and listener agree—can also support a feeling of closeness. If we listen to "Susie Asado"—try saying it three times fast—we might hear "you see as I do." In Stein's "Susie Asado", the auditory links between "sweet tea" and "sweetie," and between repeating a name ("Susie Asado") and seeing eye to eye ("You see as I do"), suggest the strong relationship between speech, sight, and human relationships. Seeing eye to eye is one way of describing the goal of chat.

A conversation can be a "nail" between people, constructing a relationship as much or more than it represents one. Our talk creates feelings of closeness because we intentionally, even if automatically, choose topics that we know are "safe" and will let us feel we are discovering that we are in agreement or have much in common. A conversation can build harmonious agreement, letting us feel in "unison" with one another—"unison" itself suggesting harmonic sound.

If we pretend that "Susie Asado" is a transcribed conversation, its structure suggests that it is about building or repairing relationships. Christine Cheepen's work on the predictability of informal conversation asserts that when there is a topic loop—for example, "sweet sweet sweet sweet sweet tea" occurs both at the beginning and the end of this text—then "interactive trouble *must* have occurred" within that loop (117). Within "Susie Asado" are several likely sites for that interactive trouble, although—as we probably all know from experience—sometimes it is impossible to tell what is going to be interpreted as criticism and cause interactive trouble. The imperative "must" can cause interactive trouble between equals. Misunderstandings (Did someone ask what "Incy" meant?) and clarifications that come across as condescending or otherwise annoying to someone ("Incy is short for incubus") can lead to trouble.

"Susie Asado" can be sounded out as the friendly overture "you see as I do," but "Susie Asado" must also be read as the name of a person, and a likely topic of conversation. If interactive trouble occurred before this conversation began, then Susie Asado herself could be a scapegoat who, in cooperation with agreement about the tea, *nail*s these speakers back into agreement and friendship.[32] She could be a sacrifice to their unity, one whom they overtly agree is a witch ("which") and silently work out to be "a told tray sure" (a told, old, gold and sure treasure)—a priceless piece of talk that smoothes relations over the tea tray. People can be linked by conversational knick-knacks that they casually mouth together—in "unison." Perhaps Susie Asado is a bauble ("bobble") passed around, one that "shade[s] and shove[s] and render[s] clean" the previous disagreement; thus the invocation of "Susie Asado" is a bauble link. Repeating the name "Susie Asado" and having it bring these speakers together is like the bobolink calling out its own name to its own kind to find a mate. Besides evoking sweets, sweet tea, and a sweetie, "sweet sweet sweet sweet sweet tea" also sounds like a bird's "tweet tweet tweet tweet tweet." The "bobo*link*" call of the bobolink seems scattered throughout this work, as do the lapping sounds of "drink pup." Both the bobolink and Susie Asado link up relationships. About Susie Asado, the speakers can say, "you see as I do." And when that scapegoating has done the preliminary and most difficult work, they can again calmly agree on the sweetness of the tea (it's always sweet to the fifth power). Then they are again sweeties.

One-sided Conversations with Shakespeare, or Tricked by Talk

Of course there are other possibilities. No matter how informally it is invoked, Incy the incubus is still a spirit, one that combines the topics of sexual liaisons and ghosts. (The same year that Stein became interested in flamenco dancing—the ostensible topic of "Susie Asado"—she visited Mabel Dodge's ghost-haunted villa, where she overheard the living Dodge and her lover in the next room.) In the spirit of spirits, the repetition of the first two lines in the next two lines—and, in part, in the last line—signals a chant to me. That conversation over tea may work the same kind of magic that a chant over a cauldron can: people can be linked (love potions), people can be destroyed (vicious gossip), and women tend to group together in both cases.

Stein's words might remind one of Shakespeare's *Macbeth*, and this would not be the first time Stein alludes to Shakespeare in her writing: "Q.E.D." (1903) begins with a long epigraph from *As You Like It*, act 3, scene 2.[33] In *Macbeth*, the witches dance around a cauldron, take turns speaking, and jointly repeat the chant: "Double, double, toil and trouble; / Fire burn, and cauldron bubble."[34] But look again at the longest paragraph in "Susie Asado": "A pot. A pot is a beginning of a rare bit of trees. Trees tremble, the old vats are in bobbles, bobbles which shade and shove and render clean, render clean must." The pot can both be a flowerpot ("a beginning of . . . trees") and a cauldron in a forest ("the old vats" in "a rare bit of trees"). Stein's words create the image of a bubbling and popping, or "bobble"-ing and "pups"-ing, cauldron in a forest clearing, witches ("which is") chanting, and a brew being prepared.

This chant over the pot opens the scene in which the witches (the old *b*ats) equivocate with Macbeth about his future, including the prediction that he "shall never vanquished be until / Great Birnam Wood to high Dunsinane Hill / Shall come against him" (4.1.92–94). Birnam Wood's "remove to Dunsinane" (5.3.2) certainly demonstrates that it is a "rare bit of trees"—or that bits of trees have been used as effective camouflage. Until her death, Lady Macbeth tries to "render clean" her blood- and guilt-stained hands; she frets, "Yet here's a spot" (5.1.30), and we see here "a pot."[35] Stein's "shade and shove" may refer to the moving trees (which "shadow" Malcolm's soldiers [5.4.5] and allow them to shove on); the equivocation of the witches who "palter" with Macbeth "in a double sense" (5.8.20), words that shade meaning and shove Macbeth toward his tragic fate; or the words that Macbeth uses to address the ghost of Banquo (called a "shadow" [3.4.107]): "The time has been / That, when the brains were out, the man would die, /

And there an end; but now they rise again / With twenty mortal murders on their crowns, / And push us from our stools" (3.3.79–83).

Stein's allusion, if we can call it that, to Shakespeare's equivocating witches reminds me of the power of their spoken words, especially the power they achieve because Macbeth forgets to understand their words in the proper context or for their full potential. He repeats their words as if they had been written in a legal contract upon which he can depend. When attempting to interpret the portentous emblems, Macbeth also struggles, and fails, to put the visual together with the verbal. Stein demonstrates that words can be interpreted in a variety of ways, and that this ambiguity can be both constructive (allowing us to build relationships in spite of our differences) and destructive (if we assume we understand each other perfectly). Stein's words are more than equivocal, they are multivocal, and while we will die still trying to understand them fully, she lets them live. If we insist on killing alternative meaning, we will be like Lady Macbeth, whose "eyes are open but their sense are shut" (5.1.23–24).

This paragraph in "Susie Asado" is not Stein's only echo of *Macbeth*. One paragraph of *Tender Buttons* (written the previous year) evokes the same metrical rhythm, the same rhyme, and even some of the same sense as a section of the witches' recipe for their brew. Compare these excerpts:

Scale of dragon, tooth of wolf,
Witches' mummy, maw and gulf
Of the ravined salt-sea shark,
Root of hemlock digged i' the dark,
Liver of blaspheming Jew,
Gall of goat, and slips of yew
Slivered in the moon's eclipse,
Nose of Turk and Tartar's lips. (*Macbeth*, 4.1.22–29)

Lovely snipe and tender turn, excellent vapor and slender butter, all the splinter and the trunk, all the poisonous darkning drunk, all the joy in weak success, all the joyful tenderness, all the section and the tea, all the stouter symmetry. (*Tender Buttons*, 35)

Stein seems to be listing ingredients for something slightly more tasty than the witches are making, but her concoction may share some of the destructive aspects of the witches' charm. The fourth line or phrase of each passage refers to poison and darkness. As the weird sisters wreak havoc on a sailor and Macbeth, Stein's weird word spells seem playful but have also been read as dangerously disruptive of our common linguistic and social orders. T. S. Eliot called Stein's writing "ominous" ("Charleston," 595), and Faÿ reports that "people spoke of [Stein] as of a witch" (62). Perhaps Stein and Toklas are twentieth-century weird sisters, in convocation with the literary past.

But all this is a long way from what I set out to prove. Unlike the weird sisters, who seem to be telling Macbeth something they are not, Stein's plays seem to say very little at all but tell us many things about the ways we communicate. Instead of disguising her real meanings, Stein has to erase all apparent meaning in order to motivate her readers to find something they weren't looking for. She knows that we're lazy, that we'd be happy to find a little chat over tea, perhaps the story of a divorce in the neighborhood or a bit of subtly expressed hatred with some background history. We don't need greatness; we'll be satisfied with a soap opera or a funny story. But none of that's there, and either we say she's wasting our time, or we keep looking and are forced to find surprises. If we stop looking for the emperor's new clothes and stop blaming the tailor for ineptitude or fraud, we'll see and start to understand the structures of the naked body.

CHAPTER 4

Talk in the Thirties:
In the Present, with the Past

THE 1930S WERE a hugely successful time for Stein as a writer and a celebrity. Toklas's Plain Edition published three of Stein's books between 1930 and 1934, and then Stein moved on to major publishers. Portions of *The Autobiography of Alice B. Toklas* appeared in *Atlantic Monthly*, and the book was then published by Harcourt Brace, which also published the abridged version of *The Making of Americans* (1933). Random House published *Lectures in America* (1935), *The Geographical History of America* (1936), and *Everybody's Autobiography* (1937). In 1934, *Four Saints in Three Acts* was a hit in New York and Chicago (where Stein saw it performed)—and Stein explained that "her idea . . . had been that of conversation between saints" because saints only "exist" and "converse" ("4 Saints"). During this decade, Stein also wrote at least one other opera, a play, and a children's book. While in the United States, Stein showed up late at a performance of the cantata "Capital Capitals," which Virgil Thompson had explained to the audience as "a conversation among the four capitals of Provence—Aix, Arles, Avignon, and Lesbaux—in the manner in which capitals would talk if they could." (A reporter adds: "It didn't make any difference whether they could or not, for no one would know what they were talking about" ["4 Saints"].) In short, Stein continued to fool around with conversation, even as she made it big.

Stein's sudden rise to fame after the publication of *The Autobiography of Alice B. Toklas* led to her tour. After thirty years of writing, Stein became "a best-selling author and house-hold name" when she was almost sixty years old (Blackmer, 243). She was on the cover of *Time* on 11 September 1933. The February 1935 volume of *transition* devoted itself to (angry) responses to *The Autobiography of Alice B. Toklas* from the very people about whom she had written. Stein also wrote (but did not publish—yet) the long works *Stanzas in Meditation* and *Four in America*. Some of the work—I think—is her most baffling, and some is her most straightforward (though surely baffling in its own ways). I do not discuss the ways the works "speak to each other"—how, as Dydo has convincingly argued, *Stanzas in Meditation* and *The Autobiography of Alice B. Toklas* are two parts of the same project. Nor do I explore the ways Stein creatively weaves an interest in conversation into her works—as in "How I wish I were able to say what I think" in stanza 17 or "She asked . . And I said . . And she said . . I said" in the first four lines of stanza 18 in *Stanzas in Meditation*. Instead, this chapter concentrates on Stein's visit to the United States after thirty-one years away. She came to speak English, hear English, and talk to Americans. To lecture, but also to converse.

Starting Conversations in America

While *The Autobiography of Alice B. Toklas* made Stein famous as a personality who rubbed shoulders with other (already famous) personalities, her lectures emphasize her roles as writer and thinker. According to Bridgman, Stein "undertook to expand those few sentences in *The Autobiography of Alice B. Toklas* which had pretended to summarize theories. The resulting defense of her art was much more satisfactory" (243–44). The lectures introduce an avid reader's ideas about the history of English literature (in "What is English Literature"), an art collector's theories about modern art (in "Pictures"), and a writer's goals in her several genres: plays (in "Plays"), her lengthy prose style (in "The Gradual Making of the Making of Americans"), short portraits (in "Portraits and Repetition"), and poetry (in "Poetry and Grammar"). Her explanations, however, struck audiences (and strike many readers) as almost as confusing as the literary works themselves. She is very clear, but very digressive; very repetitive, but not very strict with herself about defining certain oft-repeated words. When she talks about English literature, for example, she starts with (and doubles back quite often to) discussions about what it means to know something. She points out that while English literature has been written over centuries, all that one has read is always simultaneously present in one's mind; that different readers know different English literatures; that some writers serve God and some serve mammon; that American literature is English literature and yet very different, since it was not written on an island; and relatedly, how island life differs from continental life. Along the way, she offers a lovely history of English literature, largely based on how different writers chose their words (and how sound was, at some points in this history, their primary consideration).

In spite of this confusion, between fall 1934 and spring 1935, Stein was "the most feted woman in America" ("Gertrude Stein Gives Talk"; "Elite Fete"). She spent six months traveling by train and plane, talking to audiences of up to five hundred people. Arriving in New York City on 24 October 1934, she began lecturing in November—in Manhattan, Poughkeepsie, and Brooklyn, and in Princeton, New Jersey. When she lectured in New York City, "requests for tickets [came] from as far away as Kentucky and Vermont" ("Gertrude Stein Discusses Art"). From her base in New York, she made short forays to Philadelphia, Bryn Mawr, and Boston. Her "welcome . . . was so much more hospitable than she expected" that she extended her trip past mid-November, touring the country ("Literary Enigma"). She visited Chicago, Illinois; Madison, Wisconsin; St. Paul, Minnesota; Detroit and Ann Arbor, Michigan; Indianapolis, Indiana; Columbus, Toledo, and Cleveland, Ohio; Baltimore, Maryland; Washington, D.C.; Springfield, Amherst, Northampton, Pittsfield, and South Hadley, Massachusetts; Wallingford, Middletown, Springfield, and Hartford, Connecticut; Charlottesville, Richmond, Williamsburg, and Sweet Briar, Virginia; Charleston, South Carolina; Birmingham, Alabama; and New Orleans, Louisiana. After a fortnight in Chicago, where she taught a class and gave her *Narration* lectures at the university, she lectured in Dallas, Fort Worth, and Austin, Texas; Oklahoma City, Oklahoma; and Pasadena, Carmel, Palo Alto, San Francisco, Oakland, and Berkeley, California. She returned to New York for a couple of weeks and then left for Europe on 4 May 1935. During the tour, people "scramble[d] for available tickets," because Stein was considered "a wow" and the "genial apostle of the new English" ("Miss Stein a Wow"). I doubt most people understood her or loved her, but she certainly caught their attention.

During her tour, she signed books at bookstores and department stores, auctioned off autographed copies of her work for charity, gave many interviews, spoke on a national radio broadcast, loaned some of her artwork to exhibitions, and canceled any speaking engagement for which more than five hundred tickets had been distributed or admission had been charged. She had tea with Eleanor Roosevelt at the White House and went out on the night beat in a Chicago police car. She met many famous people and was greeted by "8,000 rabid devotees of [Clark] Gable" when she landed in Dallas—they thought it was his plane ("Multitude Greets Highbrow"). She was interviewed by Walter Cronkite when he was a student at the University of Texas at Austin, published some articles on the American scene with the

Herald Tribune Syndicate, chaired a college debate (between the University of Chicago and Willamette University) on international munitions control, and attended a University of Chicago honor society meeting devoted to the topic of literature and propaganda.[1]

The *Time* cover story asserts that Stein was "very democratic, proud of being a plain American, she likes people, [and] is always accessible to strangers" ("Stein's Way"). When she arrived in the United States, she told reporters: "I like people, you see. I like to talk to people, I am always wandering around the streets having conversations with people. I like single human contacts" ("Gertrude Stein Home"). The *New York Sun* reported that during her lecture, "she stood on the platform, conversing as to every person present as an individual" ("4 Saints"). She liked rubbing shoulders with people in the street: she walked from West Forty-third Street to Park Avenue and Sixty-second to deliver her first lecture at the Colony Club; she walked the seventy-two blocks from her hotel to 116th street to give her second lecture at Columbia University ("Gertrude Stein Discusses Art"; Alsop, "Gertrude Stein Says"). At least one reporter found Stein's tone condescending when she gave her lectures (Murray), but most found it sincere and conversational.

I like to think that Stein had other goals besides "la gloire" and money when she visited her native land. I imagine she hoped to start some conversations, something like those that were inspired by the 1913 Armory Show in New York, which Mabel Dodge called "the most important public event that has ever come off since the signing of the Declaration of Independence" (Dodge Luhan and Stein, 157; see also Blackmer, 228). Van Vechten describes the effect of the show on the population of New York:

> It was the first, and possibly the last, exhibition of paintings held in New York which everybody attended. Everybody went and everybody talked about it. Street-car conductors asked for your opinion of the Nude Descending the Staircase, as they asked you for your nickel. Elevator boys grinned about Matisse's Le Madras Rouge, Picabia's La Danse a la Source, and Brancusi's Mademoiselle Pogany, as they lifted you to the twenty-third floor. Ladies you met at dinner found Archipenko's sculpture very amusing, but was it art? (Blackmer, 228–29)[2]

In short, everyone was talking. As Blackmer concludes: "When it came to interpreting modernist art, virtually everybody from elevator boys to society ladies was on the same rudimentary level, with no conventional critical perspectives to guide them," and "audiences rather than artists had the responsibility of interpreting their works according to their own lights, . . . [and] modernist writers and artists indirectly forced their audiences to examine the prejudices and preoccupations that informed their aesthetic judgements" (229). That new art got all sorts of people to step back and reconsider, and to talk about it with everyone else. Whether or not it was Stein's goal, did anything like this happen as a result of her American tour? Did Stein start a nationwide conversation?

The short (disappointing) answer is "No," although I'd like to qualify that with a "Kind of, maybe." In chapter 6, I describe the kind of conversation Stein would later advocate, but that idea seems to have come to her during the decade after her trip. Still, Stein took pleasure in confusing people, and one reason might be that confusion—or "mental chaos," as the *Boston Evening Press* called her effect on audiences—is a first step toward thought ("Gertrude Stein Baffles"). After Stein's success with *The Autobiography of Alice B. Toklas*, Lansing Warren traveled to Paris to interview Stein for the *New York Times* and observed: "When she laughs, as she often does at the mental confusion produced in her auditor by many of her remarks, her face and body become mobile, and there is something impish in her expression." Stein likes to make remarks that will get a rise out of her listeners—perhaps even make them jump up and state their own opinions, listen to themselves, and rethink some of their assumptions.

For example, in this same interview she says "that Hitler ought to have the peace prize . . . because he is removing all elements of contest and of struggle from Germany. By driving out the Jews and the democratic and Left elements, he is driving out everything that conduces to activity. That means peace." Warren doesn't try to figure out what this means, and in the next paragraph he says "her provocative side" is limited to her "experimental" writing and "does not appear in her everyday life." Couching her ideas in plain English, however, Stein is being just as provocative in her theorizing about Hitler and the Nobel Peace Prize. Edward M. Burns and Ulla E. Dydo deduce that Stein's proposal is "ironic, a point of black humor" (Stein and Wilder, 414), and they are surely right. But it is also thought-provoking: if Hitler can in any way appear to be bringing peace, then we need to rethink our ideas about peace. Might peace as an end in itself be overrated? Might it in some situations be a deadening complacency? Might dissent be more valuable than we assume? And might Stein lead her listener even to question the appeasement of Germany in the interest of peace? In a later conversation, she makes her views on peace clearer. She refers to recent purges in "peaceful" countries and asks: "What's the difference between getting killed in war or getting killed in peace? . . . Peace! P-s-s-s-t—and they shoot you. I'd rather be killed in war than in peace" (Buchalter).[3] If that's peace, who (aside from tyrants) needs it?

Stein speaks in "conundrums" which go "unanswered" ("A Painting Is a Painting"). A *New York Sun* reporter calls her surprising comments "little nifties," appreciates her "American colloquialisms," and says that, in spite of "her common representation as a lady who is very hard to understand, . . . for fifty-nine minutes in any hour you will think her altogether charming, and as transparent as a bartender's laugh" (McClain). Another journalist describes her "slow, conversational tone . . . interspersed with the crisp sentences of cryptic meaning—some bordering on the startling" (O'Connell). In Texas, a *Dallas Morning News* reporter found her "perplexingly clear" ("Multitude Greets Highbrow"). But audiences seemed to be struck by her "sincerity," in spite of her mixture of "epigrams," "extremely astute remark[s]," and comments that seem "thoroughly absurd" (Murray). In "Miss Stein Speaks to Bewildered 500," the *New York Times* reports: "At the end of the address there was obviously no unanimity of opinion among the audience as to its meaning or significance." That's good, for people will have to think, discuss. The newspaper's editorial page the next day suggests that Stein's "ingenious publicity man" is the real hero, since the "bewildered" audience just sat there with a "splitting headache and holding their breath" ("Devoted Band"), but Stein's lecture tour was primarily advertised by *The Autobiography of Alice B. Toklas* and cobbled together by friends and her own whims. There is something compelling, even enlivening, about being confused and provoked, and people went for it. In spite of the audience's "exchanging covert smiles," some listeners thought to themselves, or whispered "begrudgingly, 'A good basic idea'" (Winsten). Stein's ideas are "esoteric," but they are "not without the grain of shrewd good sense" (Alsop, "Gertrude Stein Likes").

Not everyone appreciated Stein's rousing the minds of her audiences. A *New York Post* writer comments: "It seems to have become more or less obligatory to express one's self upon the subject of Gertrude Stein" (Brickell). Columnist Evelyn Seeley wishes Stein hadn't come to New York, because then "we wouldn't have had her to argue about." Seeley implies that the argument is open-ended, unending, but she has reached her own conclusion: Stein is too much an outsider, too "Bohemian," too much like most people are in their youth, and Seeley "wishes she would come down for a while and see the America we see." Stein may have come to America, however, to let her compatriots see *her* way for a moment, to let her listeners imagine a difference.

Stein ended her lectures by asking, "Are there any questions?" When a woman in one audience came out with a "la-di-da" question, Stein's response was "a flat slapping 'What?'" which suggests her suspicion of posturing and her desire for straight talk (Winsten). In fact, sometimes she chose to stop reading her lecture to talk directly to her audience ("Gertrude Stein Explains Work"). At Princeton, there were no questions—which we could optimistically read as audience members having come to think for themselves, but I doubt it. According to the reporter at the Princeton lecture: "Few if any even came close to assimilating Miss Stein's literary theories. The audience was amused but otherwise unaffected by the obscurities which Miss Stein considers axiomatic" ("Princeton Dazed"). While Lewis Gannett of the *New York Herald Tribune* thought Stein was "jolly, bright-eyed, wholly natural, [and] likeable," he still wasn't compelled to think: he said her words tended to be "utterly meaningless" and her opera "was a big fat zero," and, to a passage from her weirder work, he can only say, "Pooh!" Some reviewers, such as Harry Hansen at the *New York World-Telegram*, refused to go see her. Stein started conversations among some people, but other listeners were just turned off.

And some people she must have purposely sent packing, perhaps because they were too stubborn to make any effort worth the trouble, and also because she was "intransigent on principle" ("Gertrude Stein Arrives"). One writer thought: "If you come up to her and say 'I don't understand anything you write, but I want to know something about you,' [Stein was likely to] be frank and friendly and helpful" ("Literary Enigma"). But James Marlow's interview with Stein sounds like a comedy routine or an interview with Bob Dylan. She starts with "Who are you?" and "What do you want? Sit down," and then she leaves the room for a while. Marlow asks questions and gets answers he doesn't understand; he says, "I do not mean that," and "I mean," and "I know, but," and "What I am trying to find out is . . ." Stein interrupts him, contradicts him, and accuses him of having the wrong type of mind: "It [my writing] does not stammer. It may seem that way to you because you have that kind of mind"; and "You haven't an ear for the way people talk"; and "You have too many ideas in your head at the same time"; and "That is the trouble with you"; and "Your choice of words is very poor." (He says, "Is what?" and she answers, "Very poor." He says, "Oh.") She also cuts him off several times with "You will have to talk louder. I can't hear you"; or "Do I what? I can't hear you." Then she turns to another interviewer: "What do you want?" Perhaps she's telling Marlow to be more open-minded, but she's not demonstrating much of an open mind herself.

Stein refuses to be drawn into a debate. One *Chicago Daily Tribune* reporter says that "Gertrude Stein never answers attacks"—but answering attacks isn't quite conversation ("Paris Aroused"). When she was a moderator at a college debate on munitions, she said (unsupportively, considering the circumstances): "All they are taught is debate. They have never learned to think" ("Miss Stein Lets"). Her position seems to be that "we have wars because people want wars"—a position provocative enough to be defended on the editorial page of the *Daily Tribune* and to cause at least one reader to reply with a different opinion—that, in short, people with children don't want war and "talk is cheap, but lives are dear" ("Miss Stein Lets"; Frey). The newspaper appreciates Stein's facing facts, but the reader replies with clichés. Debate, but not conversation, can occur when people won't think beyond, or even about, their cherished phrases.

What They Might Have Talked About

"What is art?" and "Is this art?" was one debate spurred by Stein's tour. A *New York Times* editorial mentions B. F. Skinner's critique of Stein's "unconscious prose" but argues for a different position: that the nonsense of *Tender Buttons* is "ravishing." Defending Stein's prose poetry, the editorial writer asks: "Why should 'meaningless' poetry be on the eligible list and 'meaningless' prose be excluded? Is Mr. Skinner deaf to music and obdurate to magic?" ("Two Steins"). The *Springfield Daily Republican* was all effusion: "Her highly concentrated style embraced this subject with characteristic efficiency," "a literary style which may still be considered bewildering because of its many facets . . . [and] the sudden blossoming forth of vast panoramas of information, too concentrated to be grasped without careful analysis, and too odd in form . . . to convey more than a total impression of a great erudition, powerful personality, fearlessness" ([W. Rogers?], "Stein Gives Talk").[4] Or perhaps she just spouts "the most absolute rubbish on earth" (Laurie). Whatever it all means, however she did it, however much her tour resembles "a circus tour," the editors at the *Cleveland Press* are willing to credit Stein with "20 years ago . . . [giving] license to experimenters in all the fields of all the arts to try to say what they wanted to say in their own way, regardless of how anyone else had ever done it." The editorial concludes:

> She pulled a cork. She took a lid off. Scads of criticism, ranging all of the way from serious incomprehensible attempts to define her old serious incomprehensibilities, to some of the fanciest writing produced by the lunatic fringe of her followers, still do not explain just how she did it.

But she did. And a whole generation of quite comprehensible vital artists of our time was released into birth. ("About Gertrude Stein")

Thumbs up or thumbs down, understandable or not, serious or a joke, even art or not—escaping most attempts at definition—Stein's writing started noisy debates (and perhaps some quiet conversations) on all these topics: What is art? What is meaning? What is important?

A feature in the 19 November 1934 *New York Sun* printed this letter from Helene Marer: "'What do you think of [*Four Saints in Three Acts*]?' It seems to me a lot of words, thrown together, meaning nothing. But, maybe I'm wrong. May I have somebody's opinion of it?" During two weeks of letters on this topic, Dian Deene on 22 November responded that she loved Stein's opera, even though it was indeed "a jumble of words": "There was a time I would have derided Miss Stein's 'method' in no uncertain terms, but I am beginning to realize how little I know and that maybe she is way ahead of me or something." In a more pretentious letter, on 23 November, Prudencio de Pereda defends Stein more specifically but less open-mindedly. He calls Stein a member of "the cult of temporary unintelligibility" because "effort brings a handsome reward." Rhoda Lawner is critical of Stein, however, calling her in a 26 November letter "a nonunderstanding authoress of non-understandable books." Mrs. L.B.W. wonders in her 3 December letter if Stein is "playing a hoax" or "spoofing us"—which was a common third view, though third views aren't always that common. If people started imagining their own limitations, as the first letter writer did, or started imagining the ways that art was being critiqued, as this last writer did, then Stein started some people thinking.

This debate spawned another one: about the primacy of words and their sounds. A reviewer of the Hartford, Connecticut, premier of *Four Saints in Three Acts* passes on the rumor that Stein "apparently uses words for sounds instead of meanings" and quotes Virgil Thomson's confirmation of it: "Miss Stein . . . clothed [the] story in a sound-pattern of words vaguely suggesting the atmosphere" of seventeenth-century Spain. The "All-Negro Cast" was said to have been chosen because "they had better diction" and they "projected the vocal lines with [a] startling clarity and beauty of phrasing" ("Stein Opera Sung"). Her lectures are described as "the sound within a sea shell" and "intricate, definitely lyric verbal rhythms"(Winsten; Alsop, "Gertrude Stein Says"). But a *New York Times* editorial, missing her valuation of spoken words, is disappointed in her ideas on punctuation: "Does the eye need to take a breath?" In fact, choosing to criticize Stein from the opposite direction than the paper usually takes, the editorial says Stein has not gone far enough: "She should have given us the New Style, absolute and flawless, instead of patching up the Old" ("Perfecting Language"). But Stein was interested in the real English language.

Stein's lecture tour also changed the way people talked, although not in very important ways—at least as far as the news reports tell it. The *Boston Daily Globe* says she was "contagious," and the "Radcliffe girls" started "stuttering" just like her: "Are you going out with me tonight, tonight are you going out with me, with me tonight, tonight with me?" ("Radcliffe Giggles"). As Stein's tour went on, the news headlines mimicked her repetition more and more often: "Gertrude Stein Is Here Is Here Is Here Here Is" (Dush); "A Painting Is a Painting Is a Gertrude Stein Axiom on Art"; "Greeted Greeted at Airport" (O'Hara); "A Snub, a Snub, a Snub." But copying some of the symptoms of deep thought, as opposed to thinking deeply, was not going to get Americans very close to creative thinking.

Stein's words, both spoken and written, seem especially thought provoking if we contrast them with the sentimental and formulaic poetry that appears alongside the news articles about her tour. One begins: "I know I shall be lonely just at first, / Until your step grows fainter on the stair, / And I have learned to look without swift tears / Across the room at your dear, empty chair" (Welshimer). Another begins: "In the first months when they were wed / Glamour so softened care and duty / He thought he loved her, but he fled / The moment Time had stained her beauty." It ends: "He thought he loved her, but he tired / And from his life forever thrust her / When he discovered love required / More strength of will than he could muster" (Guest). These do not represent even good twentieth-century American poetry. But if this is what people are reading in the newspaper, then we can thank Stein for stepping into the news and getting herself, her words, and her ideas discussed. These poems say what everybody knows, but Stein gets people thinking about what they don't know, what they might try to know, and even what might not be knowable.

Stein and Einstein

The very issue of "meaning" was thrown into question by the chance juxtaposition of Stein's and Albert Einstein's lectures. The 1933 *Time* magazine cover story begins with a poem that links them in a way they continued to be linked.

I don't like the family Stein.
There is Gert, there is Ed, there is Ein:

Gert's poems are bunk,
Ed's statues are punk,
And nobody understands Ein. ("Stein's Way")

Even this silly poem points to the way that the audiences for literature, science, and sculpture are confused. An editorial comments that Stein's writing is "harder to understand then the mathematical hieroglyphics of Einstein's theory of relativity, yet she is hailed as a great literary pioneer" ("Fancy Writing"). Why are the practitioners of both science and literature so baffling to their audiences? What does it mean—about past assumptions, about this moment in history, about these particular thinkers—that the audience feels left behind, grasping at straws? Is the proper response a commonsense outing of nonsense, or is it patience, yearning, deep thought, revision, and work?

The audience's tendencies in their responses to Stein and Einstein were usually quite different—and some people remarked on the contrast. John McClain of the *New York Sun* noted some unfairness in the way Stein was quizzed for explanations, since "it is a matter of record that Prof. Einstein and other protagonists of slightly baffling theories have entered and left the port for years without being called upon to defend themselves." Under a photograph of the physicist and headlined "Einstein 'Explains' Theories to Reporters," the caption reads: "In his lecture he gave additional proof of a theorem advanced by him in 1905 that energy and matter are two different forms of the same thing." Except for the quotation marks in the headline, there's nothing dubious about this report.

At the end of December 1935, Stein's and Einstein's lectures are both covered by the Washington, D.C., *Evening Star.* On 29 December, Stein (with her second cousin and a large white dog) is pictured a few pages away from an extensive article on Einstein. The next day, the paper ran a picture of Einstein and his colleagues, and Einstein's white hair and his placement in the composition of the photo make him look like the white dog in the picture of Stein! Thomas Henry reports that during Einstein's lecture, he apologetically repeated, "But this is so elementary I will not trouble you with it," and "at one rather knotty point, at which some lofty brows were puckered, he remarked, 'This is so infantile I must not delay over it.'" Like Stein, Einstein is a bit uncooperative sometimes. When a reporter asks if he enjoys talking about anything besides science, Einstein replies, "Yes, but not with you" (Henry). One short article begins: "The tradition of only 12 scientists understanding Einstein is upset completely" ("Science Understands"). And when Einstein's colleagues assure a journalist that *they,* of course, understand Einstein, he seems to trust the experts' consensus. Instead of doubting him, Einstein's nonscientist audience believes they would understand if they had bigger brains. This reporter depicts Einstein as a lone genius, concluding one story: "Prof. Einstein now does most of his thinking in his sloop off Watch Hill, R.I. He sails alone" (Henry).

Stein was more difficult to categorize. Headlines included: "Gertrude Stein Too Much for Harvard and Radcliffe; She Wonders If It Is Necessary to Stand Still to Live" (Fessenden); "Princeton Dazed by Gertrude Stein: . . . 'The Making of the Making of Americans' Befuddles Even Most Erudite Erudite"; and "Gertrude Stein Tells All About All but Audience Just Can't Take It" (Evans).

Stein noticed that new scientific ideas got more general acceptance than did her writing. She described her art as called for by "the movement of [her] time," just as "Edison's time forced on him the electric light and on the Wright brothers the airplane," but, "because inventions are practical things, people don't make a fuss about them" (O'Hara). While Stein was getting at representing the essence inside the working parts of a car, one of Einstein's colleagues explained his theory of energy as "a new part for an auto," although the part it's replacing still works ("Science Understands").

Stein tries to buck the theory of relativity, stating that if "a movement were lively enough it would exist so completely that it would not be necessary to see it moving against anything to know that it is moving" (*Lectures*, 170). In spite of this antirelativism, Conrad Aiken links Stein to Einstein in the *New Republic* when he dubiously reports that "in Miss Stein's work we were witnessing a bold and intricate and revolutionary and always consciously radical experiment in style, of which the results were to be of incalculable importance for English literature. Like the splitting of the atom, or the theory of relativity, Miss Stein's destruction of meaning was inevitably going to change, if not the world, at any rate the word" (38). Unlike Aiken, Mina Loy celebrates Stein's potential power:

> Curie
> of the laboratory
> of vocabulary
> she crushed
> the tonnage
> of consciousness
> congealed to phrases
> to extract
> a radium of the word (94)

Although Loy is probably referring to something more all encompassing, this "tonnage / of consciousness / congealed to phrases" certainly also can describe the psychological complexity of short exchanged phrases—what I see as Stein's exploration of conversation. Curie extracts a physical or material element, eighty-eighth on the periodic table, and Stein the essence of what happens between people.

Both Stein and Einstein seem to be contributing to a movement that demanded a "new mode of thinking," as the *Washington Daily News* reports on 28 December 1934. Citing the way Einstein's theories "disarranged the old-fashioned laws of time and motion," the plan is that "the new thinking blasts the idea that 'a thing is what is' or that it is identical with itself in all respects. For example, you are not the same you that existed a second ago or a year ago" ("Scientists' Meeting"). Stein would probably agree with that notion: it is one assumption behind her ideas on repetition and copying. Alfred Korzybeski is the "leading expositor" of this new type of thought, and while Einstein's famed ideas may have led to its newspaper coverage, Stein's ideas parallel Korzybeski's, too. To change the way people think, Korzybeski and his colleagues believe—in a re-dyed nominalism—that all names should be dated or numbered ("apple No. 1" and "apple No. 2") "to avoid the fallacy of false identification" (ibid.). Korzybeski also advocated avoiding the use of the verb "to be." Whether we think these changes feasible or not, these scientists—and Stein—seem to think that a change in the way language is used will be necessary to effect a change in underlying assumptions that affect human thought.

The Closed American Mind

Stein did not start a nationwide conversation. Her wish for small venues and free tickets, while democratic in spirit, contributed to her drawing a limited audience: members of museums and clubs, "grey-haired, gray-faced women . . . [and] comparatively few men"—at least at Columbia University (Winsten). She spoke to members of the "exclusive and intellectual" arts clubs, students and professors at thirty-five colleges and universities, women's clubs, the John Reed Club of Indianapolis, several audiences of museum members, and other "invited audience[s]" (Butcher; "Gertrude Stein Speaks"; "Youth Understands"). At the University of Chicago, she met with "chosen students," but "the curiosity seekers [were] kept out as firmly as nonmembers are banned from an exclusive country club golf course" ("Paris Aroused"). At one lecture, she sat on the stage at the Ritz Tower with Mrs. William Randolph Hearst, and Cole Porter was present, along with other "intellectuals" and "fashionables" ("Miss Stein Uses Saints"; Flutterbye). She only sometimes spoke to more general audiences, as at the Town Hall in Toledo and a bookstore in Cleveland.

While Stein argued that style and content "can't be divorced. They are one" (Winsten), news headlines all over the nation were increasingly likely to parrot Stein's style and maintain their closed-mindedness when it came to content. Only six days into her tour, the *New York Times* subtitled its story "'The Making of the Making of Americans' Befuddles Even Most Erudite Erudite" and ended with the speculation that the audience has realized "that their education, their education had been sadly neglected, neglected" ("Princeton Dazed"). Less than two weeks later, a *New York Times* review of *Portraits and Prayers* titled "But a Stein Is a Stein Is a Stein" asserts: "There is nothing in this book to merit more than five minutes' attention of a reasonably honest and intelligent mind." By February 1935, the *New York Times* was claiming that both Stein *and* the proletarian writers were snobs: "'Appreciation' of the unintelligible poets . . . was a form of self-flattery"; "the intelligentsia were sure they were good because the man in the street couldn't make head nor tail out of them"; and Stein seems to "continue to function . . . [as if she's] protecting a vested interest, like a losing trolley line that keeps going because it has a franchise." And the Communist writers were snobs because "if you aren't a workman . . . you and your thoughts and feelings just don't count" ("Literary Snobbery").

While everyone seemed to like Stein the person, they couldn't take her ideas seriously. The *New York Times* could do little but editorialize in the negative. For John Chamberlain, Stein's work is as silly as yoga, she is just "talking nonsense," and she's running a "racket" that takes advantage of our love of "goggling, gaping, and gazing." But for the reasonable person, he goes on, "those who have a no doubt irrational prejudice against vacuity, Miss Stein can only serve as an irritant." He even likens her writing to "the Chinese water torture." But the newspaper of record is looking for points, not ideas, and, in Chamberlain's view: "The trouble with the Stein game is that no one ever scores."

In short, this "stormy petrel of belles lettres, high priestess of the cult of scrambled words," and "word wrangler" didn't open everyone's minds (O'Hara; Evans). "The literary rebus whose unorthodox style of writing the English language has made her glorified and ridiculous alike" was asked closed-minded questions such as "What inspired you to begin doing tricks with the English language?" Sometimes she snapped at her "nosey inquisitors," and sometimes she behaved "patiently, graciously" (O'Hara). In San Francisco, a reporter claims that the audience did not understand "one single sentence, one single word, or one single syllable of Miss Stein's tiresome, and, if you ask me, rather impertinent address." This journalist, Annie Laurie, cannot understand "why Americans are such dumb driven cattle when it comes to listening to" what (she estimates) adds up to "the most absolute rubbish on earth." Laurie asks: Why didn't anyone "boo" or "hiss"? Why were they all so "polite"? She praises Americans for being so open-minded that they'll "put up with manners and customs of the crocodile on his native sandbar," but she thinks that when someone "of our own species" tries to tell us something clearly wrong, clearly "a bit thick," and probably insulting, Americans shouldn't take it sitting down. Another journalist is inspired by Keats and Coleridge to describe an audience as "left . . . palely loitering; mere metaphysicians meandering along the stream of consciousness, measureless to man, down to a psychopathic sea" (Evans). The tendency either to "scoff" or to "worship" disables thought in both cases (Murray).

In a world that wants points—wants brief pragmatic answers—Stein's mysterious miscellany was difficult to recognize as a position in itself. For example, when asked what she thought of Roosevelt, Stein said, "I think many things about him," but the answer was discounted as a nonanswer, likely to have been inspired by the sudden distraction of a camera's flash (O'Hara). Most people wanted—and still want—adamancy, not complexity.

Writing and Speaking in Stein's Quirky Defining

Stein's lectures did have points to them, however, and most of these depended on the difference between the sights and sounds of the English language. Attention to this distinction permeates many of the definitions set forth in her lectures—especially "What Is English Literature" and "Plays" (in *Lectures*) and "What Are Master-pieces and Why Are There So Few of Them"—as well as other works of the thirties, such as *The Geographical History of America* (1936), *Everybody's Autobiography* (1937), "My Debt to Books" (1939), and *Four in America* (written 1932–33, published in 1947). Stein discusses "writing" and "saying" in a variety of contexts, revealing that these visual and auditory media play an important definitional role for her. Her concepts of speaking, listening, writing, and reading figure into her definition of human nature and the human mind, her ideas of genius and masterpieces, and her method of picking up a person's internal rhythms and writing a portrait.

Stein told her audiences in the United States "to look at plays in relation to sight and sound rather than in terms of story and time" (Evans), and in

Everybody's Autobiography she reminds her readers to investigate the difference in her works between writing and speaking. In that book, Stein describes an exchange she carried on with a man during her lecture tour.

> On the airplane leaving there was a young man he was from Stanford University and I had spoken twice there, and he wrote questions on a piece of paper and I wrote him back the answers, . . . *he wanted to know what I meant by the difference between writing and speaking* and we spent all the time handing papers forward and back, perhaps he has kept them and so he knows what I answered him, I naturally do not, but it was interesting it always is interesting to answer anything. (294; my italics)

In the absence of these (no doubt) only enigmatically illuminating paper napkins, I have pieced together the answer to the young man's question from Stein's works in the thirties.

For Stein, speaking does not always mean talking, and writing does not only mean putting pencil to paper. For example, when Stein writes "writing," she only sometimes means spelling words onto paper; other times, "writing" refers to a state of heightened attention and consequent creativity. According to Dewey: "All discourse, oral or written, which is more than a routine unrolling of vocal habits, says things that surprise the one that says them" (*Experience*, 194); Stein thinks "writing" is when we pay enough attention to our own words that we register this surprise. When Stein says a genius can talk and listen at the same time, the auditory medium is less important than the genius's ability to escape routine and be an attentive audience for his or her own words—whether written or spoken (see *Lectures*, 170). This heightened attention can create written masterpieces, but it also makes for a rich and playful conversation:

> If the same person does the talking and the listening why so much the better there is just by so much the greater concentration. One may really indeed say that that is the essence of genius, of being most intensely alive, that is being one who is at the same time talking and listening. It is really that that makes one a genius. And it is necessary if you are to be really and truly alive it is necessary to be at once talking and listening, doing both things, not as if there [they?] were one thing, not as if they were two things, but doing them, well if you like, like the motor going inside and the car moving, they are part of the same thing. (*Lectures*, 170)

This "motor going inside and the car moving" should be reminiscent of the "essence" of what happens in conversation. Someone who talks and listens to himself might be considered narcissistic, but that speaker is in communion not so much with himself as with his words. And the loving existence of Narcissus seems preferable to the deadening repeating of Echo. Stein is often said to be repetitive, but perhaps she is instead gloriously insistent. Insisting (which three decades earlier she called "repeating") is a method of satisfying one's "will to live"—saying, "I am here now and I am different now!" Now, repeating (which earlier she called "copying") is succumbing to a kind of death—saying only, "I'll second that!" Insisting, not repeating or copying, leads to existing or living in the fullest present participle, which, for Stein, is genius (*Lectures*, 169, 170).

The rhythm of this insistence is one thing that Stein hears when she listens to a person talking and that she attempts to capture in her portraits. She writes that she tried to express "the complete conception" of a person, "the complete rhythm of a personality that I had gradually acquired by listening seeing feeling and experience" (*Lectures*, 147). In trying to express this independent existing, Stein's "portrait writing began" (*Lectures*, 171). Stein must have savored the paradox of her listening and recreating sounds in order to create something called a "portrait"—a word that most commonly suggests the primacy of sight. But "portrait" stems from "portray," which means "to draw forth"—which can be done in conversation, as well as in the visual arts.

Speaking and writing are also important in Stein's distinction between human nature and the human mind, the agent of genius (see *Geographical History*, 68–69, 96–97). In Stein's paradigm, human nature "use[s]" language by using ordinary speech; the human mind "plays" with language, which is done in the best writing (*Geographical History*, 190, 91–92). Human nature imagines an audience when it communicates, while the human mind is its own audience when it plays games by maneuvering words. Stein discusses—while demonstrating—human nature, human mind, masterpieces, and conversation in a section of *The Geographical History of America*:

> But really what I would like to know is why the very good things everybody says and everybody knows and everybody writes are not master-pieces I would really very much like to know why they are not. And when I say identity is not yes there is something in it all the time that there is not.

If not why not.

So many words to use.

Oh do not say that words have a use.

Anybody can tell what everybody knows but what does that disclose.

Oh dear what does that inclose.

After all what everybody knows is not a master-piece but everybody says it is.

Do they.

Oh yes everybody says it is.

But everybody knows what everybody knows.

And human nature is what everybody knows and time and identity is what everybody knows and they are not master-pieces and yet everybody knows that master-pieces say what they do say about human nature and time and identity, and what is the use, there is no abuse in what is the use, there is no use. Why not.

Now listen. What is conversation.

Conversation is only interesting if nobody hears.

Hear hear.

Master-pieces are second to none.

One and one.

I am not frightened but reasonably secure that whether it is so whether it is so whether it is so.

Master-piece or none.

Which is one.

I ask you which is one.

If he had not been frightened away he might have drunk at water but he finally did.

This is as good an example of a master-piece as there is. (190–91)

Elsewhere, Stein links the human mind, writing, and masterpieces so closely that it may be surprising to hear her ask why everything that is written is not a masterpiece, "why [are] the very good things everybody . . . writes . . . not master-pieces." But if we here understand "writing" to mean the physical act or legible product, then we can easily agree with her: certainly not everything printed on paper is a masterpiece. Stein has also connected "knowing" with masterpieces, writing, and the human mind, so we may also be surprised to hear that "the very good things" that "everybody knows" do not always create masterpieces. It turns out, however, that "everybody knows" about "human nature and time and identity," and that these topics are uninteresting. For example, she writes: "human nature is not interesting and what the master-pieces tell about human nature in them is not what makes them everlastingly interesting, no it is not" (*Geographical History*, 166). As Booth says in *King Lear, Macbeth, Indefinition, and Tragedy*, what makes a masterpiece is the complex texture of overlapping false expectations created by each phoneme and incomplete pattern, rather than character and plot. If the human mind creates a masterpiece, it's in spite of, not because of, these uninteresting pieces of information.

When Stein ends the first paragraph, "And when I say identity is not yes there is something in it all the time that there is not," she seems to change the subject. Asking about masterpieces, she suddenly discusses identity. But identity is a product of human nature, and neither of them can create a masterpiece. One of the defining characteristics of identity is that it causes one to make positive assertions about oneself. Stein says that one's true self (one's "entity," to borrow a term from *The Making of Americans*) cannot conform to a positive assertion—it "is not yes"—and if one makes a positive assertion about oneself, then "there is something in it [the assertion] all the time that there is not" in one's true self. The "yes" invariably asserts something that is not true. And then following her own instructions for a masterpiece, she asks herself a question about what she has just said: "if not why not." In other words (and I have explored this in *The Making of Americans* and will again in *Ida*), why is identity "not yes"?

While pondering that question, Stein wonders about the way an answer would be formed. The answer would use words—there are "So many words to use"—and while she perhaps first meant that there were so many words to choose from, she notices her own use of the word "use" and remonstrates with herself: "Oh do not say that words have a use." At the end of the next long paragraph, Stein returns to the issue—"what is the use"—and seems to decide that "there is no abuse [of the word "use"] in what is the use." This judgment may depend on the fact that she has uttered "use" in a question or, more likely, that—by asking, "what is the use"—she idiomatically means that "there is no use." "No" and "ab-" are both negatives, reputed to cancel each other out, but we have to notice that "There is use in what is the use" does not have the same meaning as the original sentence. Using "use" with a negative, and making her readers' minds fool around with its possible meanings in this way, is not the same as using the word.

Stein asks, "Anybody can tell what everybody knows but what does that disclose." Repeating what we all know does not uncover anything very interesting or new. But Stein recognizes a worse result of this complacent repetition of common knowledge: "Oh dear what does that inclose." She critiques conventional rhetoric not only because it fails to divulge anything new, but also because it can effectively build a fence around, contain, and keep from our awareness potentially new perceptions. It seems that there is a missing question: why would people keep doing this if it did not create masterpieces? The answer: "After all what everybody knows is not a masterpiece but everybody says it is." It is not the kind of masterpiece that Stein envisions, but perhaps it is a masterpiece of a different genre, one that can contain and control. It is a masterpiece in that it exerts mastery, but for Stein a masterpiece must break that mastery into pieces of less determinacy. "Oh dear," she sincerely says, realizing the truly greater danger, the way clichés cost us dearly. And "Oh dear" may also register an insincere expression of concern: "Thank you my dear for bringing me this lovely cliché as a gift," and "Oh dear! I've dropped it, and it has broken into a great number of (much more lovely and interesting) pieces." Gertrude Stein did have a "weakness for breakable objects," after all, and "a horror of people who collect only the unbreakable" (*Autobiography*, 13).

After holding this conversation with herself—asking questions, starting to answer them, moving on to related topics, and wondering about her use of certain words and their often unintended significance—Stein begins to wonder about conversation itself. "What is conversation," she asks, and she answers, "Conversation is only interesting if nobody hears." She thus points to private conversation—with ourselves, say, or in playful and intimate circumstances—the kind of conversation in which we happily game with one another. Here we can more cheerfully wonder and wander than when we are trying to demonstrate our knowledge by giving authoritative answers.

With her "Hear hear," Stein characterizes the way listeners endorse speakers, shouting to others to agree with the speaker because he has the right answer to all their questions or problems. Even alone, "hear" can be spoken as an imperative, and as an order to give consent. In a similar way, "Hear hear" describes the way we endorse what other people know and say instead of coming up with new and difficult questions. Her "Hear hear" may also be a playful way of supporting and undermining her own positive assertion in the previous sentence: "Conversation is only interesting if nobody hears." (Stein's voice is always most assertive when she is making statements with paradoxical, ambiguous, or apparently nonsensical meanings.) "Hear hear" may also tell us to define "hear" as "agree," as in: "Conversation is only interesting if nobody [agrees]." In other words, conversation is interesting only if people constantly question or check one another.

Unlike the listener who shouts, "Hear hear" to second the speaker, "Master-pieces are second to none." They refuse to "second" someone else parliamentarily. They say what they say, and they are counted "one and one" instead of rated in relation (or addition) to one another. Something is a masterpiece or not ("Master-piece or none") and exists alone instead of in relation to others. "Which is one" could be a statement which insists again that a masterpiece is one, but Stein makes it into a question in the next paragraph with "I ask you which is one," which asks something like, "How do we recognize a masterpiece?" and recalls the question with which this section began.

Ending with the claim "This is as good an example of a master-piece as there is" makes the reader thrill at Stein's flippant self-confidence, as well as wonder just what "this" is. *The Geographical History of America?* This particular sentence? This section? The previous sentence? For the moment, let's interpret "this" as the previous sentence: "If he had not been frightened away he might have drunk at water but he finally did." This sentence is not quite a non sequitur, since it follows from the word "frightened" in the actual (because first?) non sequitur in the excerpt "I am not frightened but reasonably secure that whether it is so whether it is so whether it is so." Considering the context, Stein may be declaring that her writing is either a masterpiece or it is not ("whether" suggests that there are two choices, and the next paragraph gives "master-piece or none" as the two likeliest options). She may mean that while some people would be scared—or at least uncomfortable—not knowing if something is one thing or another, she feels secure in this position of duality. The other sentence has "frightened" in it as well, but this time it is a "he" who is frightened, and as a result he cannot drink water until later. This paraphrase doesn't make any sense to me, it does not repeat any knowledge that I already had, and the verbs are strange enough that it does not even call to mind any situation that I can imagine taking place. With this final sentence, Stein may have created a masterpiece by not using words to answer a question, not saying something that everybody knows, and not using declarative verbs that afford certainty. She has successfully broken to pieces my mastery of this section of her work.

Our human minds are thrilled, of course, but by choosing another option, we can soothe our human nature. The "this" in "This is as good an example of a master-piece as there is" may refer to the whole section, which exemplifies the kind of conversation that can make a masterpiece: playful verbal exchange with oneself, paying attention to words and the many meanings they mean beyond those meanings one first intended. Stein demonstrates the kinds of questions that can make a masterpiece. They cannot be questions about human nature and the mind and time; they are the questions that arise along the way, often in response to the words one first "uses" but then sees and hears and considers. A masterpiece elicits heightened consciousness on the part of the writer and reader.

Stein does not react only to the words she wields; she also notes the sounds between those words. Although she does not use the word "masterpiece" in the "Henry James" section of *Four in America*, Stein here also distinguishes between two types of creation, one of which seems to correspond to that definition. The two ways of writing are when "you write" and when "You write what you intend to write" (*Four in America*, 124).[5] Stein contrasts Shakespeare's sonnets and Shakespeare's plays, saying that the sonnets are an example of writing what is intended (written by human nature) and the plays are an example of right writing (masterpieces of the human mind).[6] She writes that any two consecutive words in Shakespeare's plays "mak[e] three sounds, each word makes a sound, that is two words make two sounds and the words next to each other make not only a sound but nearly a sound" (129). Her assertion supports my practice of saying a series of Stein's words out loud and paying attention not only to the sounds that the words make, but also to the "nearly sounds" that are automatically made during the transitions between words. But it's possible for both writing and talking to be products of the human mind. Talking and listening at the same time, the essence of genius, and the essence of lively open chat, is talking with the playful human mind. That lively talking and listening is what Stein somehow writes.

Learning about Listening through Reading Borrow and Smollett

As I suggested when discussing *The Making of Americans*, a writer is also in indirect conversation with previous writers. In addition to Shakespeare, two other British authors, one from the eighteenth and one from the nineteenth century, also may have suggested to Stein ways of thinking about talk and print. Obviously, one cannot accord as much significance to books that Stein liked as one does to books that she wrote and in which she chose every word, but Stein mentions *Lavengro* more often than any other book title, and Stein and the author George Henry Borrow (1803–81) seem to share many interests, including a suspicion of masters.[7] Borrow's partly autobiographical novels may have particularly interested Stein because *Lavengro* discerns relationships between words based on their sounds and folk etymologies. Borrow's novels describe the material and intellectual adventures of a "word-master," or philologist. What is remarkable about this philologist is that, rather than reading dictionaries of dead languages, he learns from experience and conversation. Inspired by what he gleans in conversation with gypsies who speak Romany, a businessman who speaks Armenian, and friends who speak Scots and Irish, he ponders (often aloud, within these same conversations) how relationships may exist between words in different living languages, how these relationships suggest latent meanings in English words, and how these latent meanings can subvert our assumptions about binarisms, as well as cast into doubt our ability to communicate without ambiguity.

For example, one conversation inspires Lavengro to wonder "if divine and devilish were originally one and the same word" (Borrow, 114). Here the philologist glimpses irony within the sounds and possible histories of ordinarily oppositional English terms. "Duvel" and "devil" and "divine" and "duvelskoe" sound somewhat alike, and those sounds suggest a possible semantic relationship among them. If "divine" and "devil" are derived from the same word, then what might that mean about the relationship between the savior and the tempter of humankind? This is the kind of question Stein seems to appreciate, one that upsets our assumptions and, while having an answer in this case, makes us keep asking questions.[8]

While Borrow champions folk etymology and provocative ideas, Tobias Smollett emphasizes the creative humor in nonstandard spelling, diction, and pronunciation. Stein mentions reading Smollett at age fifteen, and, in *The Expedition of Humphry Clinker*, Smollett highlights the additional play in language afforded by sound homonyms and visual homomorphs.[9] In that book, both Tabitha Bramble, the overbearing manager of her brother's household, and Winifred Jenkins, her good-natured servant, have primarily experienced the English language auditorily. Their limited visual experience with language leads them to make mistakes in spelling and diction that exponentially increase the semantic possibilities of their epistles.[10] Reading Smollett may have encouraged Stein to notice that the gap between written and spoken words contains significance worth exploring. The rerealized or rediscovered network of meaning between the visual and auditory mediums enables more movement and play in language and allows freedom to express more, and more complex, meaning than our already word-ful and meaning-capable English language can.

Smollett, like Stein, plays with the homophones "rite," "write," and "right." These homonyms are emphasized in an epistolary narration of one character's defense of his native Scotland in *Humphry Clinker*:

To prove that [the English] had impaired the energy of our language by false refinement, he mentioned the following words, which, though widely different in signification, are pronounced exactly in the same manner—wright, write, right, rite: but among the Scots, these words are as different in pronunciation, as they are in meaning and orthography; and this is the case with many others which he mentioned by way of illustration. (200)

Tabitha and Winifred are obviously English, because in their letters they substitute "rite" for "write" (44, 107) and for "right" (71, 220, 338). All three words sound the same to them. Tabitha's mistake occurs in the context of complaining that her written commands to the servants at home are ignored, but that her brother's uneconomical advice is always followed; what right/rite/write does he have to give away her very productive cow (44)? While the novel makes it clear that the reader is to understand her brother as generous and usually wise and Tabitha as greedy and lascivious (not just thrifty and lonely), the woman's orthographic mistakes are playfully thought-provoking. Winifred reports that the "thieving and tricking" cook in Bath says "it was her rite to rummage the pantry" (71), which may make us wonder if this right by proximity and opportunity is any more or less right than the ones afforded to educated men—or are they just habitual rites? Winifred describes Christianity as ritual rather than the rightful truth when she wishes "some of our family be not fallen off from the rite way" (220). And Winifred also questions the ritual of patriarchal name distribution when she writes about Humphry Clinker's "rite naam" being "Mattew Loyd" (338). She subverts his "rite naam" by spelling the first one incorrectly, but this issue is also complicated by the fact that Humphry Clinker was named after his father Matthew Loyd. The elder Loyd had taken his mother's name when he inherited her property, but after selling that land and in order to inherit his father's estate, he "resumed [his] real name," Matthew Bramble (318). When Matthew Bramble calls it his "real name," there is no commentary on that name—it is a matter of fact and not to be pondered on. But Winifred's calling it a "rite" name leads to speculation about maternal and paternal rights, patriarchal rites, and even assumptions about right and wrong. If the male prerogatives—his rights—are a rite, than perhaps they can be questioned as arbitrary; if these rights come from his ability to write, then perhaps they can be superseded by education for women. These spelling errors suggest that the ritual of writing, in addition to other rituals, affords educated males an authority—a right—that uneducated women do not have.[11]

Stein's Reading and Writing of "Rights" and "Rites"

Stein's writing is so unusual that a reader would be hard-pressed to tell whether Stein had substituted a homonym or not, but she also plays with "rite," "write," and "right." Instead of relying on misspellings, Stein places homonyms close to one another, which induces a reader to play with substitution in those cases and suggests the possible fruitfulness of substitution elsewhere in Stein's texts. Her treatment of these homophones throughout *The Geographical History of America* suggests her interest in conversation and theorizing. Enigmatic as ever, Stein writes: "I am right because I write this" (*Geographical History*, 78). But she doesn't approve of "being right," because it is too limiting and ends discussion. As with "writing," Stein defines "right" in at least two ways. "Being right" is a job for human nature and saying, and it involves claiming certainty—and Stein implies that self-delusional certainty is the only kind:

> Write and right.
> Of course they have nothing to do with one another.
>   (*Geographical History*, 227)

Then again, "right" appears in the phrase "right writing" and is the kind of physical writing that successfully attends to and plays with language. Right writing is not the same as "being right." This "right" modifies "write" and denotes the ideal kind of writing that forms masterpieces:

> The human mind can write what it is because what it is is all that it is and as it is all that it is all it can do is to write.
>   Yes that is right. (97)

The human mind "is all that it is," in contrast with human nature, which claims to be much that it is not. Because the human mind just is and has no intention of presenting itself as something else (or even presenting itself at all), it can write. Because "The human mind has no resemblances" (which involve memory), it can write: "if it had [a habit of memory] it could not write that is to say write right" (91). These different definitions of "write" and "right" confuse the issue quite a bit but highlight the mind at play with language.

The following paragraphs continue that same game and exemplify others:

They say I am not right when I say that what you say is not the same as what you write but anybody try to write and they will say that this is so.

When you write well when you write anybody try to write and they will say that I am right.

What you say has nothing to do with what you write. . . .

They say that when I say it is not what they say but what they write that has to do with the human mind they say when I say this that I am not right but I am right because I write this and I do not say this. When I say it it is not so but when I write it it is so. Anybody can know that this is so. (*Geographical History*, 78)

Several word games are going on here. "They say" and "I say" have literal as well as idiomatic meanings, and Stein lets the idioms push her ideas along. "They say" suggests the big anonymous group that determines public opinion (discussed more fully here in chapter 6), and Stein disagrees on general principle with this generalized "they." They are also *saying*, which suggests human nature is at work, rather than the human mind. The word "well" functions in two ways: as a pause or filler word and as an important qualifying adjective for the kind of writing one must do in order to discover Stein is right.

In "Volume two" in *The Geographical History of America*, Stein frustrates readers, because she doesn't provide what we think we need to understand her. We think we need to know what the question is, and we think we need to understand an unequivocal answer. But a different kind of expression might have undermined her "message" by making it equivocal in a different way. Again playing with "right" and "write" (I've added punctuation to signal how I separate the phrases):

Volume two

I have been writing a political series just to know as well as to know that I am always right that is I am always right when I say what I say and I always say something that is what I am doing I am always saying something but as I am never writing what I am saying when I am writing I am as it were not saying something and so then[,] there it is[,] that is what writing is[:] not saying something[,] content without form[.] but anyway[,] in saying anything there is no content but there is the form of question and answer[,] and really anybody can know that a question if there is an answer[—]or an answer if there is a question[—]is almost always almost human nature[.] which we do know[—]we are not right about it[,] but we do know it[,] know that it is not at all interesting. (227–28)

Stein's ideas align themselves in two categories, one that has to do with writing and one with saying. "Saying" corresponds to "being right" and having "no content"; it takes the form of questions and answers. The part of us that deals in questions and answers is our human nature. (Since it is also our human nature that usually speaks, and usually wants some closure, this idea that saying takes on the form of questions and answers is consistent.) Our human minds cannot be right about human nature, since rightness is not a quality of the human mind.[12] The human mind can know, which is different from being right, and all that the human mind seems to know for sure about human nature is that it is not interesting. Writing corresponds with knowing and "content" and can be "without form." "Content" seems to be a matter of significance, something that "right writing" holds. "Form," though, seems to be a false signal for content. For example, we are used to the format of questions and answers, and we assume that format holds something important, but in Stein's opinion it does not.

Stein is not alone in opining that form can disguise a lack of content. Neil Postman in *Amusing Ourselves to Death: Public Discourse in the Age of Show Business* criticizes contemporary public discourse for having "little content, as this word used to be defined" (112). He asserts that questions and answers in the form of crossword puzzles, quiz shows, and the game Trivial Pursuit are invented contexts "in which otherwise useless information might be put to some apparent use" (76). Combining terms from Stein and Postman, human nature may be what tempts us into being amused, what appreciates the images and the speed of modern "news," but the human mind appreciates "such larger abstractions as truth, honor, love, [and] false-hood [which] cannot be talked about in the lexicon of pictures" or, Stein might add, within a prearranged format (Postman, *Amusing Ourselves,* 72). In *The Geographical History of America,* Stein explains that human nature deals in questions and answers, and she suggests that while this may make a person feel right, it does not give him knowledge. Instead, questions and answers may lead to a false sense of understanding; they are part of a rite we enact when we try to understand our world and ourselves, but that formula only misleads us into thinking we know something. If you have an answer to a question (or even a question for an answer), then that issue seems re-solved; the questioner and answerer know what is important about that field of inquiry and forget that original discovery occurs through observation and wonder, not questions and answers. As Henry Adams points out: "Nothing in education is so astonishing as the amount of ignorance it accumulates in the form of inert facts" (379).

On the other hand, right writing somehow escapes this particular question-and-answer form. Writing has content without this form, and if we look at Stein's writing, we learn that content often consists of phrases that may or may not be accurately called questions—they don't have question marks and they don't have answers. Stein says that the best modern writing, because it has content instead of form, must be done by a woman, and that she is doing "the important literary thinking" herself (*Geographical History*, 210, 214). If we understand content to mean questions without answers, and if we believe the widespread claim that feminine writing—like women's sexuality, the argument goes—is willing to be open-ended, inconclusive, and less authoritative, then there may be something to what she says. Stein writes that "it is always interesting to answer anything," but (as we saw on the airplane) she does not seem to care if she remembers the answers. The activity is more important than the product.

What have been reported as Gertrude Stein's last words—"What is the answer . . . in that case what is the question?"—are so appropriate that the story seems apocryphal. If so, it was made up by someone who understood issues that Stein worried to death. Instead of the repetition and certainty of the questions and answers in the catechism or just the reassuring answers of Christian last rites, Stein wonders, as she leaves the world, not only about the truth but also about the way to truth.

When Stein dies, she asks for "the answer" and Alice responds with silence. It's possible that Stein is referring to the circumstances of their conversation: Stein is dying of stomach cancer and insists on an operation even though the doctors have said the risks are too great. The dilemma may seem obvious: either she dies of stomach cancer or she dies from the operation, so there is no good answer. But "What is the question?" is a good question. Thus far perhaps they have assumed the question, probably something like, "How am I going to stay alive?" But is that the most interesting question? Perhaps the question is "What is the best way to die?" Or maybe Stein isn't thinking about the best way for her physical form to expire. By asking "What is the question?" Stein may wonder about and accomplish the most affecting exit from her physical form, riding her intellectual hobbyhorse into the sunset. One reviewer comments that Stein "wonders in rhythm and in cadences and she rouses wonder in you and she never answers your

wonders because that would end it, that would be death" (Winter, 83–84).
Her dying words are her characteristic way of refusing to die.

When in 1934 Stein says, "Language as a real thing is not imitation either of sounds or colors or emotions it is an intellectual recreation" (*Lectures*, 238), she celebrates Ferdinand de Saussure's 1916 conception that the "relation of words to their meanings is fundamentally arbitrary" (Lehman, 94). But Stein adds that language as it "has come to be spoken and written," holds in it "all the history of its intellectual recreation," which suggests that the semantic tradition has an interesting history of its own which influences the multiple connotations of words.[13] Stein's friend and publisher Daniel-Henry Kahnweiler emphasizes freedom and self-determination when he writes that Stein's "entirely new use of [English] vocabulary" frees the words from "any law antecedent to the act of creation" and "abandon[s]" those words to their "interior logic" (xii). The problem with German, Stein says, is that there is too strong a connection between words and their meanings: "the german language as a language suffers from this what the words mean sound too much like what they do, and children do these things by one sort or another of invention but this has really nothing to do with language" (*Lectures*, 238). According to Stein, then, the poor Germans don't get "intellectual recreation" from their language. The good thing about a language such as English is that there is no intrinsic connection between words and meanings but there are an infinite number of connections between words and words, and these connections create a jungle gym for the exercise of our intellects.

Not only does this network of meaning allow "intellectual recreation" as in playful fun, but "intellectual recreation" also suggests we can recreate our language and our meaning as we move onward. Derrida playfully deconstructs, but Stein's play is an intellectual reconstruction. Connections are made by noting visual and auditory similarities between words that we usually understand as semantically different. Stein disposes words in unusual arrangements such that her readers are disposed to notice their sights and sounds, make recreational connections between them, and produce unusual arrangements of meaning. Stein's word arrangements demand that words do more than they usually do. She writes: "I like the feeling of words doing as they want to do and as they have to do when they live where they have to live that is where they have come to live which of course they do do" (*Narration*, 15). Words can do what they want to do only if we are listening to them as they come out of our mouths, or watching them as they land on the paper in front of us—if we read creatively instead of dogmatically.

While Stein demonstrates these conversations in *The Geographical History of America* and in her lectures, most of her listeners in the United States walked away wondering what she meant. They tried to follow along with her words instead of participating in a free exchange of ideas and letting meaning develop as it could, as it does.

CHAPTER 5

Talking Boundaries into Thresholds in *Ida*

S TEIN PREFERRED NOT to be introduced before her lectures; reports state that she just walked up to the stage (usually down the center aisle, through the audience) and started talking without any introduction or introductory remarks ("Miss Stein Speaks"; "Princeton Dazed"; Schriftgiesser). She liked to meet people straight in, in her own terms. But Stein became an American icon during the tour, and she was happily but uneasily aware of her fame. In a December 1934 letter to Carl Van Vechten, she expressed her amazement and pleasure at being identifiable to someone who very probably would not be attending one of her free but often exclusive lectures:

> a reporter girl, told me and she swears she did not make it up here in Toledo that she went to the station to meet us on a train we did not come on and she asked the gate man if we had come through and he looked blank and a shabby citizen leaning on the wall said no she did not come through and the ticket man said who and the shabby man said sure I know her I never saw her but she would not get by here without my knowing her and then he said to the porter, you know her the one who said a rose is a rose is a rose is a rose you know her. (Burns, 368)

Aware of the complications of fame even before setting foot in the United States, Stein describes in *How Writing Is Written* (1936) its dangerous effects on subjectivity:

> One never gets quite used to unexpectedly seeing one's name in print no matter how often it happens to you to be that one; it always gives you a shock of a slightly mixed-up feeling, are you or are you not one. No matter how often it happens there is always this thing, but what is that, imagine what is that compared to never having heard anybody's voice

speaking while a picture is doing something, and that voice and that person is yourself, if you could really and truly be that one. It upset me very much when that happened to me, there is no doubt about that, if there can really not be any doubt about anything. ("I Came and Here I Am," 68; my italics)

What does it mean to look at the self from the outside? From a perspective of time and distance? "Are you or are you not one." If you are hearing yourself speak, and watching your lips move while you talk, which one are you? Can you be two, speaking to yourself?

Ida and its title character act as sounding boards for various possibilities about the self, and these ideas contribute, with much of Stein's other writing, to a theory of personal subjectivity and social cohesion that depends upon conversation. In the novel, Stein is still interested in some of the details of speech, but here that interest is compounded with an analysis of the self. Stein wonders why a self is so fragile, who makes it, and how to avoid letting others break it. She seems finally to perceive the self as a formation of the interactional conversations that take place between voices within and voices without, but a problem arises if any of the voices become too hardened by expectation or reputation. She recognizes fame as a dilemma for the famous and even begins to see it as a troublesome phenomenon among the fans; she will explore this issue of the public as a political mass in similar terms in later works. Stein sees the cessation of verbal intercourse as an individual's living death, but she also depicts true death as the end of reciprocal conversation, petrifying the deceased into the subject of a summary monologue.

There are (of course) some thought-provokingly mysterious sections to the novel, but Ida speaks in standard phrases, at least one of which she exchanges for another in a new setting. She agreeably begins many of her sentences with "yes" (*Ida*, 628, 692), and Stein tells us that she says "nice little things" such as "all right" (628), "You are very welcome," and "very well I thank you" (625). Ida "liked to thank" and "she liked to be thanked," although Stein suggests that Ida "was not really interested" in much, including "Anything that was given to her": "she [just] liked to thank" (692). After many exchanges of "how do you do" (623, 625), Ida moves house and notices that people in her new town say, "How are you?" so "Ida learned to say it like that. How are you" (661). Later, when Ida is "resting" so often that she appears to be ill, she learns that some people (nurses, probably) say, "well how are we today," or "well and how are we today" (701). In describing the way Ida never answers this question, no matter how many people ask it,

Stein offers up an axiom on a conversational routine: "Ida would have nothing to say. She had not answered the first one and if you are resting you cannot hurry enough to catch up and so she had nothing to say," because "you always have to answer the first one before you answer the second one" (701). That is, if you want to avoid offending anyone.

Ida herself, like the earlier Stein, is interested in food and talk: "She liked to see people eat, in restaurants and wherever they eat, and she liked to talk" (*Ida*, 624). But Stein seems to have become intensely interested in how people become themselves, and how they stay that way—an interest she had begun to explore in *The Making of Americans*. In *Ida*, she demonstrates how the self is endangered by the constrictions of fame. Listening to what "they say" can alter (or freeze) the sense of self, so celebrity offers an intensified instance of a common problem. The problem is especially complicated by the fact that living people with real being are flexible and, like Ida, "change all the time" (629). How do we genuinely remain ourselves without getting stuck and staying too much the same? How do we insist instead of copy? Possibly the only solution is to maintain a give-and-take relationship with oneself and others. We must keep up the interactional conversation of mutual discovery.

I choose the word "self" because Stein's specific understanding of the word "identity" (in a pair with "entity") makes that word impossible to use in a general sense. I mean "self" to represent the varying proportions of (formal, intentional, sometimes false) identities and (basic, internal, often ignored but necessarily true) entities a person experiences as self—at particular moments, but also across a lifetime. Identities are simple, performative, and singular; entities are complex, inherent, and singular; but the self is multiple, more than an idea, and dependent on experience and the interaction between external and internal forces. In fact, Ida may represent that very mix, Ida-entity.

Conversation may also be the place where the self is most evident in the moment, demonstrating the provisional, transient, evanescent agreement our different sides and multiple external influences have reached with each other, the ongoing compromise we've reached with our potential selves and the world we inhabit. The self is perhaps best manifested in the moment of speech when each utterance is the result of countless conscious and unconscious decisions about the relationship between our unique selves and the others! Each decision in which we negotiate our way through our own desires and the forces of external expectation makes us a combination of self and other. Stein might agree that we are what we eat, but she would also add that we are what we say. By our fruits ye shall know us, and the fruit of all this silent dialogue is our uttered conversation. We carry on a running multisided dialogue as we try to get a sense of who we are, and the answer is somewhere in between, in the dialogue itself (like meaning in modern semiotics). If I am not just one but two, if I am not just I but you (and it, that there), then I am formed by the conversation held between me and myself, me and you, us and it—the conversation among all. I exist within what my selves and yours (who are just as multiple) all end up saying to each other. But *Ida* is not really about single utterances. *Ida* seems to be more about the negotiations than about the uttered conclusions we reach.

I use the word "conversation" because that's what is taking place on real and metaphorical—audible and inaudible—levels. If the self is the shape I just described—multiple and influenced by other selves—then conversation within and without is of primary importance. Certainly we talk to ourselves, within ourselves, as much as or more than we talk to others. Perhaps silent and internal debate is only conversation in a metaphorical sense, but it mimics the exchange between differently embodied "real" voices. The most metaphorical of these conversations—since one side can't use language—is between the nonhuman environment and ourselves, yet whatever we notice about that environment we internalize, turn into words, and thus enable to participate in our silent internal conversation. Sam Hamilton—who, like many other characters in *Ida*, appears only to speak and disappear—says, "I like everything I say to be said out loud" (627), which suggests that much of the other conversation in the book takes place silently. Sam likes to speak "out loud," but much that the characters "say" in this book is part of their own silent intrapersonal communion, most obviously when Ida-Ida writes to Ida, and when Ida writes to Winnie.

In *Ida*, then, Stein is less interested in the mechanics or "essence" of small talk than in the conversational nature of subjectivity, an idea that might have come naturally to her, or that could have been inspired by George Herbert Mead, who called thought "inner conversation" ("Social Self," 146). Individuals are always conversing—with other people's words, with impressionistic memories of those words (the way other people's words have become internalized), and among aspects of the self whose origins are so complex that it's impossible to determine whether they originated "in here" or "out there." Our public and private selves vie for primacy, our old and new selves disagree about how we should spend our time, our angelic and devilish selves make decisions inconsistent with each other, our skeptical and creative selves cooperate (we hope) to determine the kind of work we do, and so on. Sometimes one voice might "win," but usually the voices have to coexist and keep talking. Stein seems to envision subjectivity as a product of all that gets said in serious colloquy, gossipy prattle, or deep communion among voices originating both within and without.

Like utterances, subjectivity is "context-shaped" and "context-renewing" (Heritage, 242). Subjectivity is changed by, and changes, the subjectivities (and even the nonhuman environments) around it. To borrow and amend an idea and phrase from Neil Postman, who calls his field "media ecology," Stein explores the social ecology of self. Postman argues that the environment in which contemporary humans in the developed world find ourselves consists most evidently of the media around us; language is our primary environment. Stein's ecology of the self necessitates mutual adaptation through language exchange.[1] That's a fancy way of saying that if a person talks and listens, she changes and is changed, but it also suggests that a person has a self from which to speak and adapt. We do not start with nothing; our peculiar elements express themselves and react with others in all-their-own ways.

A self and that which is not part of that self may be less distinct than we assume, and a creative and perpetual dialogue takes place across or through the permeable boundary between them. Referring, inevitably, to inside and outside, self and other, I am using the very Cartesian distinction that Stein muddies; my plain English can't quite escape the intellectual bonds that Stein's "cuckoo" writing can. Stein writes in *Ida*: "Once upon a time way back there were always gates," but then "little by little there were no fences no walls anywhere. For a little time they had a gate even when there was no fence. It was there just to look elegant and it was nice to have a gate that would click even if there was no fence. By and by there was no gate" (626). Once upon a time there might have been distinct properties, distinct selves, but then the fences disappeared and the gates were just ornamental. Now, she posits, none of that is left or is even necessary. Ida's preference is "People should be there and not come through a door" (690). It might look as if Stein is still tearing apart the distinction between self and other, but really she's already building something else in its place. Some people might be worrying about how to handle the loss of the individual and apparently independent self, but Stein imagines a new (or just newly recognized) sense of personhood arising from the acknowledgment and celebration of messy inner subjectivity and its analogies to a wider human network.

"Who is any one said the wife to the husband"

While it is possible to read *The Making of Americans* as a psychomachia in which Stein takes herself and Americans apart and puts neither back together, it is impossible to read *Ida*—particularly "First Half"—as anything but the subject's separation into pieces. Ida is many people: she is one ("I" looks like "1") and two ("da" sounds a bit like "deux") and possibly the Freudian "id" negotiating with voices different from the predictably conscientious superego and the mediating ego. (None of her parts know their part; perhaps they are too vital for that). "Da" is also Russian for "yes," one of Ida's favorite words. Ida is an "I" and an "idea" that "I" thinks. She is probably not Stein's ideal, but it is also a mistake to understand Ida as abnormal—as having a multiple personality disorder, for example. Unlike Edmund Spenser, Stein does not characterize a self with "a thousand yong ones" in its mouth as a dangerous and monstrous Errour ("Faerie Queene," 1.15–18).

The novel explores Ida's relationship with herself, and her different selves necessarily communicate with each other through various kinds of conversation. In *Everybody's Autobiography*, Stein writes that "real ideas are not the relation of human beings as groups but a human being to himself inside him" (206). In *Ida*, Stein explores these "real ideas." Ida talks to named aspects of herself: Ida-Ida and Winnie, for sure, and perhaps others (since self and other can be so easily be mistaken here). Stein's report that Ida "was just going to talk to herself" and so "she no longer even needed a twin" suggests that these twins represent Ida's multiple voices (*Ida*, 634). And this suggestion remains, in spite of the fact that Winnie herself—as far I can tell—never says anything but only inspires reactions from the people around her. Their communication hardly turns psychological drama into action, so it is more likely that it represents Stein's understanding of the self as formed by conversation—internal and silent conversation, as well as external and aloud.

Both types of communication form and inform Ida's sense of self, because internal conversation is influenced by her affiliations with the people around her. By blurring the distinctions between them, Stein depicts the mutual dependency of individual selves. When Ida converses with named aspects of herself, the reader has to guess who is internal and who is not. While Winnie and Ida-Ida are almost certainly internal (the beautiful parts of Ida that make her famous), Andrew is a mystery. We are first told: "Everybody knew that Andrew was one of two. He was so completely one of two that he was two" (*Ida*, 661). Either Andrew is a twin, too, or he is one of Ida's selves (she's gotten rid of her other twins by now), or he is two different things: a person in his own right *and* an internalized voice. Perhaps he is both an externalized self (a real person with whom Ida identifies) and an internalized other (a voice within Ida that has been inspired by that of an external, "real" person). Andrew continues to be identified by contradictions: he is there but he never seems to begin being there, he does "not notice Ida but he saw her," he takes lots of walks but "in a way was never out walking," and "Ida called him but she really never called him" (662, 663). He is "always there," but Ida says, "How do you do" to him when she meets him, although Stein adds that "she did not really meet him nobody did" (663). In these ways, he just seems to *be* there, to be there *always*, and perhaps even to be inside, reachable through silence and always observing. Andrew's case suggests the difficulty of determining whether a character represents an alien aspect of oneself (an otherness that is internal; a facet of oneself that does not feel homogenous with the rest of the self); or a very familiar other with whom one identifies (an external self, an extension of one's being). When self and other are so easily confused, real (oral, aural, public, exterior) conversation and metaphorical (silent, private, interior) dialogue are indistinguishable. In spite of the presence of Ida Ida, Winnie, Andrew, an officer, men with orange blossoms in their hats, five aunts, and a married couple, among others, *Ida* may be a book with one character. Ida exists between and among these other personalities, and they seem to exist mainly within her, as well.

Stein's analysis of human types, and her exploration of the ways that listeners can influence the self-perception of the speaker, lead her, even as early as *The Making of Americans*, to the possibility that the only definable difference between inside and out is an arbitrary epidermic perimeter. She writes of a particular type of person who is "being independent dependent being in completely fluid condition and being a whole one only, and always being one, by having a skin to hold it in and to separate it so from every one and make it so an individual one" (*Making*, 398, and see 387). Other characters and types have "being" in them "in a more solid concentration," and *The Making of Americans* does not explicitly delve further into the subject of the indeterminate self. (Although, because it's so difficult to remember which is which of the two main types—"dependent independent" and "independent dependent"—she may implicitly be discussing this indeterminate mutual dependence.) *The Making of Americans* already suggests, then, that the differences between self and other are very minor: if we are all made up of the same components in different proportions—an unknown ratio of attacking and resisting, say—then the main difference between self and other is a thin layer of skin.[2] When we are defining ourselves as unique, perhaps we are really only gerrymandering to form an appearance of consistency.

Stein's fame, which came to her long after she wrote *The Making of Americans*, may have radicalized her thinking but did not qualitatively change it. *Ida* continues her thoughts on fluid, interpenetrating being. That which exists outside a person's skin can influence a person's self—that which is outside comes inside—and, by the time she writes *Ida*, Stein has felt this public influence so strongly that she only approximately draws the line between self and not-self in that work. The influence of these outside voices on Ida is so significant that the boundary between self and other is almost indistinguishable. We feel we know the difference, of course, and Stein seems to have successfully divided her sense of self from her reputation, but the turbid area around Ida's personal boundary makes definition very difficult.

Everything and everyone a person attends to becomes part of the self's experience and being. In *The Dialogical Self: Meaning as Movement*, Hubert J. M. Hermans and Harry J. G. Kempen bring together the ideas of Giambattista Vico, John Dewey, William James, George Herbert Mead, and Mikhail Bakhtin to grapple with Descartes and the Cartesian basis of Western thought about the self. Hermans and Kempen explain that while the French structuralists resist the Cartesian distinction between mind and body, subject and object, and they "decentralize" the self, their idea of a multifaceted human self is subject to "impersonal structures and processes." In this constructivist model, the self is at the mercy of the inhuman world. The pragmatists, however, and Hermans and Kempen, "stress *inter*subjective transactions and practices" (32; my italics). Citing John Dewey, Hermans and Kempen define the subject as an "agent-sufferer" or "embodied agent . . . living between two centers: the subject as acting upon the world and the world acting upon the subject. The interaction is so complex that the environment is in a way *in* the subject" (31).[3] While the French structuralists see the self as subject to the other, the pragmatists see the other as part of the self, and see them as having a reciprocal relationship. Perhaps I exaggerate only a little when I say that what is "out there" has to come "in here" to be noticeable.

This analysis suggests, among other things, that human interaction—which tends to occur through conversation—greatly influences subjectivity. Understanding subjectivity through dialogue "acknowledges both the existence of pre-existing structures and the subject as an innovative agent" (Hermans and Kempen, 47n1).[4] Starting with the (false) assumption that there is a single, stable self from which we speak, it is quite easy to accept the theory that this self was developed in relationship to the other selves around it. (Indeed, how—or where—else is language acquired to describe the self or anything else?) Acknowledging that the self continues to interact with other people, and to participate in a wide range of relationships, recommends the further axiom that the self is constantly under renovation and even develops multiple, coexistent, and sometimes contradictory forms. We are in dialogue with the world. Indeed, each of us multiplies into a we when encountering the multiplicities of the social world.

The characters in *Ida* are only vaguely distinguished from one another, which makes us wonder who they are, specifically, as well as who *anyone* is. Ida creates Winnie as a separate being, but everyone else thinks they are the same person. For example, one man sees Winnie, follows Winnie, rings the bell and asks for Winnie, but "of course there was no Winnie," and "he could not ask for Ida because he did not know Ida. . . . Well in a way he did ask for Ida" (*Ida*, 623). Midway through *Ida*, a married couple discusses possible husbands for their houseguest Ida, a discussion which produces an overwhelming question: "who is any one said the wife to the husband" (655). Inherently a deep question, its exchange between spouses complicates the issue even further. The marriage service would have husband and wife be "one flesh." Are the two participants in this dialogue separate people, or two halves (or even smaller fractions) of the same person? And how does either state of affairs explicate the question, "Who is anyone"? This reminder of the binding of two people in marriage also suggests further divisions in Ida: she marries several times, and her husbands—other parts of herself, though she doesn't seem to pay any attention to them—keep disappearing from the novel. So we are left wondering: who is any one, or anyone? Stein's answer: perhaps there is no such thing as "one."[5]

Fame and the Public: Alienation from the Self

From early on, Ida feels divided within herself. The novel begins with her mother trying to keep Ida from being born. That birth leads to a further birth, because "as Ida came, with her came her twin, so there she was Ida-Ida," which suggests a plausible psychoanalytic scenario in which an unwanted child develops dual selves to separate good and bad characteristics (*Ida*, 611). Ida separates herself from her appearance: she creates a beautiful and famous twin, to whom she writes letters and from whom she often feels quite alienated. Another creation story for this twin arises when Ida tells her dog, Love (who is "almost blind"), that Ida is "tired of being just one" and so she is "going to have a twin yes I am Love" (613). When this twin dyes her hair, it is Ida who will be called "a suicide blonde" (613).[6] Stein's "Ida often wrote letters to herself that is to say she wrote to her twin," and in these letters she touts her twin's appearance: "I think that you could be a queen of beauty . . . they go everywhere and everybody looks at them and everybody sees them" (618). Ida thinks of the beauty queen as someone separate from herself, as modern sports figures and politicians refer to themselves in third person by name. But others see the everyday Ida (the speaker or subject who knows herself) and the famed Ida (the object or thing known) as one. "Nobody knew anything about her except that she was Ida but that was enough because she was Ida the beauty Ida" (619). The twin is (a part of) Ida but feels alien.

Having become (or having one part of her become) the beauty queen, Ida feels lost: "she was a beauty, she had won the prize she was judged to be the most beautiful but she was bewildered" (*Ida*, 620). Ida never has any sense that she is the beauty queen. Stein tells a strange tale which suggests that the lost Ida develops a third internal other who may mediate for, or just be confused between, the other two. On the way home to a place different from the home address she gives out, Ida

> saw a woman carrying a large bundle of wash. This woman stopped and she was looking at a photograph, Ida stopped too and it was astonishing, the woman was looking at the photograph, she had it in her hand, of Ida's dog Love. This was astonishing.
>
> Ida was so surprised she tried to snatch the photograph and just then an automobile came along, there were two women in it, and the automobile stopped and they stepped out to see what was happening. Ida snatched the photograph from the woman who was busy looking at the automobile and Ida jumped into the automobile and tried to start it, the two women jumped into the automobile threw Ida out and went on in the automobile with the photograph. Ida and the woman with the big bundle of wash were left there. The two of them stood and did not say a word. (620)

If we think of the two women in the car as Ida and her beautiful twin, then the Ida walking home is a third Ida, lost between her famous persona and her (imaginary but convenient to call it so in this schema) originary self. (The two women in the car could also represent the two names Ida has given her more famous persona: Ida-Ida and Winnie. The walker would then be our alienated Ida.) This walking Ida is literally "go[ing] a long way round" between the address she gives out (as the beauty queen) and her private home (that of the first Ida) (620). The photograph of Love is probably available to the woman looking at it because it depicts the dog of the famous beauty queen, but the lost Ida can't understand why a picture of *her own* dog has been published.[7] The woman with the photograph is far enough outside her own self to be staring at a picture of a stranger's dog, and to let someone steal the picture when the beauty queen in the car takes her full attention. She is so blinded by what she's supposed to see, so enamored of the picture, that she cannot see the real Ida right there with her. The lost Ida wants to get into the car and take back control. But once begun, the role of "publicity saint" moves on its own, like an automobile, and the saint herself doesn't have to (or can't) do anything but "rest."[8] The famous Ida regains the driver's seat, and another aspect of Ida is silenced: she and the woman "did not say a word."

There isn't much to the beauty queen—whom Ida eventually names Winnie—but the attention she gets makes her interesting. Attention breeds more attention, and the people who give it have lost their will to attend to whatever idiosyncrasies interest them most. In one episode: "The place was full, nobody looked at Ida. Some of them were talking about Winnie. They said. But really, is Winnie so interesting? They just talked and talked about that" (*Ida*, 622). They can't see Ida—who looks just like Winnie, who *is* Winnie in at least one sense, but who probably doesn't carry herself the same way—because the *idea* of Winnie is so strong in their minds. "They said" is one of Stein's ways of pointing toward a group mentality, a loss of individuality and personal discrimination. Stein asks us, "But really, is Winnie so interesting?" and perhaps the crowd is wondering the same thing, except that as they talk and talk, they prove that they do find her "so interesting."

Winnie becomes a precursor to Don DeLillo's "most photographed barn in America" (12). Stein describes one of the "many things [that] happened to Winnie:

> Once there were two people who met together. They said. What shall we do? So what did they do. They went to see Winnie. That is they went to look at Winnie.
>
> When they looked at her they almost began to cry. One said. What if I did not look at her did not look at Winnie. And the other said. Well that is just the way I feel about it.
>
> After a while they began to think that they had done it, that they had seen Winnie, that they had looked at her. It made them nervous because perhaps really had they.

One said to the other. Say have we and the other answered back, say have we.

Did you see her said one of them. Sure I saw her did you. Sure he said sure I saw her.

They went back to where they came from. (*Ida*, 622)

For lack of something better to do, these two people go to look at (not necessarily see) Winnie, the beauty queen. Their incomplete expression about what would happen if they chose not to look at Winnie suggests first the hypothesis that she would not exist without spectators and also the likelihood that these people are not quite thoughtful enough to think that thought in its entirety. Neither of them seems sure that they see Winnie, but their shared experience allows them to believe that they have. As Murray Jay Siskind, DeLillo's "visiting lecturer on living icons," says about visiting the barn: "Being here is a kind of spiritual surrender. We see only what others see. . . . We've agreed to be part of a collective perception" (DeLillo, 10, 12). While Ida, Ida-Ida, and Winnie are distinct but communicating personas within one person, these two physically distinct interlocutors share a point of view. They agree on everything, however vaguely, which may suggest that they serve as external selves for one another. And they are not changed by their experience: they saw what they set out to see and then "went back to where they came from."

If the barn were a "living icon" like Winnie, then Siskind's questions would address even more of Stein's concerns about the life of a living sign; he says, "No one sees the barn," and he asks, "What was the barn like before it was photographed?" (DeLillo, 12–13). He concludes: "We can't answer these questions because we've read the signs, seen the people snapping the pictures. We can't get outside the aura. We're part of the aura" (13). So imagine Ida's bewilderment, trapped inside the aura of her own double's fame.[9] Can she escape? Can she assert herself? Since she's essentially passive, is passivity her one recourse for self-expression? And can that self-expression really live underneath, or in any way revolt from, Winnie's fame?

Ida is herself, interested in herself, and perhaps too self-absorbed, too much interested in sitting, resting, and being satisfied with that. She wants mainly to talk to herself, a situation in which she feels nobody can interrupt her (*Ida*, 634). But her self-absorption has some social benefits: she will probably not become like these men, who need reassurance from others about their own experiences. Ida's unlikely to become part of the anonymous "they." She's a complex person who cannot become a cog in a political wheel (though her passivity is likely to make her irrelevant). She will not accept authority; as soon as someone knows even her twin's name, Ida leaves town. Names, the ones we call ourselves or the ones others call us, are a form of power. One of Ida's husbands meets a chief of police who can't catch fish; the chief says: "Well I caught a trout the other day and he got away from me. Why didn't you take his number said Arthur. Because fish can't talk was the answer" (631). The fish is uncatchable without a name, or without a voice to participate in this transaction with the police chief. In fact, pointing forward to a problem faced in ecocriticism, Stein suggests that the fish does not inhabit names at all; the problem is not only choosing the *correct* voice to impose on the fish, but imposing *any* voice on the fish. As a talking person, however, Ida has to work to avoid identifying herself, to avoid letting herself be mastered by an identity. Nor will Ida become an authority over someone else: she wants to remain childless because she doesn't want to "tell [her children] what to do" (634). This is an example of her interest, first, in her relationship with herself, not with others and, second, in interactional instead of transactional conversation. (Ida's tendencies are also related to Stein's antiauthoritarianism, which I discuss in the next chapter in greater depth.)

The Self and Its Trappings

Ida addresses often unrecognized influences on the self from which we speak, including the bodies we both are and feel we inhabit. Our bodies have a say in our subjectivities, and other people's bodies speak to us before the people start using words. Ida wishes to be free of these restrictions, which may explain why she runs away from Winnie, who represents Ida's appearance. She does not like to be recognized. Stein points to the way the physical body influences the mind, ideas, and subjectivity:

> A woman said to Ida, I only like a white skin. If when I die I come back again and I find I have any other kind of skin then I will be sure that I was very wicked before.
> This made Ida think about talking. (624)

A contemporary reader is surprised that this woman's words don't make Ida think about racism, but Ida's thoughts encompass the problem of racial prejudice. The woman speaks from her (probably) white-skinned body, which points to "the role of the body in the process of knowing itself" (Hermans and Kempen, 9).[10] Like most thinkers influenced by the legacy of Descartes, though, this woman does not acknowledge the ways her body influences her views on skin color (and probably on other topics); she assumes that if she were reborn as a person of color, she would still believe as her white-skinned self did. A reader also wonders why this woman makes this comment to Ida, and Ida's own skin color becomes important to understanding the exchange—but we don't really know Ida's race. If Ida is white skinned, then the woman may be assuming that Ida agrees with her. If Ida is a person of color, the woman is chastising her for wickedness. This conversation also makes a reader notice that Stein never describes Ida. In fact, *Ida* must be one of a very few novels in which the female main character is assigned no physical characteristics.

Issues of identity upset Ida, perhaps because they tend to influence what people say. They make interactional conversation less free-form, more predictable, and perhaps slightly more transactional. So Ida chooses to converse with people of indeterminate identity: officers without their uniforms (who may or may not be officers) and people who have not introduced themselves by name (624–25).[11] Stein writes: "This makes conversation with them easier and more difficult" (624). Ida does not want an officer to tell her his name because "if I knew your name I would not be interested in you, no, I would not" (625–26). Ida likes to speak to people about whom she knows as little as possible; without roles to fulfill (except, of course, the female one that she carries with her always), Ida—like Stein, who would not speak to officials—can specialize in interactional conversation. She can speak without predicting the consequences and thus perhaps being tempted to alter what she says.

In spite of her dislike of roles, and even though she eventually murders Winnie, Ida recognizes the difficulty of losing a pose:

> Ida said to this one. When you put your uniform away for the summer you are afraid of moths. Yes said the officer. I understand that, said Ida, and she slowly drifted away, very thoughtfully, because she knew of this. Alone and she was alone and she was afraid of moths and of mothballs. The two go together. (*Ida*, 626)

Trying to free herself from Winnie is a task about which Ida feels mixed emotions. She wants to escape her public persona and be a private, freer self, but she is attached to the fame and beauty of that twin. She and the officer are afraid of moths because moths can destroy the uniform (and uniformed) side of themselves, the side they show to the world and for which they are known, but she is also afraid of mothballs because they tempt her to protect Winnie, which can only perpetuate the overshadowing of whomever she sees as her real(er) self. Ida is afraid of losing her socially constructed or performative self—but also scared of the poisons involved in trying *not* to lose it.

A public persona argues with the internal felt self in an attempt to find the real self and work from there. But the persona is what others tell one about oneself. It starts outside in the environment (and that's a simplification too, since one did or is something that gives this impression), but one internalizes it and it becomes a voice in the internal dialogue. (The external world can, after all, say almost nothing unless one listens, pays attention, brings impressions inside, and says them to oneself.) The environmental influence on the self is also felt through the body—the skin, the epidermis itself. Outward appearance encourages one to feel certain ways about oneself, because of pains or pleasures, other people's reactions, advantages or disadvantages conferred.[12] Like the beautiful Ida, one may not at first see the disadvantages of this persona; like her, one may want to both erase and retain that image. It is easier to be aware of external influences when one is aware of audiences, one knows them and what they want to hear (or not), and one finesses one's utterances. In this way, developing a self is like choosing what to say: one has personal agency, one can say whatever one wants, and at the same time one is heavily influenced by forces from all directions.

Stein at Night Means Delight

The placement and content of Stein's obituary in the *Nation* reveals her impact on Americans. An observation on Gertrude Stein's death appears two weeks after she dies, on the third page of the magazine's opening section, "The Shape of Things," surrounded by commentary on Senate approval of the Morse resolution, the stalemate between Truman and the Seventy-ninth Congress, India's extrication from the British Empire, the "cost padding" of war contractors, and the Senate decision to fund physical but not social sciences. The anonymous writer begins: "Hearing that Gertrude Stein is dead is like hearing that Paul Bunyan has been eaten by his ox Babe." This writer goes on to assert that Stein made herself into

> an American legend more lasting than anything Barnum himself ever created. . . . she sat in Paris as the Pythoness used to sit at Delphi: everybody in the world, from Picasso to a sergeant of marines, came asking for a sign, and went away happy with some oracular utterance which he could finger as if it were a Chinese puzzle. (If you believe in yourself

hard enough, the world will beat a path to your door—especially if you live in Paris.) . . . in our secular, commercial, and merciless age, she came somehow to stand for Wisdom, which doesn't sell itself in the streets, but gives itself away at home, in cipher. ("Shape of Things")

Stein herself had become a sign (and was sometimes misunderstood as "the essence of mockery"), but this author (and some portion of his or her audience) saw Stein as a sign for "Wisdom" with a capital W.[13] And this sign makes signs like an oracle.

Stein's status as a sign put her in stasis. An obituary in *Saturday Review* calls her a "monumental and enigmatic figure," whose "strong, almost masculine face, with its close-cropped, wiry gray hair was magnificently sculptural and timeless" (Smith). She might not have anticipated this particular summary of her life, but while traveling throughout the United States reading newspaper stories about herself, she would have perceived that these were prevalent impressions of her. Continuing to be human, writing from her human mind, would be difficult for anyone who notices her own "monumental" reputation and "sculptural" image. Timelessness implies a constancy Stein could not, and would not want to, achieve. Brinnin reports that *The Autobiography of Alice B. Toklas* was "a scintillating public success, [but] also a relentless personal trial. Nothing was natural after its appearance" (312). But Stein's valuation of unique individuality must have been complicated by her growing realization of just how little one can control one's own identity; identity can even influence entity. It is generally accepted that after her U.S. lecture tour, Stein found it difficult to resume writing. The fame she had sought disturbed the entity from which she liked to think she wrote. Once Stein discovered herself to *be* a sign—to stand for "Wisdom"—she had to learn to write with signs all over again.

Ida was written several years after Stein recovered from her dilemma, and here Stein personifies common signs in an attempt to understand—or reclaim—their inner life. As unlikely as it may sound, Stein explores the conflicting desires to have and not to have a public persona through a dispute among a spider, a cuckoo, a goldfish, and some dwarves. They are arguing with each other, but the reader can also note the way each one is conflicted within. In a conversation among Andrew (who asks questions), Ida (who doesn't speak), and "a man," Stein depicts signs speaking for themselves, reminding readers that the sign is not merely what it signifies. "Somebody one afternoon" explains:

Spider at night makes delight.
Spider in the morning makes mourning.
Yes said Andrew.
Well, said the man who was talking, think of a spider talking.
Yes said Andrew.
The spider says
Listen to me I, I am a spider, you must not mistake me for the sky, the sky red at night is a sailor's delight, the sky red in the morning is a sailor's warning, you must not mistake me for the sky, I am I, I am a spider. (682)

A spider at night and the red sky at night both signal coming "delight"; a red sky in the morning and a spider in the morning are negative signals of warning and mourning. But a spider and a red sky are themselves quite different things and want to be remembered as such: "I am a spider, you must not mistake me for the sky." Stein also imagines the cuckoo, the goldfish, and the dwarf speaking for themselves, asserting their separateness from what they mean to other people. This section of *Ida* is a fable to resist fables (and thereby, paradoxically, anthropomorphism).

These sign beings begin to squabble with one another because each claims not to believe in the further implications of the others. Once again mentioning a dish ("bubble and squeak" is fried cabbage and potatoes) and highlighting sound (the dish is called that because of the noises it makes while it cooks), this story's narrator says that the "goldfish suddenly began to swish and to bubble and squeak and to shriek" about how he believes in nothing but himself, "I I" (685). His "I I" sounds like "aye aye," the nautical "hear, hear" or "yes sir," and thus the goldfish demands that his listeners agree with him. The cuckoo says:

Oh you poor fish, you do not believe in me, you poor fish, and I do not believe in you fish nothing but fish a goldfish only fish, no I do not believe in you no fish no, I believe in me, I am a cuckoo and I know and I tell you so, no the only thing I believe in which is not me is when I see the new moon through a glass window, I never do because there is no glass to see through, but I believe in that too, I believe in that and I believe in me ah yes I do I see what I see through, and I do I do I do.
No I do not believe in a fish, nor in a dwarf nor in a spider not I, because I am I a cuckoo and I, I, I. (685)

"The spider screamed . . . everybody believes in me . . . bah. I believe in me. . . . I I. I" (685–86). In short, each creature does not believe in the further meaning of the others; he believes only in himself and in his own further significances (not just "I" but "I I" and "I I I"—which are insistently self-promotional but also resemble the roman numerals for "two" and "three"). The cuckoo's reference to the (invisible because dark) new moon (not) seen through (transparent or missing) glass is a mystery, although it suggests that the cuckoo tries to remember that real stuff is there even when it cannot be seen, which may be similar to remembering that he really exists even when nobody acknowledges that part of his existence. The goldfish, who says, "listen to me I am stronger than a cuckoo stronger and meaner because I never do bring good luck I bring nothing but misery" (684), tries to outdo the cuckoo by having more significance. But the cuckoo grants the fish only his being, not his signhood; he's "nothing but a fish." Like many iconic celebrities, these signs want their being to be acknowledged, but they are too enamored of their signhood to let anyone forget it. In other words, they insist upon having the moths and the mothballs.

The fight among the signs probably alludes to the lasting split between two of the most famous modernist sign creators: Stein the "cuckoo" writer and Matisse the painter of goldfish. In 1910–11, Stein wrote the portrait "Matisse," in which, in the middle of admitting that "some" think one thing and "some" another, she seems to assert the painter's greatness: "he was clearly expressing what he was expressing. He was a great one"—and part of what he is expressing is his "struggling" (278). But even this early work hints that Matisse is stuck, unchanging: he tells the same story "again and again and again," his story is so repetitive that people stop listening to it, and people want to imitate him—a potential problem, since it may increase the likelihood of his imitating his own work, as well as his own story (280). When Stein ends the portrait with the opinion of "some" people who think Matisse is "one not greatly expressing something being struggling," she suggests that his struggle is over, that he's become (or he's becoming, or he might become) the static kind of "great man" (281). And when she writes, "This one was one," she might not just be throwing in some of her playful (or annoying) redundancy; perhaps she means he is *only* one, not the several that make up a complex person with an active and "struggling" being. In *The Autobiography of Alice B. Toklas*, Stein gives some idea of the financial pressure Matisse may have felt, which—even if Stein is right about Matisse's work—explains his choice to stick with what sold and start teaching. Later, in the 1938 work *Picasso*, Stein says Matisse got stuck in the past: he and "all the others saw the twentieth century with their eyes, but they saw the reality of the nineteenth century" (512). In Stein's opinion, Matisse ended up seeing as others have seen, not as *he* sees, uniquely and individually.

In *Ida*, Stein's comments about Matisse are coded, but the author (the cuckoo) certainly comes off better than the painter (the goldfish). The cuckoo sends good luck to an author who "had written a lovely book but nobody took the lovely book nobody paid her money for the lovely book they never gave her money, never never never, and she was poor and they needed money oh yes they did she and her lover" (*Ida*, 683).[14] But a painter "bought goldfish and any day he made a painting of us," and "he turned goldfish into gold because everything he did was bold and it sold, and he had money and fame but all the same we the goldfish just sat and waited while he painted" (684). The fish tells the strength of his signhood, which is a curse:

> They buy me because I look so pretty and red and gold in my bowl but I never bring good luck I only bring bad, bad bad bad. . . .
> One day, crack, the bowl where we were fell apart and we were all cracked the bowl the water and the fish, and the painter too crack went the painter and his painting too and he woke up and he knew that he was dead too, the goldfish and he, they were all dead, but we there are always goldfish in plenty to bring bad luck to anybody too but he the painter and his painting was dead dead dead. (684)

Stein suggests that Matisse was ruined by his own fame and even associates him with Midas, whose profitable wish turned to a curse (these are *goldfish,* not carp). (Similarly, Stein said of William Saroyan: "He cannot stand the weight of being great" [Steward, *Chapters*, 105]). The fish bring bad luck and, like a broken mirror, destroy the man on whom they pretended to reflect so well (and vice versa). This author and this painter make signs—and signs, in some sense, make them. The silly dialogue among the signs parallels a common internal dialogue. Who they feel like inside argues with who they are identified as externally, each complicating assertions about self. Those who become signs in themselves must continue to assert themselves as beings in order to continue existing and working. Stein may feel superior—though sympathy would be more becoming—because she probably imagines she has successfully avoided having her wish for fame ruin her.

Stein was more sympathetic to others in a September 1934 *Vanity Fair* article, where she contemplates her own recent loss of identity:

> What happened to me was this. When the success began and it was a success I got lost completely lost. You know the nursery rhyme, I am I

because my little dog knows me. Well you see I did not know myself. I lost my personality. It has always been completely included in myself my personality as any personality naturally is, and here all of a sudden, *I was not just I because so many people did know me.* . . . for the first time since I had begun to write I could not write and what was worse I could not worry about not writing and what was also worse *I began to think about how my writing would sound to others.* . . . And then all of a sudden I said there that it is that is what was the matter with all of them all *the young men whose syrup did not pour, and here I am being just the same. They were young and I am not but when it happens it is just the same, the syrup does not pour.* ("And Now," 63–64; my italics)

People knew her, and she thought she knew what they wanted from her writing, and so the interaction between Stein and others became more transactional than interactional. Expectation or even entitlement superseded discovery and innovation. Again using a metaphor of liquids and solids, Stein depicts the solid state that an exterior definition can impose. The self becomes a fetish of the self, a stable and controllable piece of personhood that spares one from dealing with one's whole complex humanness. This fetish carries useful social symbolism but gives a false encapsulation of the self. When a sign maker becomes a sign, the signs he or she produces are likely to be imitations. Creativity dries up unless a person continually reasserts his or her self as a living, changing being. Awareness of the audience, thinking about how one's "writing would sound to others," teaching (which is often performed by repeating what one already knows instead of being fully present and thoughtful), and doing the same thing over and over because it sells, all are ways to keep the syrup from pouring, to stop creativity itself, as well as the creation of a unique self.

Standing in the Window

Conversations take place in all sorts of settings, among people of different sexes and gestures and postures, and these details make a difference. Even children know what it means when they have to sit down and someone self-righteously towers over them. Imagine an academic conference (on Stein, say) where informal groups of people discuss Stein's writing while sitting around a swimming pool, or while playing catch or boules, or while chopping vegetables and setting a table together. It would be different from a formal conference setting, and different things would get said. Doing handwork side by side and chatting is different from receiving handouts and a lecture, even of the most conversational kind.

One early reviewer of *Three Lives* saw Stein and Henry James as having "analogous method[s]": "James presents us the world he knows largely through . . . conversations," and Stein's "murmuring people are as truly shown as are James' people who not only talk but live while they talk" ("Curious Fiction Study," 12). In *Four in America*, Stein asserts "that there are two ways of writing and Henry James . . . has selected both" (138). Henry James is a notoriously subtle writer, and he takes advantage of what people knew about polite conversation to express much that goes unstated in his novels. The climactic chapter of *A Portrait of a Lady* depends on the reader's knowing that a man would not sit in the presence of a standing woman unless the two were intimately acquainted. Mrs. Isabel Osmond (née Archer) walks in on Gilbert Osmond (her husband) and Madame Merle "musing, face to face" (H. James, 376). Merle is standing and Osmond is sitting; when Isabel enters, Osmond quickly stands too. "Their relative position, their absorbed mutual gaze, struck [Isabel] as something detected," and James devotes a subsequent chapter to Isabel's "meditation" on how this scene alters her understanding of herself and the people around her (376, 389).

Ida may lightly allude to this scene. Ida visits a married couple, and the names of the husband and wife—William and Edith—help support this leap of attention to a different author. Henry James seems to me to be a likely cross between William James and Edith Wharton. In *The Autobiography of Alice B. Toklas* (written in 1932 and published the following year), Stein has Toklas say that "only very lately Gertrude Stein reads Henry James" (78). Stein probably read Henry James much earlier than she admits, but if she was reading (or rereading) his work around the time she wrote the *Autobiography*, then James's writing would have been fairly fresh in her mind when *Ida* was being composed.

Ida walks into the room (or house) as Edith and William discuss possible husbands for her, and Edith and William go silent (in light of her possible anxiety of influence, this is perhaps wishful thinking on Stein's part):

> all right they would talk about Ida and Ida came in, not to rest, but to come in. They stopped it, stopped talking about her.
>   So Edith and William did not look at Ida, they started talking. What do you think said William what do you think if and when we decide anything what do you think it will be like. This is what William said and Edith looked out of the window. They were not in the same room with

Ida but they might have been. Edith liked an opportunity to stand and so she looked out of the window. She half turned, she said to William, Did you say you said Ida. William then took to standing. This was it so they were standing. It is not natural that if anybody should be coming in that they would be standing. Ida did not come in, Edith went away from the window and William stood by the window and saw some one come in, it was not Gerald Seaton [the most likely suitor for Ida] because he had gone away. (*Ida*, 657)

Although Stein has not made it clear whether Ida came into the room or not, she has managed to make it seem that something portentous has happened, and I can't help thinking of the scene and its sequel in Henry James's *Portrait of a Lady*. Stein may have been struck by James's sensitivity to conversational setting, and perhaps also by his ideas about the construction of the self. In both Stein's and James's scenes, a man and woman are talking, but when another woman enters they become silent. In both cases, the couple is plotting something to do with women and marriage. At some point in both scenes, everyone is standing in a way that is "not natural."

Ross Posnock makes a convincing argument for Henry James's interest in the self as social construction: "What James discovers in America is that a fluidity of identification instills a capacity for a mutuality that is the basis of vital citizenship." Further: "Implicit in Henry James . . . is the belief that the subject 'is an artificial reality imposed on material not intended to receive it,'" and that "freedom is 'not reducible to the freedom of subjects; it is at least partly the release of that which does not fit into the molds of subjectivity and normalization'" (23, 50).[15] Hanna Pitkin describes Henry James's idea of citizenship as maintaining "mutuality within difference" and patriotism as "a redefinition of self, an enlarged awareness of how individuality and community are connected in the self" (qtd. in Posnock 255, 256).[16] While Stein is heavily influenced by William James and values individualism above all things, her idea of the complex, nonindependent individual parallels Henry James's ideas.

In *Portrait of a Lady*, Isabel's musings on Gilbert Osmond supply Stein with a metaphor relevant to the issue of internally and externally influenced character. Isabel is surprised to learn that "she had never seen any one who thought so much of others" as Osmond, and that "he had looked at it ['this base, ignoble world'] out of his window even when he appeared to be most detached from it" (H. James, 396–97). For Isabel, Osmond's stance at the window means he is paying attention to what's out there, what "they" think. She realizes that Osmond, who insists that she "think of him as he thought of himself," hates her because she has "a mind of her own" (396, 398). Not only do Edith and William take turns standing at the window in *Ida*, but a few paragraphs after their mild perturbation, Stein suddenly injects: "It was a pleasant home, if a home has windows and any house has them anybody can stand at the window and look out" (*Ida*, 657). In this way, Stein may refer back to their discomfort and continue a discussion of Edith's question: "who is any one." The statement "anybody can stand at the window and look out" may allude across novels to Osmond's tendency to perform himself. But Stein adds: "Ida never did. She rested"—and we remember that Winnie's fame continues on its own even if Ida just sits in the room without looking out the window (657). When fame comes, it stays, whether Ida aids it or not.

Also Known As, or The Metaphor of Sight

Standing at the window limits, stultifies, and makes one's individual creativity stop pouring, but letting a dog tell you who you are is just as bad. *Ida* is full of aliases or misperceptions. More specifically (and more eccentrically), the novel is full of mistaken dogs—dogs who are named for things they are not, and dogs who mistake one thing for another. Everything appears to be something else. For example: "There was a Pekinese named Sandy, he was a very large one, Pekineses should be tiny but he was a big one like a small lion but he was all Pekinese." Not only does this dog look like a lion, but "Sandy was his name because he was that color, the color of sand." And this dog who looks like a lion and sand misidentifies other things: he hates to climb mountains, but "they were not real mountains, they were made of a man on two chairs" (*Ida*, 668). Another dog is named "Chocolate because he looked like a chocolate cake or a bar of chocolate or chocolate candy," but instead of being sweet, "he was a monster" and "he was awful" (670).[17] We'd be wrong to eat Chocolate or sunbathe on Sandy, just as it is a mistake to base judgments on appearances.

Clouds are not bunnies, either, but when Ida and her friend (or double) Andrew have visitors who tell what they see in the clouds, Stein is probably commenting on a couple of issues other than (but related to) false appearances. Our individual sight is an important measurement of uniqueness. These friends

> would come in and say this evening I saw a cloud and it looked like a hunting dog and others would say he saw a cloud that looked like a dragon, and another one would say he said [*sic* (saw?)] a cloud that

looked like a dream, and another he saw a cloud that looked like a queen. Ida said yes and Andrew said very nicely. They liked people to come in and tell what kind of clouds they had seen. Some had seen a cloud that looked like a fish and some had seen a cloud that looked like a rhinoceros, almost any of them had seen a cloud.

It was very pleasant for Ida that they came and told what the clouds they had seen looked like. (*Ida*, 699)

A favorite instance of subjectivity, and borrowed subjectivity, is Hamlet's discussion of clouds with Polonius:

HAMLET. Do you see yonder cloud that's almost in shape of a camel?
POLONIUS. By th' mass, and 'tis like a camel indeed.
HAMLET. Methinks it is like a weasel.
POLONIUS. It is backed like a weasel.
HAMLET. Or like a whale?
POLONIUS. Very like a whale. (3.2.339–44)

Clouds are clouds, really, not camels or whales or weasels. Hamlet says what he sees in them, and Polonius says what Hamlet sees. Polonius is not a genius, or even much of an individual. If we see how others see, we are not ourselves. But the alternative perceptions of clouds in *Ida* and *Hamlet* also suggest the projective and metaphorical quality of human knowledge. These qualities are present in and confuse our perceptions of ourselves and one another.

Over and over again, in many different works, Stein associates dogs with false, limited, or static (or otherwise lacking) identity. In her lecture "What Are Master-Pieces and Why Are There So Few of Them," presented at Oxford and Cambridge Universities in 1936, she says that "mostly people live in identity and memory that is when they think. They know they are they because their little dog knows them, and so they are not an entity but an identity. . . . The second you are you because your little dog knows you you cannot make a master-piece and that is all of that" (153). The dogs in *Ida* have one thing in common: they mistake parts for wholes, which leads to terrible misidentifications. For example, "any shadow was a rabbit to them," one dog "chased sheep . . . thinking they were rabbits," and "Another little dog was so foolish once he always thought that any table leg was his mother, and would suck away at it as if it was his mother" (*Ida*, 671). Dogs see that which is inaccurate and partial; they see identity. As a (sometimes) deliberately formed creation of selfhood, identity is only a shadow, only a false goal, only a wooden consolation.

When a reader of *Ida* begins to wonder if Andrew is a person or just one facet of Ida, Ida is "left alone," and this reader expected Ida to think about herself in a way that would reveal whether Andrew is internal or external; but instead "she thought about her life with dogs" (667). Is Andrew a dog? Probably not, but Ida reads and Andrew doesn't, and in Stein's paradigm, the human mind (genius, being) reads and human nature (limited) does not, so maybe Andrew is *like* a dog (663). At one point, Andrew voices his independence but is still overcome by Ida; he says, "Kindly consider that I am capable of deciding when and why I am coming," but "He came all the same" (664). Andrew speaks up, and he says that unlike a dog he won't come when he's called, but he comes like a good dog nonetheless. Stein ends the first half of her novel:

> And now Ida was not only Ida she was Andrew's Ida and being Andrew's Ida Ida was more that [*sic* (than?)] Ida she was Ida itself.
>
> For this there was a change, everybody changed, Ida even changed and even changed Andrew. Andrew had changed Ida to be more Ida and Ida changed Andrew to be less Andrew and they were both always together. (664)

As "Andrew's Ida," Andrew's gaze has changed Ida, but she is still Ida and not just a holograph of Andrew's desires or expectations. Andrew is somehow confirming without being limiting. He makes Ida more herself, perhaps parallel to the way good relationships make people feel like who they really are and—even better—like someone they like. But why is Andrew less Andrew? Is he too busy being an alter ego to be an ego?

Andrew and Ida fold in and out of one another even more in the second half of the novel. "Andrew's name changed to Ida and eight changed to four and sixteen changed to twenty-five and they all sat down," but very soon after, "You see there was he it came to be Andrew again and it was Ida," and "it made gradually that it was not so important that Ida was Ida" (*Ida*, 666). If Andrew becomes part of Ida, then there are half as many people (four is half of eight), but if Ida had four sides before, she suddenly has five. This mathematical function suggests that if Ida contains four selves, she also contains the personalities that each one forms in relation to the others and to itself (four squared is sixteen); when she contains five selves, she also contains the sides of those selves that they reveal to and develop in relationship to the others and itself (five squared is twenty-five). And suddenly, "There was no Andrew" (666). In the very next paragraph, Andrew exists enough to be doing things: he "stayed at home and waited for her," and he "could walk and come to see Ida and tell her what he did," although Ida could "not tell Andrew that she had been walking" (666–67). Later, after Ida thinks about dogs, and after she seems to die and then comes "back to life exactly day before yesterday," "Ida was almost married to Andrew" (674, 676). She dreams that the wedding becomes a funeral for Andrew, which suggests that when two people become one, one of them has to die. After so much ambiguity, and even more, the last page of the novel reads:

> Little by little there it was It was Ida and Andrew.
> Not too much not too much Ida and not too much Andrew.
> And not enough Ida and not enough Andrew. (703–4)

Their melding together hasn't killed either one. They have shared themselves, such that each has been influenced by the other. Their coupling seems inevitable and commonsensical, but it also seems a diminishment; there's not enough of either one of them. Ida is still "one" (or just an idea of one), and Andrew is just "and," an addition rather than an identity. Love is a dog that won't hunt for a real self.

The Death of Conversation, or The Monologue of Death

In the shorter "Second Half," Ida incessantly rests. No longer just sitting and being, now Ida seems to be sick and less comfortable in herself. Here, in at least one instance, when Stein says, "What happened," she may refer to the way that Ida doesn't do anything when she is sick; the sickness just happens to her (*Ida*, 694). After meeting a family that brings bad luck, she "never went out to see any one" (681). She has a hard time imagining herself young (677), dreams of Andrew's death and a funeral (676), cries for the first time when she hears of someone else's death (673), predicts another man's death from meningitis (675), and even seems to die (674).

But "what happened" is also that when Ida dies (if she dies), her conversations are over. In "Second Half," Ida's conversations are less apparent; she seems to go on walks with Susan Little instead of with Andrew, and they don't sing and they don't talk (666). When Ida goes on walks, she cannot tell Andrew about them; he is the only one who can talk about walks (667). Suddenly when people said, "how do you do . . . it did not matter" (667).

"Part One" of "Second Half" is largely devoted to Ida's "thought[s] about her life with dogs," and what Stein says about dogs suggests that this section of the book will be devoted to the drying up of the vital self. Here the self succumbs to the stasis that comes with death instead of the kind that came with fame. The dogs in this section are identified by their inaccurate, appearance-based names and their misconceptions (as noted earlier), but Stein also mentions their deaths (they all die, often by getting run over by cars) and their relationships with each other. Basket and Never Sleeps play together, but Lillieman and Dick ignore each other completely, even when "on the same lawn together" (673, 669). In fact, except for the two playful dogs and the many allusions to dogs "making love," "tempt[ing each] other," and doing "what they should not" (669, 670–71), several of the dogs are antisocial: Polybe "never barked, he had nothing to say" (672), and Mary Rose is not interested in her puppy Blanchette (670). The dogs who are interested in each other are separated: Mary Rose leaves Polybe; her favorite puppy, Chocolate, gets "run over"; and Lillieman dies and is separated from Dick, who now "went on running around making love to distant dogs" (669). The dogs represent a limitedness, and their relations with each other are narrowly defined by certain games or by a refusal to interact. They are the way they are, and they see humans as having the same simplicity; they do not change, and they don't let their views of us change: "Dogs are dogs" (670).

A repeated allusion to moonlight shows that things look different in different lights, and it leads to the way that death itself, the unchanging fact, can appear different depending on who dies. This second half begins with a reference to the way "a white dog . . . looked gray in the moonlight and on the snow," and the end of the dog section alludes to the moon again: "the moon scarcely the moon but still there is a moon" and "Very likely hers was the moon" (*Ida*, 665, 673). The moon makes things look different than they are; appearances are relative. And then Stein tells us:

Ida knew she never had been a little sister or even a little brother.
Ida knew.
So scarcely was there an absence when someone died.
Believe it or not someone died. (673)

Ida is relative, too; her lack of relatives makes it appear as if her death was not a death. But here, actually, a young man dies, a person with parents, and Ida mourns him, although "Ida had never cried before" (674). Ida begins to see the use of fame, and she uses this knowledge to reassure other people as they come to see her: "one by one somebody said Thank you, have you heard of me. And [Ida] always had. That was Ida"; and "Even Andrew had he had heard of them" (674). If they have to die, at least they are remembered in their fame.

Stein seems to have Ida die and immediately come back to life in her fame. "One day, she saw a star it was an uncommonly large one and when it set it made a cross, she looked and looked and she did not hear Andrew take a walk and that was natural enough she was not there. They had lost her. Ida was gone" (*Ida*, 674). But in the next paragraph she goes to bed more "carefully," in the next she comes "back to life," and in the next her life is patly summed up in terms of how many times she married and what her husbands did (674). W. H. Auden captures the difference when he writes of Yeats's becoming what he means to others: "But for him it was his last afternoon as himself, / . . . [and when] The current of his feeling failed; he became his admirers" ("In Memory"). When Ida comes back to life, in someone else's monologue instead of her own conversation, it is with a different self.

In other words, that summary of husbands is not Ida's being, which is better expressed through some short poetic lines of Andrew's, here excerpted from the conversational setting, in which they are interlarded with laughter and interruptions.

> At a glance
> what a chance
> That she needs
> What she has
> And they have what they are
> And they have what they are
> And they like where they go
> Which is all after a while
> (*Ida*, 656, ellipses and paragraph markers omitted)

In other words—which are completely different and perhaps make too brutal a revision—we are what we see and do in the moment, the minor decisions we make, the gestures and movements and detours and attitudes. The moments are our chances to be us, and we have to be us, have what we have, do what we do. That's all there is.

Stein almost (but not quite) tolls the death of the independent self. One critic concludes that "*Ida, A Novel* simultaneously testifies to an impossibility to remember . . . the laws of the traditional novel . . . and to a memory of the impossible . . . i.e. writing a novel" (Tomiche, 275). *Ida*, then, may be a memorial to the novel as a genre (as "Lycidas" is to pastoral elegy), but it is also a memorial to a no-longer-viable (or probably always mythical) singular sense of an independent self, as well as a beacon that spotlights another possible model of being. I believe this model to be true and good, but, in the second half of *Ida*, Stein seems to recognize the difficulty—the impossibility—of remaining a true self after death. If we live in our reputations, we can live on after death, but in rejecting that ancient solution to selfhood, Stein (and Ida) disappear when they can no longer just be. The only possible consolation seems to be uncertainty: "She knew she would be away but not really away," and "If Ida goes on, does she go on even when she does not go on any more. No and yes" (*Ida*, 702, 704). All she can do is stay herself until there's "not enough Ida" left. Only until death can she be where she is, continue to "Thank them," and say, "Yes" (704). We die when we cannot participate in the conversations that create us.

Human Intertextuality

Merging like her characters in *Ida*, some of Stein's texts are differentiable only by title and binding. The more one reads, the more puzzling Stein's work becomes, and one reason for this difficulty is that Stein leaves pieces of her writing around the house of her complete works. In *Ida*, for example, Stein refers to or rewrites sections of *Paris, France*; "Preciosilla"; *The World Is Round*; and *Blood on the Dining Room Floor*. *Ida* has a permeable identity in the corpus of Stein's works—one more correspondence to Stein's strong implication that people get meaning from outside themselves.

Not only does Stein's treatment of identity correspond to whole texts, whole bodies of work, but also it corresponds to words, and here we come full circle. Emphasizing the general "postmodern" instability or uncertainty in *Ida*—and choosing not to decide whether Ida and her twin represent "contradictory desires," "a split between public and private selves," conscious and unconscious, action and "unactualized potential," ego and alter ego, or even self and mother figure—Berry writes that "Ida wanders among possibilities that remain open, nomadizing in order to stay in the same place, the place where she is always just Ida" (164, 155). My discussion has depicted the twins as representing a public and a private self, though I have meant this division to suggest further divisions, and I have meant other divisions (Andrew and Ida, Ida and her various husbands) to represent multiple participants in Ida's entire self. Ida's nomadic partnering, influencing others and being influenced by them, might recall the square dance of words (sometimes in fours and fives) noted earlier. Encouraged to explore the multiple meanings of single words and the way they reflect on one another in odd groups, readers of Stein's writing cannot be content to settle for single meanings for those words any more than Ida can settle down and accept a single meaning for life. Ida wants to avoid fame, but she also wants to avoid the anonymity that threatens when she marries Gerald Seaton and "they lived almost as if Ida had not been Ida and Gerald Seaton had married any woman" (*Ida*, 659). Similarly, Stein's writing avoids static determinacy *and* does not settle for being complete nonsense. Neither Ida's nor Stein's words are satisfied with one meaning. Nor do they want *no* meaning, though our mental programming tends to resist too many simultaneous, multiple alternatives. As we tend to be suspicious of promiscuity, we tend to be suspicious of polysemy.

And so, Stein's words are independently dependent, her character Ida is independently dependent, and her works are independently dependent in relation to each other. For William James, "*My experience is what I agree to attend to*" (*Principles*; his italics, 380), and Stein tries to get us to agree to attend to much more complexity about the development of the self than we might otherwise. In describing the self in a different way, she practices a kind of "utopian politics or revolutionary science" that involves "redescrib[ing] lots and lots of things in new ways, until you have created a pattern of linguistic behavior which will tempt the rising generation to adopt it, thereby causing them to look for appropriate new forms of nonlinguistic behavior" (Rorty, *Contingency*, 9). Imagining ourselves as permeable and impermanent changes who we are, as well as how we think. Perhaps we human beings can evolve and adapt to let ourselves be as complex as the dynamic that creates us, as flexible as the language through which we know ourselves, all and each of us.

CHAPTER 6

Expressing a State of Mind: Conversation, Politics, and Individuality in *Mrs. Reynolds* and *Brewsie and Willie*

THE PEOPLE IN *Ida* who look at Winnie and depend on each other for reassurance as to what they are seeing are early manifestations of a type Stein critiques more fully in her works of the forties. Since the people agree with each other without really understanding what they are agreeing to, and they agree to approve of something they can barely appreciate on their own, they are primed for a mass movement. After *Ida*, Stein's attention shifts from mass culture to its manipulations in politics. Perhaps Stein's path of thought follows the same trajectory as that of somewhat later thinkers on the subject of tyranny: reviewing Benjamin Alpers's *Dictators, Democracy, and American Public Culture*, Louis Menand concludes that "the critique of totalitarianism by writers like [Hannah] Arendt is of a piece with their critique of popular culture, which they attacked as culture manufactured for the mass of unindividuated individuals, atomized beings able to feel alive only in their frenzied response to empty celebrity" (85). Alpers himself writes: "Although [Arthur] Schlesinger [Jr.], [George] Orwell, and Arendt disagreed on many things, they each presented totalitarianism as a nightmarish iron trap that destroyed all vestiges of individuality in its subjects" (Alpers, 253). Stein's work moves from cute psychological speculations to acute political negotiations under the repression of Nazi expansion. Stein saw that history had, in several ways, come to meet her.

Stein was always mainly interested in the individual, hating all mass movements about equally. Eric Sevareid, who met Stein in 1937, writes in *Not So Wild a Dream* that Stein "thought in terms of the human individual and was quite lost when she considered people in groups. . . . She did not understand Fascism; she did not understand that the moods and imperatives of great mass movements are far stronger and more important than the individuals involved in them. She knew persons, but not people" (90). Stein resisted distinguishing among political movements because they all seemed anti-individualist to her (as indeed they tend to be). Totalitarianism certainly is, but even progressive movements, according to Daniel T. Rodgers in *Contested Truths: Keywords in American Politics Since Independence*, turn all talk of factions and interests—of multiple ideas—into talk of procedures, management, and efficiency (see Posnock, 264). But according to W. G. Rogers, an American private first class befriended by Stein and Toklas when he was on leave in Nimes in 1917, and who remained a friend for the next thirty years: "When political issues were clarified by the eventual line-up of powers in the second World War, . . . it was as plain to Miss Stein as it was to all the rest of us that there were no two ways about it, it had to be democracy, it couldn't be totalitarianism" (222). When the European war was won, however, Stein could start worrying about the winners, too.

The primacy of individualism for Stein does much to explain her apparently mixed-up political views. The best summary of Stein's politics is DeKoven's:

> Stein's position in relation to twentieth-century democratic, egalitarian leveling, like the positions of other modernists, was as equivocal as her position in relation to female self-assertion. She hated Roosevelt and the New Deal, distrusted "big government," and allied herself politically, if at all, with an anarchic but generally right-wing American "rugged individualism." She was a close friend in the thirties and forties of the collaborationist Bernard Faÿ. . . . But, on the other side, "The Winner Loses, A Picture of Occupied France" is a tribute to the *maquisard* Resistance near her home in Belley, she excoriates Hitler as "Angel Harper" in *Mrs. Reynolds*, and, most importantly, [in "Composition as Explanation"] she links to the egalitarian-democratic principle of "one man, one vote" her notion of the "twentieth-century composition" as having no dominant center, in fact no center at all: each of its elements is as important as every other element and as important as the whole. (*Rich and Strange*, 200–201)

Right-wing "anarchy" and "rugged individualism," however, are not that far from the *maquisard*, who were fighting for their own lives, the self-determination of France, and freedom from Fascist "big government." The high expectations Stein has for individual people parallels her treatment of single words. The shape of her texts—their informal networks of association—models her ideal political body. In other words, as she declines to write formal verse, she resists the formalities of political concretion, with its hierarchies and disciplines. In her writing, and in the world as she imagines it, there is "no center at all: each of its elements is as important as every other element and as important as the whole." It is this very characteristic of the French Resistance that Jean-Paul Sartre emphasizes:

> There is no army in the world where there is such equality of risk for the private and for the commander-in-chief. And this is why the Resistance was a true democracy: for the soldier as for the commander, the same danger, the same forsakenness, the same total responsibility, the same absolute liberty within discipline. Thus, in darkness and in blood, a Republic was established, the strongest of Republics. (499–500)

Stein's politics may not weigh in very impressively in twenty-first-century American ideological retrospect, but in Vichy France her political preferences, always informed by the value she places on the individual, become recognizable, as well as defensible.

In her war writings especially, Stein advocates renewing our American individuality, and thereby the political and social character of the United States, by changing the ways we speak. She inspires her readers to become individuals, asserting our own powers of thought and doubt and saying what we see. She argues that we should listen to ourselves—our own selves and our compatriots—closely enough to hear more than the functional meaning intended by the speaker, and that listening to ourselves will lead us to speak in new ways. Earlier, in "Meditations on Being about to Visit My Native Land," contemplating her imminent lecture tour through the United States, she wrote:

> I love to ask questions and I do not dislike answering them, but I like to listen and I like to have others listen, and there is something that I can not remember not really remember did they listen in that America that I remember did they listen to the answer after they had asked the question. I always listen to the answer after I have asked the question and I hope that in that as in other things I am a good American and that they did and still do listen to the answer after they have asked a question. That would make America more than pleasant, it would make it interesting, it would make it more than interesting it would make it exciting. (*Painted Lace*, 255)

Excitement comes of paying attention to one another's possible answers, and answers can come in several forms. As an example to us, Stein's writing moves between ruthless pithiness and a doubt-filled processing of ideas.[1]

Stein's love of questions suggests that she believed a good national characteristic would be to wonder instead of to "state." One Nazi slogan, meant to discourage inquiry, was "He who thinks has already doubted," meaning that a soldier asking an honest question reveals mistrust of his orders, or of the order of things (J. Young, 70). Stein would agree with this premise, but not with the discouragement. She demonstrates the way even half-hearted, only half-doubtful questioning leads to thinking, as it does in *Brewsie and Willie*. Jo wonders:

> I wonder, said Jo, why now everybody that is all of us call America the States, in the old days that is before now, Americans always call it America or the United States, it was only foreigners who called it the States, and now just as natural as anything we each one and every one of us calls it the States just like some foreigners like the Limies used to. I wonder, said Pauline, I wonder does that really mean anything does that mean the beginning that we are beginning to feel poor, call it the States instead of America, do you think, said Pauline, do you think it does really mean anything. Everything means something, said Donald Paul, dont you know that, havent you heard, that's what's called psychoanalysis, dont you know that, that says anything always means something. (58)

If "everything means something," then idle questions mean something, too. Saying only "the States" could mean that Americans no longer express, and no longer hold, a vision of a united continent; the phrase is plural, without the unifying "United." "The States" also emphasizes assertion over questioning. "The United States," however, suggests multiplicity that mitigates the solidarity and assertiveness also implied in the name.

Like the texts discussed in previous chapters, *Mrs. Reynolds* exhibits Stein's interest in auditory and visual allusion on the level of the word.[2] In *Mrs. Reynolds*, Stein juxtaposes "fathers and feathers" (94), and "whether" and "weather" (152). She indicates that Joseph Lane's historical counterpart is Joseph Stalin by writing, "his name was Joseph lane, steal him" (114), and she implies that Joseph Lane is a "done cough" (*dummkopf*)—or that the Germans think so—when she writes that he "might cough did cough would cough" (96). Openly alluding to near homographs, Stein writes, "Eats and oats said Mrs. Reynolds can easily be confounded in printing" (136).

Directly fooling with sound, she writes: "Date rhymes with hate, murmured a man. Yes said Mrs. Reynolds it does and so does cloud rhyme with outloud" (141). Mrs. Reynolds also likes to read out loud (160), she thinks it would be valuable "to help Joseph Lane to read out loud" (238), and "She pronounced Manitoba delightfully" (157).

But Stein goes beyond looking and listening to individual words either on the page or vibrating over the airwaves. And in *Mrs. Reynolds* and *Brewsie and Willie*, she even goes beyond watching and listening to how people speak whole conversations. In *Mrs. Reynolds*, Stein contemplates how everyday conversation is both influenced by its greater context and, even more importantly, how it resists the pressure of the political situation in which it takes place. Both novels consider the characteristic speech patterns of totalitarian leaders and contrast these with the kind of talk Stein prefers. In *Brewsie and Willie*, Stein inquires into the likely cause behind the proliferation of "yes and no job men" who encourage totalitarian speech by accepting it, expecting it, and propagating it in their own talk. She concludes not only that industrialism has spoiled interesting conversation, but also that it has adversely affected original thought, and that, conversely, improved speech patterns will revive thought, which will in turn cure economic and political ailments.

Talking under an Angel Harper Cloud

One way—the main way—that Stein understands politics is through its effect on everyday life and conversation. Someone who appreciates playful, free, "cheap" talk would notice the strain put on such conversation by propaganda and fear. During her extended sojourn in Vichy France during World War II, Stein observed the ways political context circumscribed conversation, but also the ways speakers can resist that influence.[3]

Mrs. Reynolds is a novel that follows Mrs. Reynolds as she wanders around her village and the nearby countryside, speaks to the people she meets, and, upon returning home, recounts these conversations to Mr. Reynolds. In the distance is an ominous threat to their well-being, represented in the novel by worries about Angel Harper, vague hopes that Joseph Lane will do something helpful, fears of starvation and "drowning," and the presence of soldiers and refugees. Out of desperation, Mrs. Reynolds puts her faith in Saint Odile's prophecy, which she understands as predicting the end of the war. Often she discusses this prophecy; sometimes she reads it aloud to people. Interlarded with these conversations are updates about Angel Harper's age and descriptions of his childhood memories.

Stein wrote *Mrs. Reynolds* to convey the experience of a private person emotionally devastated, but not personally destroyed, by World War II's happening all around her, as she explains in her epilogue:

> This book is an effort to show the way anybody could feel these years. It is a perfectly ordinary couple living an ordinary life and having ordinary conversations and really not suffering personally from everything that is happening but over them, all over them is the shadow of two men, and then the shadow of one of the two men gets bigger and then blows away and there is no other. There is nothing historical about this book except the state of mind. (331)

This "state of mind" could be that of anyone who lives in a maelstrom of alternating silence and propaganda, daily rituals of pleasant-as-possible survival and rumors of world-changing tragedies. The French countryside may be overrun by German soldiers, and refugees may pass by every day, but every night Mr. and Mrs. Reynolds discuss when to go to bed: "Oh dear she said let us go to bed and they did" (214); "well said Mr. Reynolds let us be asleep first and they were" (216); "now they would go to bed and she said yes they would go to bed and they did they put out the lights after they went to bed" (217); "Mr. Reynolds said all right but night is night, and so good night and they went to bed and slept tight" (222); "Mr. Reynolds said it was time to go to bed and it was and they went to bed" (225); "And Mr. Reynolds said it was exciting but tomorrow was another day to be excited in so that they might just as well go to bed now and they carefully did they carefully went to bed" (227).

Wanting to go to bed earlier than they feel they should, however, is a dilemma throughout the novel, one that signals that their private lives have been infected by their moment in history. Their bedtime discussions might sound like the irrepressible Samuel Pepys, who ended many of his journal entries with references to bed: "After that to bed"; "and after a bottle of wine we all to bed"; "and so at night to bed" (42, 44), but it also suggests the syndrome of depressives who tend to sleep more than they should. Mr. and Mrs. Reynolds cannot speak openly, and sleep is the easiest form of silence. Sleep tempts them when they have run out of things they can say and want to avoid saying things they shouldn't. Bedtime would be a familiar ritual that could help them forget the war, if it weren't something they desired so much more than in peacetime. While the word "conversation" was sometimes used between the fifteenth and eighteenth centuries to refer to sexual intercourse, these bedtime conversations are not so much playful

anticipations of what's to come if they go upstairs as they are hesitant suggestions about whether or not they would be cowardly if they escaped awkward
wakefulness so early.

The main cause of their discomfort is that the daily life chronicled in
Mrs. Reynolds is overshadowed by the existence of a man whose name
is a household word—one that the book's characters often choose not to
speak, but that is indicated obliquely and always understood. Foremost in
everyone's mind is "Angel Harper," who "is clearly a version of Adolf Hitler"
(Bridgman, 319). The shared initials (pointed out in *Mrs. Reynolds* itself,
131) cannot be the only reason for Stein's choosing to call Adolf Hitler Angel
Harper. She writes: "It was a long way to wait and in the meantime every
day there was a dark cloud, a very dark one. An Angel Harper cloud said
Mrs. Reynolds" (90). If Adolf Hitler is a cloud over their lives, then Stein
may (sarcastically?) associate him with paintings of clouds and angels, or
perhaps she sees him as the angel of death. Hitler's harping voice may
have had something to do with it, too. Stein also writes that "Mrs Reynolds
remembered fie fie fie for shame everybody knows his name" (293), which
reminds me of the giant's refrain in *Jack and the Beanstalk*: "Fee fi fo fum,
I smell the blood of an Englishman!" Adolf Hitler's own attempts to sniff
out—and snuff out—Jews (and England) may associate him in Stein's mind
with this terrible giant in the clouds. Finally, as Lloyd Frankenberg argues,
Angel Harper is not so much Adolf Hitler as he is "everybody's fears and
thoughts and dreams" about Adolf Hitler (xii).[4]

The name permeates *Mrs. Reynolds*: "the name Angel Harper was the
name was one everybody knew too well" (224); "Nobody not even Mrs
Reynolds asked any one if they had ever heard of Angel Harper. Everybody
had and everybody knew that this year he was forty-eight" (144). Angel
Harper's shadow is present even when his name is not expressly invoked:
when Mrs. Reynolds says "he," she expects Mr. Reynolds to know of whom
she speaks (215). Mrs. Reynolds likes to say "who" when someone mentions
Angel Harper's name, but it is a sour joke: "Mrs. Reynolds never laughed
but she said who and when she said who she was making fun of Angel
Harper" (94, 134).

The repetition of Angel Harper's name stands out, because, with the
exception of Mr. and Mrs. Reynolds, most of Stein's character names appear
only once, such as "little Valery Hopkins," who says, "I am the same age
as Angel Harper." Stein adds: "That is the first time that the age of Angel
Harper was something to compare with something" (126). This comment
signals Stein's recognition that Angel Harper's person has come to occupy
their minds as much as his troops occasionally occupy their countryside.

"There is said Mrs. Reynolds no escaping hearing his name"; and "in the Bible it says that the poor are always with you but that said Mrs. Reynolds oh dear me that is nothing compared to Angel Harper being fifty" (139, 197). Angel Harper's existence is as evil as the persistence of human poverty, and, less patly, the idea of Angel Harper, his position as a cloud in their lives, is as much a persistent shadow as the knowledge of human suffering. His sweet name might also be a jab at the idealization of Hitler by his followers. Angel Harper's name is snapped, muttered, growled, hissed, whispered, and conspicuously omitted from conversations as often as Mr. and Mrs. Reynolds discuss whether it is late enough to go to bed.

Clearly, Stein has been listening to herself and others talking, and not talking, in occupied France. Beyond the constant repetition and avoidance of a powerful man's name, she notices what people do not have to say and what they are unwilling to say. She observes the convenient vagaries allowed by conversational communication, which can leave difference unspoken, and sometimes unrecognized, by all parties. She sees the endurance of pleasant conversation throughout the war, and she perceives how reassuring verbal (and nonverbal) habits can be. In "The Republic of Silence," Sartre writes: "We were never more free than during the German occupation. We had lost all our rights, beginning with the right to talk. . . . every word took on the value of a declaration of principles. . . . every one of our gestures had the weight of a solemn commitment" (498). Adolf Hitler in the guise of Angel Harper may be tearing the distant world apart, but the characters in Stein's novel manage to entrench themselves in—and assert themselves through—the protective comfort of daily ritual. Hitler may have infiltrated everyday greetings in Germany and among Nazi sympathizers and sycophants elsewhere with the obligatory "Heil Hitler," but people in Mrs. Reynolds's village still say, "How do you do."

Angel Harper's notoriety enables and encourages some resistant speakers *not* to say his name. "Mrs. Reynolds sometimes read about [Angel Harper and Joseph Lane] in a newspaper but she never talked about them to any one" (*Mrs. Reynolds*, 117). At one point, Mrs. Reynolds says about Angel Harper, "It would . . . make my teeth hurt to hear his name," Mr. Reynolds says, "What," and she says, "you know what I mean." "And indeed he did he did know what she did mean," Stein tells us (139). When Nelly asks Mrs. Reynolds, "is Angel Harper married," Mrs. Reynolds abruptly rejects that topic of conversation: "Mrs. Reynolds said I am telling just as I told you before I do prefer potatoes and I do not need butter, lard will do it. Now if you have anything to say she said to Nelly say it to my husband. And if you want to wait until He comes in you had better not go away" (79).[5] Mrs. Reynolds resists letting Angel Harper's political presence make her talk about him, and her refusal to speak in this situation also reveals her dislike and distrust of both Angel Harper and Nelly. Of course, refusing to say his name is an influence in itself. Whether one speaks about one's politics or not, others can discern one's feelings: "Gradually everybody came to know what they thought about everything some because they expressed their opinions and some because they were afraid to say anything, so one way or another way every one came to know how they felt" (97).

Choosing not to speak may be a form of repression, but it can also be revelatory. When Mrs. Reynolds "met the sister of her uncle's brother" ("Not a real uncle of course"), "she said well, and the sister of her uncle's brother said well and they both laughed together. It was quite dark and the evening was dusky and they did both laugh together" (131). The placement of the conversation within the novel, surrounded by situations of worry and sadness, hints that Mrs. Reynolds and the other woman could say much to one another about the state of occupied life, but their preoccupation keeps them from speaking at the same time that it lets them communicate without words. Perhaps they are laughing because neither of them is really "well."[6]

Sometimes in *Mrs. Reynolds*, people cough instead of saying what they believe (163), but sometimes *not* saying something requires saying something *else* instead:

> And now Angel Harper was fifty and it was getting pretty serious, nobody saw anybody they used to see and it was getting pretty serious, oh dear me said Mrs. Reynolds and when she said oh dear me she wanted to say to Mr. Reynolds that it was getting pretty serious but she did not say that it was getting pretty serious she did not say it just then she only said that she was not seeing any one she used to see no not any one, and Mr. Reynolds said and what then but what he really meant to say was that he still saw her and she still saw him, so what then. (181)

The struggle between Saint Odile and Angel Harper is in full force; Angel Harper must stop dictating, stop winning, and stop living very soon for Saint Odile's prophecy to be correct. But Mrs. Reynolds does not always want to describe her feelings about the war and occupation, nor does she want to mention Saint Odile (158). Instead, she says that she no longer sees the same people she used to see, a seemingly banal comment about her social life, but one that intimates their inability to travel, their distant friends' long absences, and their neighbors' fleeing as refugees. Mr. Reynolds says, "and what then," which could mean so many things and leaves out what he really means (and what would remind them too clearly of their own desperate situation): at least *we* are still together.

Both men and women inhibit their speech in these conditions. Mrs. Reynolds and Mrs. Ellen discuss whether or not men are more selective than women about what they say: "Mrs. Reynolds said, pooh, you know what men say, they scare each other so none of them can say what they want to say" (206). This comment may be an indictment of men who don't say what they see. On the very next page, though, Mrs. Reynolds demonstrates that women do not always say everything either. In the following, "something" is an evasive euphemism for a domicile—either staying where one is, going away, or "not having any place to stay": "Naturally she never said anything about this something because if she did well she would change it to something else that was the only way not to be frightened all day" (207). If she spoke of it, this vague something would become a more distinct—a more pronounced—threat.

Sometimes speakers do not plan their evasions far enough ahead, and they have to trail off in order to avoid certain words or topics: "I wish said Mrs. Reynolds and she did not finish her sentence" (297; see also 174, 184). Stein's portrayal of her characters' avoidance helps readers notice that the novel is also evasive; the avoidance of horrid facts and dire possibilities characterizes Stein's writing of the novel itself. "Enough said" sometimes appears in a sentence by itself, signaling Stein's unwillingness to verbalize the situation of her own occupation (302).

The spoken and written words that Stein and her characters in *Mrs. Reynolds* do not express often correspond to the thoughts they choose not to think. For example, they keep saying "drowned," when it seems likely that people have been *killed* (182–83).[7] One night, Mrs. Reynolds dreams an entire conversation that she must have avoided having with herself when awake.

> While Mrs. Reynolds was sleeping she heard herself saying, why did the lamb die, and she heard a voice that answered because he was hungry and then she heard herself asking and why was he hungry and she heard the voice answer because he had nothing to eat. And she woke up and she woke up Mr. Reynolds and she said to him is it so, and he said is what so and she told him and he said well perhaps not now but perhaps later and then she let him go to sleep and she went to sleep to sleep herself. And when she woke up she said to Mr. Reynolds and I did dream it and he said you did and she said and you said perhaps not now

but perhaps later did you mean it and Mr. Reynolds said yes perhaps he meant it. (184)

When Mrs. Reynolds wakes her husband to ask about her dream, she still resists saying the words aloud. She tries to get him to answer her oblique question "is it so," and only after prompting does she explain what she means. Although Mrs. Reynolds tells Mr. Reynolds enough of the dream to get him to respond, Stein does not repeat that part to her readers (and we know her penchant for repetition). She avoids writing about the possibility of starvation except in the context of a dream about a lamb. Then Mrs. Reynolds "went to sleep to sleep" instead of to dream. The next morning Mrs. Reynolds gestures toward the question of starvation, but in the light of day Mr. Reynolds is less direct. In the night he says, "perhaps not now[,] but perhaps later," or the more reassuring "perhaps[,] not now[,] but perhaps later"; in the morning he says it again, but with one more remove, making the statement even more reassuring: "and Mr. Reynolds said yes perhaps he meant it." Perhaps he meant that perhaps later they could, perhaps, starve.[8]

Mr. Reynolds's use of "perhaps" allows him to be unclear about his meaning and is one example of how conversation can permit a desirable vagueness. Mrs. Reynolds habitually says yes, but she doesn't always mean the same thing by it. She "did not say yes just to say yes," but (and the distinction is delicate) "she said yes because she doubted very much if she knew how she felt about anything, and if she did not know how she felt about anything she said yes" (120). We hear in common parlance these days that "no means no," and that fact is supposed to solve ambiguities about appropriate levels of intimacy and consent, but what if "yes" means "I don't know"? If silence is telling because, as discussed earlier, it suggests the hearer disagrees with the speaker but is too polite or fearful to say so, then verbal signals of agreement and disagreement—"No," "I don't know," and "Yes"—have become inflated. If Mrs. Reynolds does not know what she thinks, she cannot remain silent, because that would suggest she disagrees; she must say yes.

When we agree with each other in talk, there are a variety of levels of agreement, and the speaker and listener can assume different meanings that allow them to disagree very amiably (and unknowingly or just not explicitly). Mrs. Reynolds tells Mr. Reynolds about a conversation she had with a man who "rais[ed] fish for the government" and who was very bitter:

and Mrs. Reynolds said and I told him I agreed with him, he was right
to be so bitter and Mr. Reynolds said and did you agree with him, that
is do you agree with him, are you bitter and Mrs. Reynolds said she had
not agreed with him that she would be bitter but that she agreed with
him that he was right to be bitter, and Mr. Reynolds laughed and then
they went to bed feeling just a little bit bitter. (193)

Whether they went to bed feeling "bitter" or better or both is one question
we are left with. But that Mrs. Reynolds has so many different options as
to how to agree with the bitter man lets her agreeably disagree with him.
Stein points out the difference between Mrs. Reynolds's agreeing that the
bitter man was right to be bitter and agreeing that she would be bitter in
the same situation. These degrees of difference remind me of other ways
to disagree agreeably: if that had really happened, then it made sense that
he would be bitter; since you are who you are, it makes sense that you are
bitter; if I were just like you, I would be bitter, too; I can understand why
you are bitter (but—and this goes unspoken—I would never be bitter in your
situation); or even, Mrs. Reynolds's common response to speakers, "Yes,"
which could just mean "I heard what you said but I don't know what I think
about it." Mrs. Reynolds's "yes" could mean almost anything, as could the
French use of *ma foi*: "You say anything to them and they say ma foi, that
can mean yes or oh hell, or no, or just nothing" or "to be sure" (Stein, *Wars*,
148). To maintain a level of congeniality in these difficult times, people
skid across the surface of meanings: "Of course one never asks anybody
what he means" (143). This man who "does raise fish millions of fish" (*Mrs.
Reynolds*, 193) could also be a Nazi agitator who raises fists, millions of fists,
but Mrs. Reynolds's sympathetic, noncommittal, and (only) polite agreement
is not the kind of response political propagandists are trying to evoke in their
audiences.

Perhaps to avoid too many situations in which they have to navigate
through the complications of agreement and disagreement on tricky political points, but probably to keep themselves as pleasantly occupied as possible, the characters in *Mrs. Reynolds* retain old habits of speech. Conversational rituals, like funeral rituals (*Mrs. Reynolds*, 162) and the daily rituals
of eating meals and going to bed, cycle continually through the novel.
When something startling happens ("a loud noise") and Mrs. Reynolds
"very nearly lost her way" coming home, Mr. and Mrs. Reynolds stubbornly
agree that she was not very close to losing her way, they have a "pleasant
dinner," and then "Mr. Reynolds asked Mrs. Reynolds if she was tired at all
and she said no not at all, but really she was a little tired and she went to

bed early" (125–26). Mrs. Reynolds is scared enough to get lost and scared enough by that experience to need a rest, but she is unwilling to give that fear credence by talking about it.

Other conversations are reassuring and also cheer Mr. and Mrs. Reynolds in the face of possible starvation, especially when idiomatic expressions take on ironic complications. Talking and avoiding starvation seem to be the two main pursuits of people in Stein's village, where they "all talked and talked and hunted for food . . . talk and talk and look for food" (Stein, *Wars*, 89).[9] When Mrs. Reynolds says "that she was beginning to be fed up," Mr. and Mrs. Reynolds both laugh, and she adds, "not with food" (*Mrs. Reynolds*, 223). She also comments that "it was funny that some people did continue to be stout" (224). And she creates a light refrain for the war situation: "In the spring a young man's fancy lightly turns to thoughts of love but . . . now, it turns to spring offensives" (223–24). Later, "Mrs. Reynolds said that life was just one spring offensive one after the other, she giggled . . . she could do with a spring where only the spring [w]as doing a spring offensive, she thought she said she thought that that would be a nice change" (239). Mrs. Reynolds is so eager to repeat this witticism that she wants to wake Mr. Reynolds to tell him, and she finally decides to go "out to see if she could not see some one and tell them about the spring offensive and how she did hope that there never would be another one" (239). Mrs. Reynolds so much enjoys making light of their problems in conversation—at the same time as she acknowledges those problems—that she searches for someone with whom to share the pleasurable reassurance of wordplay. Mrs. Reynolds needs to talk: "she was very ready to talk to Herbert or Carrie or Helena or Joan or Paul or Charlotte or Francis or Abel or Cain or even Andrew Soutar" (137), much as Stein in her memoir of the war describes herself as "being cheered by being cheerful" when chatting with a friend on the road (*Wars*, 232).

Mrs. Reynolds is not the only one to treat her fears lightly in polite conversational rituals. People are constantly passing the Reynolds house, and we are left to guess who these people are until Stein confirms our suspicion that they are refugees (*Mrs. Reynolds*, 169). Mrs. Reynolds talks to many of them, and in one case "three of them passed by and stopped to talk to Mrs. Reynolds. How do you do said Mrs. Reynolds when she saw them and the daughter Anabel Rivers answered for all of them, Very well I thank you, and then they went on their way" (170). Stein notices that people still adhere to conversational rituals under terrible duress, even when those rituals require that they express sentiments they are unlikely to feel.

The refugees are compelled to chat, leaving us to assume that they get something out of it. One woman with a small boy "had no time to spare but she did stay to hear all that Mrs. Reynolds had to say" (206). This woman wants to hear what Mrs. Reynolds understands Saint Odile to have said about what would happen; this prophecy may be as close as they can get to optimistic news, "and Mrs. Ellen who had no time to stay listened to her and listened to her and then she said she had to go away her little boy was waiting for her but before she went away she asked Mrs. Reynolds if she thought it would really be that way" (206). The experience of a friendly piece of gossip may comfort people who are facing the unknown or dreadful. This kind of conversation may enable people to be brave when their daily lives are haunted by vague and uninformed fears.

To some extent, jokes and pleasant talk may disarm the enemy. Soldiers might even forget their duties if they chatted ritualistically. Mrs. Reynolds sees "a pretty little soldier" and she tells of her interaction with him: "I said how do you do to him but a soldier must never answer how do you do because if he does he is not a soldier" (271).[10] But another person who lived in France at that time reports that by the third day of the German soldiers' occupation, they started "unbending," playing with puppies and waving to a child picking string beans. "After the lapse of a week, although still reserved and keeping to themselves, they had become integrated with the landscape" (*All Gaul*, 13). It is difficult to imagine soldiers who have thus "integrated" themselves in a community as able to fulfill their duties quite as obediently and with as much intimidation. In *Wars I Have Seen* (83), Stein mentions a joke that the Parisians told about Hitler and Napoleon: "the Parisians are funny, that is what bothers the Germans so, the jokes are never what they expect, no never." Conversation *with* the natives may disarm the occupiers; conversation *among* the natives has the power to disorient those occupiers.

"A queer state of living," or Resistance through Reticulation and Local Area Networks

Stein finds in the condition of everyday conversation an index of large-scale political affliction, but she also notices how people keep alive a social and political body when most lines of communication have been destroyed. In her memoir *Wars I Have Seen* (200), Stein observes: "It is a queer state of living as we are all doing, you have no news except for the radio because there are no newspapers any more and no trains no mail no telephone and even going to Belley is impossible there are twenty-three barricades between here and there a distance of seventeen kilometers. As I say we live within the village completely within it." The village is an isolated local community trying to survive, and the villagers are trying to participate in a worldwide war which they know of mainly through their necessarily limited experience and through a grapevine of anecdotes and rumors. The French Resistance, a loose political body, is kept alive by people saying what they see and repeating previous conversations to one another.

A case can be made for the likelihood that Stein and Toklas participated energetically in the French Resistance, and Wagner-Martin makes this case in her 1996 biography of Stein, but to make it now, one must first contend with the suggestion that Stein supported the Vichy government (Van Dusen) or just lay low out of fear or ignorance (Malcolm). Stein translated 180 pages of Maréchal Pétain's speeches, wrote a short introduction to them, and mailed this introduction to her editor at Random House on 19 January 1942, a year and a half after the armistice. Her introduction compares Pétain to George Washington and praises him for making the Germans keep their word on the armistice in spite of France's military powerlessness. By August 1944, however, Stein is writing of "the poor maquis many of them hungry and cold and not too favorably regarded by many of their countrymen, it was a kind of a Valley Forge with no General Washington but each little band had to supply itself with its own food its own plans and its own morale. We who lived in the midst of you salute you" (*Wars*, 234).

Support of Pétain and Vichy in January 1942, however, does not contradict later, or even concurrent, participation in the Resistance. In spite of the Jewish Statute of October 1940 and mass arrests of Jews in 1941, the Resistance understood itself as resisting Germany, not Vichy, until early 1942: "the aspect of Resistance that had grown steadily throughout 1941 . . . [was] the merging of opposition to the Germans with opposition to Vichy" (Kedward, *Resistance*, 237). In fact, the Resistance press avoided criticizing Pétain or "the internal politics of Vichy" until March 1942 (237–38), the same month that the first deportation train of Jews left France. *Confluences*, a journal that claimed to be "'above all political issues'" and for which Stein wrote, was both pro-Pétain and pro-Resistance (193–94). In December 1941, this journal "gave an enthusiastic review to Pétain's speeches"—the very ones that Stein the next month tried to get printed in the United States (193).[11] While Stein seems to have diligently worked on the translations until around September 1942, six months after the deportations began, she at some point—perhaps when she finally heard the terrible news—changed her mind about who exactly constituted the good guys and the bad guys in France during World War II. While her silence on Jewish persecution is surprising—either callous or cowardly or psychologically defensive—there is nothing very sinister in her belated shift from Vichy supporter to Resistance supporter. People throughout France only gradually became aware of the Vichy government's overenthusiastic cooperation with Germany.

In a recent *New Yorker* article, "Gertrude Stein's War," Janet Malcolm accuses Stein and Toklas of being as shallow and guilty of "callow pre-ciousness" as the "pretentious young persons" who read *The Alice B. Toklas Cookbook* in the 1960s (59). Noting the "forced gaiety" of the chapter titled "Food in the Bugey during the Occupation," Malcolm suggests that Tok-las (and Stein) should have made a point of saying they were Jewish and lesbian, and certainly should have complained more about the Germans. She adjudges that "the evasions seem egregious" (60). But Toklas does not need to state the obvious. Everyone knew she and Stein were Jewish, and almost everyone knew they were lesbian. Sexual orientation was not an open topic of conversation in those days, and even today some enlight-ened people still hold doubts about the value, the manners, and even the anti-sensuousness of talking about something as private and tactile as sex, because speaking of it belies its nature. Stein told Samuel Steward that "she and Alice had always been surrounded by homosexuals, that they both liked all people who produced—'and what they do in bed is their own business, and what we do is not theirs'" (Steward, *Chapters*, 63). Steward's opinion might have to be interpreted in light of his own sexual activities, which led to an initial five-hour interview with Alfred C. Kinsey followed by seven hundred more hours in the next decade *and* eighteen personal journals, but he goes on to say that Stein and Toklas "were very private persons, really Victorian—completely monogamous, abstemious, and on the surface more than a little reserved" (63). Homosexuality, when it was not labeled an *outrage des moeurs* (an outrage of taste or manners), was called *une affaire rose* (53), and "a rose is a rose is a rose" was probably a not-very-subtle statement of Toklas's and Stein's natural sexual orientation—in addition to all the other things it meant. During her lecture tour, Stein was repeat-edly called "mannish" and "manly" (Marlow uses both words in the same paragraph), and reporters referred to her "blocky form" and "man-fashion" gestures (P. Kennedy). After Miss Toklas tries to end an impromptu inter-view by saying, "Come, pussy," a reporter asks at the arranged session, "Do you like men?" a question explained by "the proclaimed Stein distaste for males." She grinned and said, "I like men enormously. . . . I live my life with them." Then "Miss Alice" arrived again, "with determination as well as gentleness," to end the interview ("Multitude Greets Highbrow"). These juxtapositions, the question, and the consistent labeling and relabeling of Toklas, suggest that people knew the women's relationship and respected (or just accepted) its privacy.

Very little is made of their Jewish heritage in the news reports, although *Time* magazine makes it clear that Stein is from a German Jewish family and that without her hair cut short she "would strongly resemble a fat Jewish *hausfrau*" ("Stein's Way"). Another reporter says she looks like "a young Jewish boy" (Murray). I assume that Stein assumed that everyone knew she was Jewish. People did not always announce their identities the way they often do now, and certainly any such announcement of Stein's would feel incomplete to her, if not to us.

Complaints about the Germans are understated, but certainly present, in the *Cookbook*. British World War II veterans (or even citizens who underwent the fear, the bombings, and the decade-long shortages) generally practice this kind of uncomplaining stoicism and brevity: we might want them to talk like heroes, but they fatalistically accept themselves as somewhat insignificant survivors. Trapped in the Bugey, Toklas and Stein pick "wretched beetles" off their potatoes "by hand" (216); they disdain the Germans' ignorance about butter (203), the Germans' food (212–13), and their general obtuseness (212); they struggle with disappointment at losing their beautiful and productive garden and at the need to start a new one "from scratch" (210). They try to maintain friendships in spite of the lack of food over which to socialize; they arrange black-market deals, food and gas and wine cooperatives; they learn to talk in code. They manage to keep their spirits higher than their depressed cook can, feed their imaginations by reading recipes for which they have no ingredients, are forced to house several groups of German and Italian soldiers, and celebrate Resistance and Allied victories when they can. Toklas reports that some shopkeepers "said it was their patriotic duty to sell what the Germans forbade." She asks, "was it not mine to purchase what they offered?" (*Cookbook*, 212). Self-serving, perhaps, but also a form of insurgency.

While it's fun to imagine Stein and Toklas slipping out to sabotage bridges, I can imagine Stein doing little other than walking throughout the French countryside and talking to everyone she meets. Yet these could easily have been very helpful activities. A wanderer might notice where airdrops of supplies and weapons from the Allies had landed and could alert the "addressees" where to find these shipments. While Stein was trekking through the countryside, Toklas visited town daily (although I assume this was not possible throughout the entire war) and may have been a contact for people who were getting on and off trains (Wagner-Martin, 251–52). Erlene Hubly (71), who taped and translated a 1986 ceremony at Stein's house in Bilignin, reports that University of Lilles professor Trenard said that Stein helped the Bugey through "aiding the Resistance fighters by collecting and transmitting information to them." Wagner-Martin (271) comments: "Because there are so few written records of resistance activity, however, the chief proof of her role is oral. Historians have long noted that many women—particularly Jewish women—worked successfully for the resistance because the Germans thought so little of women that they seldom suspected them." After all, women only talked. But maybe proof is oral because the work was oral too.

Perhaps orality enabled the French Resistance, and orality keeps us from knowing it.[12] At the beginning of the war, in a 1 October letter to Van Vechten, Stein lamented that "there is nothing to do to help," but she and Toklas seem to have found ways (Burns, 651). Alice cooked cakes for the Resistance and (unwittingly) "provided [a member of the Resistance] with the sheets of gelatin used for making false identification papers" (Toklas, *Cookbook*, 207). Stein's talents were in other areas; she walked and listened and talked.

An integral part of this kind of communication is retelling what others have said. In *Mrs. Reynolds*, many speakers do not appear in person, but we know their names (or something else about them), and we know what they say. In one instance, we hear news via four different conversations: a librarian told a librarian who told a widow who told a brother who is now telling Mr. and Mrs. Reynolds. In another instance, we know what "a little man quite shrunken" and his daughter say, but "Mrs. Reynolds never met them . . . her cousin told her what they said" (35). This repetition of peoples' names or other identifying characteristics creates a network of connection. Recounting the substance of earlier conversations in which words are attached to the individuals responsible for them is different from repeating what "they say," because who says what is especially important in a world where identity is political and one's politics are revealed by what one speaks—or suppresses.

The Resistance was a political movement largely organized by conversation—conversation that created a complex network of relationships instead of a straightforward, predetermined line of command. Stein reports on the German inability to adopt this more complex form of organization when the "mountain boys" cut off all their communications (*Wars*, 198–99). Just retribution, since the Germans had done the same for the French people, this strategy is also effective because the German army cannot operate in the same way as the Resistance: "The Germans are very uncertain in their minds now . . . guerrilla warfare gets on their nerves it is so darn individual and being individual is what they do not like that is to say what they can not do" (204–5).[13] People who conduct guerrilla warfare have a special way of communicating. Stein writes that "all around us there is fighting, the conversation in the village sounds exactly like the communiqués of the Yugo-Slavs in their early days of guerrilla fighting" (198). Stein also compares the Germans to ants, reputed for their instinctive submission to their social order. When their order is confused, the Germans "came in and out and about and they are exactly like an ants nest if you put a foreign substance in it, the Germans run around just like that" (214–15).

Another way Stein distinguishes German from French organization is that the Germans listened (to authority) but the French talked. Stein's descriptions of her neighbors' reactions to the radio—the one remaining medium of mass communication—demonstrate that listening to the imposing voices on radio divides communities and that give and take conversation rebuilds them. During the winter of 1939–40, Stein and Toklas took turns listening to their wireless radio (Wagner-Martin, 238). In *Wars I Have Seen*, Stein complained that while everyone else "had to stay home" and "could not even write letters to friends most of the time," "any public character can talk and talk all day long over the radio" (65). Stein describes everyone listening to the radio in the evenings, and then she immediately says that nobody loves their neighbors anymore (125). Assuming an association between the two topics, we may infer that listening to the radio contributes to this estrangement. During the war, every nation had its own broadcast.[14] The propaganda on each channel was so different that people had to choose whom they believed, or choose not to believe any of it at all:

> everybody listens to the radio, they listen all day long because almost everybody has one and if not there is their neighbor's and they listen to the voice from any country and yet what they really believe is not what they hear but the rumors in the town, by word of mouth is always the most convincing, they do not believe the newspapers nor the radio but they do believe what they tell each other and that is natural enough, all official news is so deceiving, so why not believe rumors, that is reasonable enough, and so they do, they believe all the rumors, and even when they know they are not true they believe them, at any rate they have a chance of being true rumors have but official news has no chance of being true none at all, of course not. (161)

Francis Bacon warned that the division of the church leads to atheism; Stein suggests that a lot of different propaganda leads people to disbelieve all information. For propaganda to work its effects, it has to be so total it becomes invisible.[15]

If people choose their propaganda from the radio, their choices create differences among neighbors, even among family members. They are literally on different wavelengths. For example, Mr. and Mrs. Reynolds hold very different views from Mr. Reynolds's brother and his wife.

> Mr. and Mrs. Madden-Henry admired Angel Harper because he never coughed. They knew that of him. He never could or would or did cough. Joseph Lane might cough did cough would cough but and this Mr. and Mrs. Madden-Henry knew Angel Harper never had and never would cough. For this they did very much admire him.
>
> Bat said Hope Reynolds, the wife of Mr. Reynolds' younger brother, Bat is a word that has two meanings, one that flies by night and one that hits a ball.
>
> By this she meant to express her admiration, her very great admiration for Angel Harper. . . .
>
> Mrs. Coates had greatly respected Mr. and Mrs. Madden-Henry, but when she heard them say that they admired Angel Harper because he never coughed, she began to think badly of them, and gradually she came to despise them.
>
> . . . Mrs. Coates said that she herself was interested in what any one said but nevertheless she herself was certain that Mr. and Mrs. Madden-Henry were mistaken. (*Mrs. Reynolds*, 96)

Mr. and Mrs. Madden-Henry seem to respect Harper because he's a persistent speaker who does not need to pause for anything. His *blitzkreigs* parallel his "*blitzsprechen.*" Mrs. Coates is "interested in what any one said" and thus may believe too much in what others say, but here she seems observant enough to notice that words have "two meanings" and that while the Madden-Henrys mean to praise Harper, the fact that he "never could or would or did cough" could mean he's a *dummkopf* (a dolt). Harper talks so much nobody else has to (or dares to), but beliefs that are only heard and not expressed personally keep a community divided. The Madden-Henrys are precursors of the current propagandist Rush Limbaugh's "ditto-heads"—not because of their beliefs but because the medium by which they receive those beliefs forbids them to express themselves. Ventriloquy is no substitute for individual expression.

But if people choose to believe nothing they hear from their media source, they can discuss and create rumors together, building a local community. This smaller social structure in turn is even more resistant to further propaganda, both because smaller structures resist influence from outside sources and because "Propaganda ceases where simple dialogue begins" (Ellul, 6). In this way there may be advantages to being "completely isolated" where "rumor follows rumor" (Stein, *Wars*, 145).

Stein had been made aware of the combined power of prejudice, press, and public opinion by prominent controversies during the last decade of the nineteenth century, when she was in college and medical school:

> It was around those days that three things happened that made me know about those kinds of things. There was my eldest brother coming home from the East as a member of the G.A.R., he had to grow a beard to look old enough, of course he did not belong but there were privileges in traveling and other things so he came along with them. It was then I first knew about officialdom and what one did by bribing. Of course that has to do with war, because the ordinary person that is one leading a peaceful life particularly men comes in contact with officials but in war-time, sooner or later everybody does. The second thing was the famous Oscar Wilde trial and the question of public opinion and the third thing was the Dreyfus case and anti-semitism. (*Wars*, 51)

The GAR is the Grand Army of the Republic, a society of Civil War veterans who had served in the Union forces. Stein's brother would have been too young to fight in the war, and Stein's ancestors had been Confederates. Since Stein has just made the difficult decision to stay in France instead of "pass by fraud" to Switzerland (50)—in 1943, after being pointedly warned to go—she may be thinking of the misrepresentations of self encouraged by officialdom. Stein sees a relationship between her brother, her own situation, and disguise. "The second thing" and "the third thing," also comment on the deceptive presentation of self in a hostile situation. Oscar Wilde's trial communicates a powerful message about the importance of disguises to a homosexual; the turmoil surrounding the Dreyfus case could convey the same message to a Jew. Both cases were also huge generators of newsprint, and the role of the press and public opinion (and famous writers) in the Dreyfus affair is as interesting as, though probably not separable from, the case itself.

Gabriel Tarde—who was "one of the three most outstanding sociologists of nineteenth-century France" (along with Auguste Comte and Emile Durkheim) and who influenced Franz Boas (and indirectly through Boas, other U.S. anthropologists)—was inspired by the Dreyfus case to distinguish between a "crowd" and a "public" (T. Clark, 1, 66–67, 52). Tarde defines a crowd as a group of people who are in "physical proximity";

a public is "a purely spiritual collectivity, a dispersion of individuals who are physically separated and whose cohesion is entirely mental (278, 277). A crowd is a long-established collectivity; the more recent "public" is enabled by technologies such as the printing press and improved transportation. But Stein's characters in *Mrs. Reynolds* and her friends in *Wars I Have Seen* do not collect in crowds of more than two or three people (the Germans forbade it), and they do not read a newspaper they trust, if they have access to one at all.

In *Mrs. Reynolds*, Stein demonstrates another kind of collectivity. Stein's fictional midcentury war-inspired network is built around chance meetings and polite visits during which people chat, pass on hearsay, make wishes, predict doom, or treat crises as lightly as they can. "Mrs. Reynolds liked to know what was happening so she asked everybody as they were passing" (91). At one point, Mrs. Reynolds talks to "Mrs. Chambers who happened to be walking in the same direction" (226). Mrs. Reynolds never gets to talk to Mrs. Andrews anymore, because "she was never out in her garden and Mrs. Reynolds never saw her. And if Mrs. Reynolds never saw her they could not talk together" (258–59). Most interactions occur between two individuals who meet on a road, speak over a fence, or, in the case of Mr. and Mrs. Reynolds, chat over their scanty meals. This loose-knit complex collectivity maintains individuality but enables strength and action through cooperation.

Getting Together and Thinking in *Brewsie and Willie*

Brewsie and Willie, written after V.E. Day (8 May 1945) and published before Stein's death (27 July 1946), is an informal transcription of an imagined conversation among American GIs and nurses in France. That its informal and imaginary status makes it diverge widely from the data of conversation analysts significantly undermines my choice of the word "transcription." But readers are struck by what sounds like real conversation. Hoffman writes that "Miss Stein demonstrates that she indeed had a remarkable sense of the way people sound when they talk" (*Abstractionism*, 128n), and that "the chapters of dialogue seem almost to have been recorded by a tape recorder" (*Gertrude Stein*, 102). Bridgman is more moderate when he observes that "the dialogue gives the impression of stylized authenticity" and that the soldiers from different states are not distinguished by regional dialect (336). When she wrote *Brewsie and Willie*, Stein's imagination was steeped in the language of the GIs; she soaked up their voices, slang, and personal histories with great pleasure when she met them at the end of World War II. Of this meeting, she writes: "Oh happy day, that is all that I can say oh happy day" (*Wars*, 244). When she met the soldiers, they "talked and talked" together, and their speech—especially the names of their hometowns—"was music to the ears" (246).

The impression of conversational structure in *Brewsie and Willie* is bolstered by the many paragraphs that consist of a name, a colon, and a speech act. This theatrical signature makes the novel an obvious candidate for a discussion of how Stein's writing incorporates spoken forms of English, but my intention is to discuss Stein's prescription for a kind of conversation which she expects will heal the economic and social problems of the United States—a way of bringing the victory back home. The ideas in *Brewsie and Willie* are presented by means of conversation, and much of that conversation is about politics, economics, society, and conversation itself. In *Mrs. Reynolds*, Stein demonstrates how politics and propaganda can change the nature of conversation, but in *Brewsie and Willie*, she delineates a different relationship between politics and conversation. Consistent with her critique of cautious conversation in a political landscape characterized by propagandistic harping, Stein presents open, playful conversation as an integral step toward improving the world's sociopolitical future.

Critics have seen logistical laziness instead of theoretical complexity in Stein's choice to write *Brewsie and Willie* in dialogue form. Bridgman supposes that Stein chose to write this way because "it exempted her from the need to develop her positions fully," "permitted her to interject disagreements and illustrative anecdotes," and "sanctioned the abrupt change of subject" (336). Hoffman summarizes Bridgman's position: "Stein found the dialogue form congenial . . . because it gave her the opportunity to vent her spleen without obligating her to develop any position logically" (*Gertrude Stein*, 102). While not necessarily contradicting Bridgman and Hoffman, I'm convinced that Stein chose to work with dialogue because its interjections, incompletions, cooperation, and playful listening to itself are all components of her suggestion for an American conversation.[16] As Rorty advocates: "all that matters for liberal politics is the widely shared conviction that . . . we shall call 'true' or 'good' whatever is the outcome of free discussion—that if we take care of political freedom, truth and goodness will take care of themselves" (*Contingency*, 84). In the interests of variety and dialogue, Stein probably does not value full positions on anything; Bridgman notes that she "was constitutionally incapable of sustained exposition, for her mind rapidly clogged with qualifications and objections as she proceeded" (336). Stein distrusted final solutions before she could have known about the "Final Solution."

Since Stein's characters directly state their discontents, critics have also tended to glean Stein's solution for these problems from their specific words. Jimmie says we "have to take care of ourselves" (*Brewsie*, 59); Brewsie says we "have to pioneer" (62); several agree that they have to "break down what has been built up," and Willie takes this to the limit: "do you want us to drop our atomic bombs on ourselves, is that what you want, so we can go out and pioneer, is that the idea" (83). These half-hearted suggestions lead Bridgman to write that Stein "offered no panacea for these urgent problems" and that Willie's "negative appraisal"—"there aint any answer, there aint going to be any answer, there never has been any answer, that's the answer" (*Brewsie*, 30)—"is never fully dissipated in the book" (Bridgman, 339). Bridgman concludes that the most "positive proposal" in the novel is that of "resistance," but that "Gertrude Stein's prudence restrained her from openly advocating revolution, which in any case would not be to her taste" (340). Stein can still prove relevant today, as we face more of the same "urgent" problems; instead of looking for quick answers to our complex problems, we should begin (and continue) the longer, messier processes that might form more successful solutions.

Stein's characters do not explicitly state an answer, but in their style of talk appears a suggestion. Their proposals are less-than-desirable alternatives to Stein's truly positive proposal: speak openly, converse, and at least while you try to solve your problems you will be friends (or at least on speaking terms), which will prevent interim violence. As Stein scolded Americans, with a phrase of lasting relevance: "A country can't live without friends" (qtd. in Brinnin, 393). Perhaps there is not one answer because it is impossible to clarify and simplify the complexity of the world—Willie says: "Well go on Brewsie, go on straighten things out. I'm sure straight is something that looks funny, but go on, let's straighten it out" (*Brewsie*, 55)—but in the meantime, we can chat.[17] Their half-baked wanderings also represent people rising up and meeting each other in conversation, which allows for the possibility, as William James rhapsodizes, that "we can *create* the conclusion, then. We can and we may, as it were, jump with both feet off the ground into or towards a world of which we trust the other parts to meet our jump—and *only so* can the *making* of a perfected world of the pluralistic pattern ever take place. Only through our precursive trust in it can it come into being" (qtd. in Shepherd, 251).

A statement in Stein's memoir *Wars I Have Seen* enables readers to better understand her views on the speech she represents in *Brewsie and Willie*. Writing after World War II, Stein contrasts American soldiers in the two world wars:

I began to realize that Americans converse much more than they did, American men in those other days, the days before these days did not converse. How well I remember in the last war seeing four or five of them at a table at a hotel and one man would sort of drone along mono-loguing about what he had or had not done and the others solemnly and quietly eating and drinking and never saying a word. And seeing the soldiers stand at a corner or be seated somewhere and there they were and minutes hours passed and they never said a word, and then one would get up and leave and the others got up and left and that was that. No this army was not like that, this army conversed, it talked it listened, and each one of them had something to say no this army was not like that other army. . . . now they are still American but they can converse and they are interesting when they talk. The older Americans always told stories that was about all there was to their talking but these don't tell stories they converse and what they say is interesting and what they hear interests them and that does make them different not really differ-ent God bless them but just the same they are not quite the same.

We did not talk about that then. We had too much to tell and they had too much to tell to spend any time conversing about conversation. (*Wars*, 248–49)

Stein notices that American soldiers in the forties speak very differently from the way their compatriots did in the teens. A doughboy either spoke forever, "tell[ing] stories" and "monologuing," or he did not speak at all. But the CIs know how to converse; they know how to talk and listen both. In *Brewsie and Willie*, these conversations take the form of lively interaction. The characters speak together in a dance of words and interject comments and puns. Stories, ideas, and questions are built by the group from the com-ments of individuals expressing their different perspectives.

Brewsie and Willie contains characters of both conversational styles. Brock represents the kind of talk Stein associates with the World War I doughboys; Brewsie and Willie, along with Pauline and many other char-acters, collaborate to converse and be interesting. Brock, who is "older," always tells things that have happened to him:

he liked to talk about how his father and mother moved from one house to another and what illnesses they had had and what it did to them and what flowers his mother grew and that she was fond of cooking and eating, and that he was not the only child but they did like him that is to say he was interested in everything they wrote to him and was natural enough because although he had been married, he did not know whether he was married now or not. (5)

The anataxis here suggests Brock's persistent and cumulative "monologuing." His ignorance as to the state of his marriage is to be pitied, but it also suggests an inability to sustain partnerships. Just as he forgets that a talker needs a listener, he forgets that to be a husband requires a wife. Brock also explains things (26), and, again, explanations are not the kind of talk Stein values. Brock is not the only character who cannot converse. Ed also tells what he's done: "I'll tell you just how I do it, just how old I am, just what I have done, just what I am going to do, I am just going to tell you" (32). Exemplifying the closed mind that accompanies this kind of presentational talk, Ed does not think it necessary to think and talk about improving the economic situation in the United States. His logic: his brother "lived through the depression and he always had a job" (31).

I suspect that Brewsie is a kind of ideal speaker for Stein, in spite of his tendency to sometimes get too explanatory, pedantic, and repetitive. Brewsie asks questions that inspire conversation. "I want to know why do you fellows feel the way you do" (5). "why don't the G.I.'s [sic] have the Bible around like the doughboys did" (10). Over and over, he asks, "Are we isolationists or are we isolated, are we efficient or are we quick to make up for long preparation" (e.g., 16). Brewsie is always thoughtful and disturbs complacency. He is "earnest" and "careful," and what he says rings true (32). Several times, Willie wishes for the otherwise hated Brock, because Brock's monologues would be comforting compared to all this unnerving discussion (52, 84). Brewsie begins many statements with "I been thinking," and Willie comments, "Well anyway . . . Brock never did begin that way" (68).

Stein has been characterized as an experimental writer; Brewsie is an experimental speaker. When he talks, he thinks out loud, in contrast to a speaker who makes up his or her mind and asserts a single definitive position on a topic.[18] Brewsie thinks about several topics at once, starts more than one conversation at a time, asks many questions, and changes his mind in midconversation. Julie Abraham describes the main "action" of *Brewsie and Willie* as "the spreading of doubt, the changing of minds" (516). Instead of declaring what's right, Brewsie says, "I think" (*Brewsie*, 3), which is one way of asking for a peaceful open conversation about what everybody else thinks too, or instead. Rather than store his opinions, which might let them become stale, he thinks as he speaks. When Brewsie has to leave before he says what's on his mind, Jo says, "Brewsie will remember what he wants to say for another day." Brewsie responds, "No . . . I wont remember but I will find it out again" (19). That Brewsie will have to rediscover his own thoughts next time he speaks demonstrates that he is not a pedantic "harper."

Besides Brewsie's letting thought inspire his more repetitive monologues, his explanations differ from, say, Angel Harper's, in another important way. Brewsie's presentations are often interrupted by other speakers' ideas and irreverent comments. When Brewsie presents his history of industrialism, he is interrupted by several jokes (34–35). The conversation deteriorates when his persistence in the face of interruption eventually produces an audience that listens without interrupting for a fairly long time. When the interjections come, they first suggest the gullibility of his audience. Jo responds only when Brewsie mentions historic facts: "My God yes, said Jo, we did have the depression" (36). The fact of the depression does not mean that Brewsie's analysis of economic trends is correct, and yet that is what Jo's awed interjection implies.[19] In one sense, then, Brewsie is temporarily a very minor dictator—intentionally or not—because his listeners are incapable of thinking independently enough to disagree with him or augment his ideas in any way.

Later in the novel, though, a productive conversation—one in which interesting ideas arise, however randomly—takes place among eight speakers: Brewsie, Jo, Willie, Pauline, Jane, Jimmie, Janet, and Donald Paul. While they all still think they are there to listen to Brewsie, most of them say something thoughtful. Jo calls their attention to language, wondering aloud why Americans have begun calling their nation "the states"; Donald Paul asserts, "Everything means something," and listens to himself enough to wonder if he means "something means anything"; Jimmie deduces the limitations of the two usual options, working or striking; and Donald Paul throws in issues of race and class when he "suppose[s] even in a poor country somebody has just got to be rich" and wonders if it will be African Americans (57–60).[20] These eight people bring their various questions and concerns to the conversation, creating a complex set of criteria that any "answer" would have to address (60–61). Single paragraphs, and even single sentences, contain speech from more than one character, further suggesting the ways that several speakers can create ideas together. What one speaker says piggybacks on the words of another one, in a form of innovation dependent on far-ranging talk and close listening.

Brewsie's thinking out loud makes him an important model, but he's not quite playful enough when he speaks. Stein does not dismiss Willie's value via a simplified binarism. Willie may resist offbeat thoughts and big questions, but he is another model speaker in that he is fun to talk to. Not only does Willie have the good judgment to listen to Brewsie when he is the only one thinking and trying to express his thoughts, but also Willie is smart, ironic, and alert to puns (34–35). Willie hears "missed steak" in "mistake," which leads him to consider the various costs of the U.S. Civil War. He ponders what it means that American Southerners are "lousy" and "foreigners" but not "lousy foreigners" (47). When a woman starts quoting her father, Willie insightfully and amusingly says, "It's enough . . . that we got to fight the rich men and the poor men too, but we got to stop somewhere sister, we cant take on your father, sure anybody has to have a father, that's all right but anybody can forget about a father especially in a war, especially" (38).[21] In pretending to summarize Brewsie's analysis of the effects of the Civil War on U.S. economics, Willie says, "yes we were fighting so no colored man would ever again have to say yes ma'am, thank you ma'am" (49). And he may be more insightful than he sounds; if "heil Hitler" is an insidious insertion of fascism into everyday life, then "yes ma'am" could just as perniciously and subtly maintain the system of human enslavement. While Willie seems to want to stop everyone's deep thought and expressiveness, his own irreverent idle talk provokes original ideas, too.

The French during the war learn to mistrust mass media, but so do the American soldiers after the war. In *Brewsie and Willie*, Willie wonders whom he can believe when he gets home:

> It used to be fine, said Willie, before the war when we used to believe what the newspapers and the magazines said, we used to believe them when we read them and now when it's us they write about we know it's lies, just lies, just bunches of lies, and if it's just bunches of lies, what we going to read when we get home, answer me that, Brewsie, answer me that. (19)

Willie worries about how he can assimilate back into the American public. The "bond" between people who are "reading the same newspaper" is forged by "their simultaneous conviction or passion and . . . their awareness of sharing at the same time an idea or a wish with a great number of other men" (Tarde, "Public," 278). Willie would like to think with the group, but now that he mistrusts the information in the press, he fears that it will be impossible to regain his position as an undeviating, untroubled member of the American public.

Yes-and-No "Job-men"

Nazis say, "Heil Hitler"; slaves in America say, "Yes, ma'am"; and, with less coercion, "yes and no job-men" say yes and no (not "kind of" or "mmhmm" or "let me think about it" or something else altogether) in the perpetuation of industrial conformity. Yes-and-no job-men are dependent employees instead of independent hired men (Stein, "Capital and Capitals," 75). Stein blames industrialism for the demise of open conversation and free thought. Admittedly, before there was industrialism, there were leaders who found willing followers. But if one assumes that Americans are different, that Americans are pioneers who lead their own kinds of lives and whose ancestors revitalized and instituted a rare form of government to ensure their right to pursue happiness in their own ways, then one might blame industrialism for the new kind of American who was just like the people left behind by those idealized movers and shakers: a follower.

The characters in Stein's *Brewsie and Willie* explicitly state their worries about the future, discussing outright the long-term economic effects and the immediately visible social effects of industrialism on the characters of Americans.[22] A "fat major" and a "thin major" compare the lives of European workers with those of U.S. workers. They wish that the United States would learn from Europe and give workers a day-and-a-half holiday each week, a month's vacation, and retirement at fifty instead of seventy (20–21). This fat major and thin major make me think of the major and minor premises in a syllogism. Their speech does not strictly follow the structure of syllogistic argument, but they do reason and reckon together (the etymological meaning of "syllogism"). They may sound lazy, but their wishes correspond to Willie's statement that Americans "dont think over there [back home, in the United States], they got no time to think, they got to get a job, they got to hold the job, they got no time to think over there" (108). Willie doesn't mind, because he thinks that thinking does no good, but Brewsie disagrees. He says that if you haven't had time to think, then "you'll be old and you never lived," and "industrialism makes industrials poor individuals" (108, 75).[23]

One might argue that it is reasonable to pay socio-psychological or cultural costs for economic prosperity, but Stein's characters also doubt that industrial capitalism is a viable long-term economic system.[24] Brewsie links new restrictions on immigration to the United States with the loss of a market for American-made products, and he describes the necessary alternative market: "now we got to make a club to make those foreign countries buy from us, and we all got to go home to make some more of those things that use up the raw material and that nobody but our own little population wants to buy" (36–37). He argues that "industrialism is wrong" because "it makes the country going all industrial poor" (56–57). Countries such as France that "never went industrial" manage to make "luxuries"—"what [France] sells dont cost her hardly anything to make," says Jo—but industrial countries use all their valuable resources making things that don't sell for very much, because "once industry makes luxuries it aint a luxury any more" (57). In short, the crisis of rising expectations caused by industrialism leads to economic ruin, as well as to intellectual bankruptcy.[25]

The characters in *Brewsie and Willie* are not the only people worried about the future of America. Stein herself seems particularly concerned with spiritual and intellectual decay, expecting that improvements in these areas would solve all the other problems, too. When she traveled to Germany with U.S. troops right after the war, she was troubled, she reported in an article for *Life* magazine, because the soldiers "admitted they liked the Germans better than the other Europeans" ("Off We All Went," 140). This admission suggested to her something ominous about the American character. In her article, she sees German "flatter[y]" as the source for this preference, and in her novel, Brewsie wonders whether "we like Germans because we are greedy and callous like them" (*Brewsie*, 20). Stein felt that the solution to a war-mongering Germany was to "teach [the Germans] disobedience, . . . make every German child know that it is its duty at least once a day to do its good deed and not believe something its father or its teacher tells them, confuse their minds, get their minds confused and perhaps then they will be disobedient and the world will be at peace" ("Off We All Went," 136). A U.S. Army sergeant told her that she "'confused the minds of his men,'" and she "got very angry": "why shouldn't their minds be confused, gracious goodness, are we going to be like the Germans, . . . all having the same point of view" (140). A Frenchman in Stein's play *In Savoy* is as direct: "Obedience is a curse. . . . The Germans are obedient and obedient people must sooner or later follow a bad leader" (21).[26]

A personal statement appended to the end of *Brewsie and Willie* further develops Stein's position. Once rightly and wrongly described as a "peroration on the subject of patriotism that is rampant with unblushing clichés" (Hoffman, *Gertrude Stein*, 103), this letter "to Americans" warns that

we have to have to fight *a spiritual pioneer fight* or we will go poor as England and other industrial countries have gone poor, and dont think that communism or socialism will save you, you just have to *find a new way*, you have to find out how you can go ahead without running away with yourselves, you have to learn to produce without exhausting your country's wealth, you have to *learn to be individual and not just mass job workers,* you have to *get courage enough to know what you feel and not just all be yes or no men,* but you have to *really learn to express complication,* go easy and if you cant go easy go as easy as you can. Remember the depression, dont be afraid to look it in the face and find out the reason why, dont be afraid of the reason why. . . . Find out the reason why, look facts in the face, *not just what they all say, the leaders, but every darn one of you* so that a government by the people for the people shall not perish from the face of the earth, it wont, somebody else will do it if we lie down on the job. (*Brewsie,* 113–14; my italics)

Sometimes a cliché is more than a cliché. Robert K. Martin's description of this passage seems apt to me: "Stein brilliantly mixes the clichés of popular advice ('look facts in the face'), folksy locutions ('every darn one of you'), and fragments from Lincoln's Gettysburg Address in a manner that both recalls the origins of her message in American political heritage and warns of its transformation into the blank phrases of Fourth of July rhetoric" (214). In this patriotic appeal, Stein expresses her belief that fighting "a spiritual pioneer fight"—one inside ourselves instead of on the plains of North America—will lead us to new ideas beyond communism and socialism, the most popularized alternatives to capitalism. Industrialism is the culprit (one that has been equally befriended by these three -isms), and our thoughts must lead us to other answers, to "a new way."

But industrialism is not just an economic culprit; it has formed us into people who cannot see beyond it. Stein is clearly aware of the kinds of jobs that are available to most people in an industrial society, and she concludes, with reason, that this kind of work diverts people from thinking and acting for themselves. Stein argues that Americans have to stop letting themselves be led around by limited binary false choices, have to escape the limits of "yes or no." Stein's Brewsie says:

you see I don't think we think, if we thought we could not articulate the same, we couldn't have Gallup polls and have everybody answer yes or no, if you think it's more complicated than that, . . . thinking is funnier and more mixed than that, . . . I guess job men just have to articulate alike, they got to articulate yes or no to their bosses, and yes or no to their unions, they just got to articulate alike, and when you begin to articulate alike, you got to drop thinking out. (*Brewsie,* 102–3)

If we escape being "mass job workers" and "learn to be individual," we will be able to see for ourselves instead of believing what a few leaders tell us.[27]

Stein's solution, or rather her means toward solutions, is linguistic: we have to get beyond the easy yes and no and "really learn to express complication." In the letter to Americans cited above, she advocates discovering causes of the depression, but *Brewsie and Willie* overall is more intent upon teaching people to participate in the processes of thinking and talking than upon asserting an economic theory. Stein prepares her readers for a conversation, and her primary directive is to become internally split so that we remember to converse with ourselves. We should think so much that we don't know for sure what we believe.

Internal stress characterizes the soldiers in *Brewsie and Willie*. Brewsie's talking to himself is a sign of an internal division (7). His "thinking and talking" make him "kind of foggy in the head" in spite of his quest for clear understanding (11). Brewsie says, "although rich we are poor," and "although quick we are slow" (22–23), extending his idea of riches beyond finances to happiness and freedom, and noticing that he values preparedness and attentive energy during times of peace even more than quick-wittedness and frantic energy in a crisis. Brewsie thinks enough to notice discrepancies between what he understands he is supposed to believe and what he feels he believes. In her memoir, Stein is told by "The man at the bank": "there are a great many different points of view and one single man can have quite a great number of them" (*Wars*, 81). As a Frenchman explains to an aptly named American woman in Stein's last play, *In Savoy*:

> my poor Constance you don't understand. How can you understand, no Constance you do not understand. There are so many points of view in a Frenchman, of course he cannot agree with any other Frenchman but he cannot even agree with himself inside him that is to say with the other Frenchman which is him. No my poor Constance you do not understand. (31–32).

When French people are asked for their opinions, they often start their answer with "no . . . and yes."

If American assertions tend to be characterized by constancy, Stein encourages us in *Brewsie and Willie* to learn a little inconsistency and free expression from the French. She noticed during the war that French free expression was curbed, and she missed it. One observer who lived in occupied France during World War II states that it was very striking to notice the restrictions on speech during the German occupation:

> Restraint in self-expression has never been a Gallic trait. Now that the Kommandantur has clamped down the ban of silence, it is especially hard to acquiesce. We have always been garrulous and carefree in speech, with a party openly advocating the return of monarchy, right in the bosom of the republican Parliament.
>
> We now see that both in manners and thought we were the freest, most unhampered people under heaven. All of which makes today's repression the more irksome. This looking over the shoulder before uttering an innocent remark does not fit into our picture. When shoving off the children for school, my wife used to say, "Don't get your feet wet." Now she warns them, "Sh-h! Don't speak to any one or answer questions." (*All Gaul*, 67–68)

This sudden speechlessness would make anyone notice and value freedom of expression, particularly someone as observant of conversation as Stein.

After the war, French habits of talk resume their freedom, as Stein observes: "all this time, well we did not say much but now France is free and we tell each other what we really think" (*In Savoy*, 58). In *Brewsie and Willie*, Stein depicts American soldiers as conversing more openly in France than they would in the United States:

> While they were talking they did not know what country they were in. . . .
>
> It was early in the morning, and there was anybody there, they never thought that there was anybody there even when there was. (13)

Their conversation is not restricted by where they are or, as I understand the implications of location, where their loyalties should lie. They never worry that anybody was there, even when someone was, which suggests a free and easy conversation not overshadowed by suspicions that "somebody's there" or hushed reassurances that "nobody's there." These soldiers feel free to think and talk about all sorts of things: "About it, about what it is, about how about it, about what is it about, about, what are you going to do about it, about, how about it" (66). They are less interested in the variable "it" than in the ruminative equation; the ultimate goal of this kind of talk is "to get going away from what everybody has gotten the habit of thinking"

(69–70). Willie goes so far as to say, "I don't see why I got to believe a thing only because it's true" (38).

Being "foggy in the head" might prevent violence, as well as lead to new and different ideas. Tarde believed that "psychic strain" prevented social conflict; groups could not form and clash if individuals were internally divided as to their beliefs (see T. Clark, 34–35). Note that Stein's men and women in *Brewsie and Willie* come and go freely; their circulation of ideas and information does not form a Rotary Club.[28] The free inconsistency which Stein believes will allow Americans to think and converse will also, according to Tarde, keep them out of violent conflict. Stein, too, seems concerned about violence. In discussing the burden of a high standard of living and industrialism, Jo says, "How do you get on top of anything that is on top of you, first you got to break it off you." Pauline worries, "Oh dear . . . fighting is so natural" (70). Instead of this "natural" revolutionary reflex, Stein suggests thinking about and speaking toward alternative ways of conceiving and generating change.

Other characters in the novel adopt Brewsie's wandering thought process and challenging talk. Henry says that his "mind's confused" and that he wants to remain in France to think:

> Willie, muttering mind mind, confused, get a mind, get it confused, I suppose, said Willie, you have been listening to Brewsie. No I havent, said Henry. Who's Brewsie. Who's Brewsie said Willie, that's Brewsie, well how did you get your mind confused if you didnt listen to Brewsie. Well I guess, said Henry, I got my mind confused because I just cant see any way not to have my mind confused that's all, see here Willie, you see it's about that employee mentality we're all getting to have, we're just a lot of employees, obeying a boss, with no mind of our own and if it goes on where is America, I say if it goes on, where is America, no sir, said Henry, no sir, I want to pioneer. Ah, said Willie, you been listening to Brewsie. (*Brewsie*, 63)

Henry sounds like Brewsie, but he has come to his ideas on his own power, his own willingness to "see here" and think. Willie doesn't seem to like this independence one bit. When Henry suggests, "let's all think," Willie responds (maybe sarcastically by this point), "No . . . you let Brewsie do the thinking, that's the way we are in this outfit, we let Brewsie do the thinking" (65). Willie notes that "the guys" won't let Brewsie talk anymore: "they found out from listening to him how to do it and now they all talk and talk and think it sounds just like him" (100–101). But the ideal is not to sound "just like" Brewsie; it is to speak freely and thoughtfully, as Brewsie demonstrates is possible. Willie warns, "look out Brewsie, soon there won't be a thing you can tell them" (67), but Brewsie is probably happy to finally be surrounded by people willing to "get together and think" (11).

Brewsie's kind of talk influences others, but the soldiers agree that he does not speak like a typical leader. Brewsie spends too much time asking questions and deliberating possible answers, sitting among the conferees and asking, "what do you think?" When a young nurse wonders how "the French expect to come back if they have no leaders" (22), Brewsie says that leaders don't lead, or they lead where nobody wants to go, and that the French don't want to go anywhere, they just want homes and fuel, and leaders only manage to get enough of that for themselves (22). Probably because he expects a leader to command people what to think and do, Willie says, "you're no leader, Brewsie, you just talk." Donald Paul asks, "And what do leaders do"; Jo says, "They talk too, but they talk differently" (24).

They talk like Angel Harper, who dictates instead of converses, who is supposed to have been from Mrs. Reynolds's town, and who is discussed in terms of his habits of speech. One woman "did not find him interesting," because "all she noticed about him was that he could not know what to say"; he "just rubbed his fingers and said he could not say what he had to say" (Mrs. Reynolds, 46). Elsewhere in Mrs. Reynolds, Stein writes:

> Once when [Angel Harper] was twelve he ate twenty macaroons and an apple. He liked it although he never said it. He said that he preferred macaroons to fruit, he said he preferred coffee to potatoes, that is he never said this but he thought that if he said anything about coffee or macaroons or fruit or potatoes he would say that. Just then when he was twelve he knew that what he thought he said and what he said was not what he said. (100)

Angel Harper thinks in set pieces and cannot find the appropriate way to insert his remarks into casual conversation. His awkward silences contrast with the present situation, in which he "talked and talked so everybody had to listen." Angel Harper cannot "participate in the gentle rhythm of being in relation" (Berry, 126). His desire for dictatorship may arise from his inability to speak comfortably in a conversation among equals at school. Angel Harper has created a national power structure that enables him to harp and requires everyone else to listen. Because he is unable to chat, his words have to have consequences.[29]

Throughout *Mrs. Reynolds*, Angel Harper is criticized not only for his style of speech but also for his murderousness and his lack of individuality: "how many people were suffering in summer and suffering in winter because he was fifty. . . . It is difficult to count when so many means more than everybody" (197); "how bitter it was that so many should be dead dead dead, dead because of Angel Harper of the fifty years of Angel Harper, dead dead dead, because of the fifty years of Angel Harper" (193). Over and over, Mrs. Reynolds wishes for Angel Harper's death: "it was really Angel Harper being forty-seven that made her cry and she could only try and hope that he would never be forty-eight" (139; see also 150, 188). When Mrs. Reynolds says, "I know that he will die," Mr. Reynolds says, "that will be a good riddance to bad rubbish" (98). Perhaps Harper can murder because he's not quite alive himself; using her own idiom, Stein sneers that "it is doubtful if he ever was a boy" (86). In other works, Stein questions the purpose of boys who become men: "But you know I know that if a boy is to grow up to be a man what is the use" (*Geographical History*, 127–28). In this way, she asks why the creative individualism and comfortable entity of children so often grow into adult conformity and identity.[30]

A further assertion of Angel Harper's lack of individuality and imagination resides in Stein's claim that he believes what "they say," a voice of false and brutal certainty: "So his life began and he never prayed although he believed in what they said. He always did even when everybody thought he did not. He believed in it a lot, so much so that it would have been much better not so" (*Mrs. Reynolds*, 86). Here, Angel Harper doesn't pray, which may refer to a lack of individual spirituality or creativity—or egosim—but he does put credence in what "they say." The passage may be read as a specific critique of Hitler's Jewish self-hate if we read it as implying that he omits Jewish rituals because he believes what an anti-Semitic "they say." Even if Stein has no idea of Hitler's origins, she depicts Harper as a leader who follows. Having no eye of his own, Angel Harper "never saw when he spoke" (85), and thus he cannot say what he sees.

In *Mrs. Reynolds*, "they" tends to refer to the enemy in the abstract, or to an abstract group that Stein sees as a negative force. Before Mrs. Reynolds dreams of the starving lamb, she has the following conversation with Mr. Reynolds:

And then said Mrs. Reynolds a lamb has died of hunger. What said Mr. Reynolds did I not tell you said Mrs. Reynolds the lamb of the Davilles' has died of hunger. Why said Mr. Reynolds did they not give it something to eat, because said Mrs. Reynolds they had nothing to feed it, and said Mrs. Reynolds they said, and Mrs. Reynolds felt a little queer as she said they say and Mr. Reynolds felt a little queer when she said they say, and they did not go on saying what she was going to say, they went in to dinner and that night just a little earlier than they usually did they went to bed and she did not go before he was ready, they went up to bed together. (184)

Mr. and Mrs. Reynolds may trail off because they do not want to say what "they say," and they cast doubt on the information already conveyed. Certainly they would rather not discuss the possibility of starvation, even the starvation of a lamb (if "the lamb" is even a farm animal at all). They may also be uncomfortably reluctant to believe their neighbors completely (since a lamb could also be killed to protect people from starvation). But they are also suspicious of the idea and the verbal construction of "they say." They do not want to attribute authority to a vaguely defined group, and when they say, "they say," they immediately cast doubt on the information conveyed.

The kind of conversation that Stein prescribes in *Brewsie and Willie* is not much different from the phatic communion I discuss in chapter 3. Pauline says: "wouldn't it just be beautiful if everybody stopped working, and just went out walking, and ate a sundae or an ice-cream soda and went on walking, and then just came home, and had doughnuts and a coke, and then they came in and sing a little and go to bed" (*Brewsie*, 73).[31] Pauline's idea sounds sickly sticky sweet (doughnuts *and* a Coke), but it is followed by Ed's more learned-sounding analysis of what would happen if people stopped going to work: big business would collapse and small businesses could start up. He says, "That sister aint so phony as she sounds, listen" (73). Pauline wants people to walk, eat, and talk—three of Stein's favorite pastimes—which combination may itself be the answer to economic problems. All that loose talk might lead to good answers, and a satisfactory long-term interim solution may be the conversational process itself. Interim solutions are the most satisfying ones anyway, in Stein's universe, and I think in ours. Consider the alternative.

Stein "ain't so phony as she sounds"

It sounds too simple, and too impossible, so we perhaps shake our heads at Stein's naïveté. Louis Bromfield, however, points to her "peculiar variety of naïveté which is the gift of the gods, . . . an innocence which is quite beyond the knowledge and experience of those who are known as sophisticated" (63). He imagines that Stein "was born . . . at a stage of development already beyond sophistication, endowed with that great simplicity which is interested in the value of everything and the price of nothing" (64). If Bromfield cannot make us take Stein seriously, perhaps the congruence between her ideas and those of other less playful thinkers will. For example, Stein's ideas on language and industrialism are surprisingly congruent with those of the highly influential social theorist Herbert Marcuse. In *One-Dimensional Man* (first published in 1964, but growing out of work done in the thirties), Marcuse's analysis of "advanced industrial society" echoes Stein's less systematic discussion of the social costs of industrialism. Voicing a problem and a dream, Stein's G.I. Joe complains that "we got to get on top of industrialism and not have it on top of us" (*Brewsie*, 70). Marcuse also sees a problem with "the technological processes of mechanization and standardization," and he dreams of a future in which these same processes "might release individual energy into a yet uncharted realm of freedom beyond necessity" (Marcuse, 2). Stein and Marcuse describe multiple facets of the problem: limited preprocessed and preapproved choices instead of free-ranging individual and interior thought, no free time to think, and the burden of the production and consumption of indoctrinated "false needs" (4).

Stein and Marcuse are concerned with our acceptance of very limited free choice. Stein's Brewsie worries about the "job men" who "got to articulate yes or no to their bosses, and yes or no to their unions," and yes or no to Gallup polls (*Brewsie*, 103). Marcuse expresses concern that our "advanced industrial civilization" has "reduce[d] the opposition to the discussion and promotion of alternative policies *within* the status quo" (2).[32] He expands on this idea: "Free choice among a wide variety of goods and services does not signify freedom if these goods and services sustain social controls over a life of toil and fear" (7–8). Marcuse also draws parallels between the bosses and the unions: this "integrating trend" of "the laboring class with capitalist society" "enforces a weakening of the negative position of the working class" (31n, 29, 31). In other words, a system that bridges and erases difference disallows opposition.

Stein and Marcuse both understand free time as necessary for open, original thought. Willie, insulting Brock and speaking more truth than he intends, says, "they give you work to shut you up" (Stein, *Brewsie*, 26). Willie again counterpoises talk with work when he says, "talk is good I like talk I like to listen to you Brewsie, but when we get home and dont wear this brown any more we got to have a job, job, job" (54). Brewsie responds, "that's what I want to say, industrialism which produces more than anybody can buy and makes employees out of free men makes 'em stop thinking, stop feeling, makes 'em all feel alike" (55). Marcuse, putting similar content in a contrasting style, writes that "the apparatus imposes its economic and political requirements for defense and expansion on labor time and free time, on the material and intellectual culture" (3). More directly linking free time and bold ideas, Marcuse writes: "Complete automation in the realm of necessity would open the dimension of free time as the one in which man's private *and* societal existence would constitute itself. This would be the historical transcendence toward a new civilization" (37). But industrial jobs keep us from thinking of this possible transcendence.[33]

One important step toward this great "new civilization" is admitting we haven't yet reached it. Both authors challenge the idea that consumerism is purely a liberty. What Marcuse calls "false needs," Stein calls "gadgets." Jo asks, "why we going to go home to jobs just to use up just what we have of iron ore making gadgets to be sold on the installment plan to people worried to death because they have to pay something every month and they'd be lots happier without it" (*Brewsie*, 33). Marcuse also sees constraint in the supposed opportunities of work and consumption: "unfreedom—in the sense of man's subjection to his productive apparatus—is perpetuated and intensified in the form of many liberties and comforts" (32).

These are a few of the reasons Stein and Marcuse believe that economic systems can enable or deny freedom as much as political systems can. It is clear that Stein blamed industrialism for a decline in individualism, and her characterization of the Germans as obedient followers is a fairly transparent reference to Nazism. Marcuse writes that "contemporary industrial society tends to be totalitarian. For 'totalitarian' is not only a terroristic political coordination of society, but also a non-terroristic economic-technical coordination which operates through the manipulation of needs by vested interests" (3). In these several ways, then, Marcuse's understanding of the social costs of advanced industrialism parallels Stein's.

But Stein and Marcuse do not agree only about the sociological effects of industrialism. They also agree that the solution to this problem is linguistic. Marcuse's delineation of the effects of industrialism on society includes a discussion of the way language has been affected, and he mentions ways of counteracting this linguistic disease:

> [The] *functionalization of language helps to repel non-conformist elements from the structure and movement of speech.* Vocabulary and syntax are equally affected. Society expresses its requirements directly in the linguistic material but not without opposition; *the popular language strikes with spiteful and defiant humor at the official and semi-official discourse.* Slang and colloquial speech have rarely been so creative.

It is as if the common man (or his anonymous spokesman) would in his speech assert his humanity against the powers that be, as if the rejection and revolt, subdued in the political sphere, would burst out in the vocabulary that calls things by their names: "head shrinker" and "egghead," "boob tube," "think tank," "beat it" and "dig it," and "gone, man, gone."

However, the defense laboratories and the executive offices, the governments and the machines, the time-keepers and managers, the efficiency experts and the political beauty parlors (which provide leaders with the appropriate make-up) speak a different language and, for the time being, they seem to have the last word. It is the word that orders and organizes, that induces people to do, to buy, and to accept. It is transmitted in a style which is a veritable linguistic creation; *a syntax in which the structure of the sentence is abridged and condensed in such a way that no tension, no "space" is left between the parts of the* sentence. This linguistic form militates against a development of meaning. (86; my italics)

If understood as primarily a form of communication, language becomes merely functional, "the concept tends to be absorbed by the word," and further "development of meaning" is prevented (87). Marcuse valorizes the everyday, informal "colloquial speech" of the 1960s as a genre in which people develop and choose words that express what they really mean. And Marcuse has a second, less directly stated, proposal: his condemnation of a lack of space between the parts of a sentence suggests that such space would counteract officialese. Marcuse wants us to use words in ways that allow for a "development of their meaning"—*and thus of our meaning.* He deplores the fact that when one hears a word such as "communist," one "is expected to react in a fixated, specific manner" (91). But when he says that "the functionalization of language expresses an abridgement of meaning which has a political connotation," he means only to change the way we use words that "denote things or occurrences beyond [the] noncontroversial context" of "the objects and implements of daily life, visible nature, vital needs and wants" (87). Marcuse means us to rethink words such as "democracy" and "freedom," "equality" and "peace," but Stein goes even further. Her comment about Hitler's deserving a peace prize makes us rethink "peace," but in *Tender Buttons* she not only makes us resee and rehear (over and over) her favorite concept words, such as "exchange," "change," and "arrange," but she also makes us renegotiate our understandings of words that refer to the objects, food, and rooms of daily living.

In *Tender Buttons*, Stein grants individual words the freedom to mean somewhat independently of the words that surround them in the sentence and paragraph. Stein's placement of words allows them multiple valences, and readers are encouraged (or even forced) to continue calling up connotations of words without ever exactly feeling satisfied enough to stop and declare denotational victory.[34] The close readings in previous chapters demonstrate that the multiple meanings of words enable them to react variously with different words around them, creating many kinds of private relationships. In this way, Stein leaves "space" between her words in which an organic, nonfunctional meaning can grow. Put another way, Stein allows her words self-determination and the freedom to form unique relationships with one another instead of locking them in a kind of totalitarian sentence structure. This careful placement of words in sentences, her refusal to become a totalitarian author who decrees all semantic relationships, corresponds with her desire for humans to escape from formal and informal totalitarian political structures. Developing our own networks of relationships and responsibilities through conversation is, theoretically, an attractive alternative to both tight totalitarianism and, on the other side of the political spectrum, anarchic isolationism in which we deny any interpersonal social or political connections.[35] The failure of syntax is both a symbol of freedom and a means to it.

Readers may become frustrated with what does not seem like an answer, and even frustrated with the way these writers define the problem of modern society: what's wrong, anyway, with technology, the easy satisfaction of real needs, and even the creation and satiation of "false needs"? Of Marcuse's text, a student typically complains: "Besides, he doesn't offer a real solution. Are we just supposed to feel bad about all this?" To accept Marcuse's and Stein's ideas as solutions, we have to get beyond what Marcuse calls "operationalism." Marcuse cites P. W. Bridgeman on the "wide implications of this mode of thought": Bridgeman points out that "we . . . no longer permit ourselves to use as tools in our thinking concepts of which we cannot give an adequate account in terms of operations" (13)[36] Our operationalist tendencies manifest themselves in our dissatisfaction with Stein's and Marcuse's answers. Talking and listening *are* actions or operations (they are things we can at least try to do), but since words and actions are understood as opposites in our society, the suggestion seems empty and necessarily ineffective. "What can we *do?*" is already a question with specific and limiting criteria for the answer it deems acceptable. These criteria do not accept "converse, talk, say playfully and differently" as an answer. As the action-oriented like to complain, "Talk is cheap."

Stein and Marcuse expect people to start listening to themselves, start listening to the clichés of other speakers, and, as a result, speak differently. Clichés are perpetuated by individuals who easily accept political (and other types of) slogans. This neglectful nonthinking in everyday linguistic experience parallels Roland Barthes's idea of "readerly" or "*lisible*" texts, the kind "that merely obey a logic of passive consumption" (Rabaté, 71). Barthes knows an alternative, and he defines another kind of text, the "writerly" or "*scriptible*":

> Why is the writerly our value? Because the goal of literary work (of literature as work) is to make the reader no longer a consumer, but a producer of the text. Our literature is characterized by the pitiless divorce which the literary institution maintains between the producer of the text and its user, between its owner and its customer, between its author and its reader. This reader is thereby plunged into a kind of idleness—he is intransitive; he is, in short, *serious:* instead of functioning himself, instead of gaining access to the magic of the signifier, to the pleasure of writing, he is left with no more than the poor freedom either to accept or reject the text: reading is nothing more than a *referendum.* (Barthes, 4)[37]

So one can only say yes or no to it. But writerly texts "stimulate the reader's active participation" (Rabaté, 71). Stein and Marcuse expect readers and listeners to activate their own attention, concentrating on the readerly texts (written and spoken) that are found everywhere around us in our daily lives. If we begin to approach readerly texts as if they were writerly, then we will notice contradictions and truths, and we will create writerly texts of our own (both in our writing and speaking). Reading these new writerly texts with our new writerly habits could initiate a cycle of inventiveness that might let us see beyond today's horizons of possibility.[38]

Barthes's choice of metaphor also builds on the relationship among language, politics, and economics that I've been exploring in Stein and Marcuse. Barthes uses "producers," "consumers," "owners," and "customers" as metaphors. A writerly text is produced by readers and writers who exist within a different economy from the one to which we are accustomed. The writerly reader does more than idly read, passively buying (or not) that which the author produces. Finally and relatedly, Barthes uses a loose political metaphor to describe a reader's relationship to a text. A reader of a writerly text does more than say yes or no to it, which would be "a poor freedom." Barthes links autocratic writing and passive reading, a capitalist economic system, and a lack of freedom. In a parallel way, Stein and Marcuse link active participation in the creation of texts and spoken conversations, an anti-industrialized economy, and greater individual and political freedom.

Real Ideas

When asked to teach a session of the History of Ideas, a course already in progress at the University of Chicago, Stein asked the regular instructors, Robert Hutchins and Mortimer Adler, "What are the ideas that are important?" Stein noticed that "none of the books read at any time by them was originally written in English" and that these men seemed to think that "there are no ideas which are not sociological or government ideas." Dismayed, she said, "Government is the least interesting thing in human life," and "real ideas are not the relation of human beings as groups but a human being to himself inside him" (Stein, *Everybody's*, 206). Stein was interested in "real ideas," not social systems concocted out of fear, hatred, or other perceived necessity. "Real ideas" involve thoughtful people internally divided enough to question persistently—and both seriously and playfully—the expression of ideas they encounter within and without. I have characterized Stein's valuation of individualism as a political position, but her own focus on individuals suggests that it is an antipolitical position.

The political climate in 1946 may have encouraged Stein to be more explicit about her political—or antipolitical—views. In that year, Albert Camus wrote in the Resistance newspaper *Combat*: "Yes, what we must fight is fear and silence, and with them the spiritual isolation they involve. What we must defend is dialogue and the universal communication of men" (138). And George Orwell, also in 1946, describes the era as a time when "it is broadly true that political writing is bad writing." He goes on to say that if the political writing is any good, then "it will generally be found that the writer is some kind of rebel, expressing private opinions and not a 'party line.'" Developing an image of a human automaton, Orwell goes on:

> Orthodoxy, of whatever color, seems to demand a lifeless, imitative style.
> . . . When one watches some tired hack on the platform *mechanically re-*
> *peating the familiar phrases*, . . . one often has a curious feeling that one
> is not watching a live human being but some kind of dummy: a feeling
> which suddenly becomes stronger at moments when the light catches
> the speaker's spectacles and turns them into blank discs which seem to
> have no eyes behind them. And this is not altogether fanciful. A speaker

who uses that kind of phraseology has gone some distance toward turning himself into a machine. The appropriate noises are coming out of his larynx, but *his brain is not involved as it would be if he were choosing his words for himself. . . . And this reduced state of consciousness, if not indispensable, is at any rate favorable to political conformity.* ("Politics and the English Language," 362–63; my italics)

Stein's recommendation that we say what we see may have been a necessary and important reminder in 1946 (as indeed it usually is).

Orwell continues to describe the powerful gravity of conventionality in "The Prevention of Literature" (also published in 1946): "It is the peculiarity of our age that the rebels against the existing order, at any rate the most numerous and characteristic of them, are also rebelling against the idea of individual integrity. 'Daring to stand alone' is ideologically criminal as well as practically dangerous" (368). Further: "The enemies of intellectual liberty always try to present their case as a plea for discipline versus individualism" (369). Orwell describes the political groups at both ends of the political spectrum as demanding loyal adherence in order to be stronger in opposing one another.[39] If efficiency requires conformity, and revolutionaries want quick, efficient change, then they require conformity even when it means that they become much more like the political organizations they are rebelling against. In Orwell's view: "Freedom of the intellect means the freedom to report what one has seen, heard, and felt, and not to be obliged to fabricate imaginary facts and feelings" (370). Mr. Reynolds says, "he was sure that if she felt that way that it was what she ought to say" (Stein, *Mrs. Reynolds*, 206). "Say what you see," commands Stein. But, in this age of yes-and-no job men, she wonders, "Oh say can you see" (*Geographical History*, 163).[40] For the United States to survive—as she values it—its anthem must be a true conversation.

CONCLUSIONS:

Feminine Endings

"The Woman Who Changed the Mind of a Nation"

AFTER THE WAR ended in Europe, in October 1945, Stein started "another opera" with Virgil Thomson; she wrote Van Vechten: "it is to be around Susan B. Anthony and Daniel Webster, that is if it comes off, I think Susan B. Anthony is a nice character for an opera . . . and the title is to be The Mother of us all" (Burns, 2:795). (After Stein's complaint about "too much fathering going on" in the thirties, "the mother of us all" may have seemed like a nice antidote, or at least an alternative.) A nurse in *Brewsie and Willie* reads a book about Anthony, and by mid-November 1945, Stein herself had read Rheta Childe Dorr's biography, *Susan B. Anthony, the Woman Who Changed the Mind of a Nation* (Burns, 2:798n). The subtitle summarizes my own understanding of Stein's potential: if things had somehow been different—if more people had read her innovative work, instead of stopping at the autobiographies and the hearsay—Stein could have changed people's minds such that they could really see, and could even say what they saw. She might have changed the operating systems of the American mind.

Several critics have noted the biographical parallels that Stein drew between Anthony and herself.[1] Of Anthony's lecture tours, Dorr writes: "Although she shocked every community she had a genius for making people think" (249). One newspaper article classed Anthony as "a revolutionist aiming at nothing less than the breaking up of the very foundations of society" (qtd. in Dorr, 246). But the most striking parallel for Stein may have been that Anthony fails to meet her goals and is ridiculed by many prominent people, but stays staunchly herself and gets a hero's welcome when she visits Europe and at her later appearances in the United States. Bridgman says that in *Brewsie and Willie*, Anthony "was offered as a model of self-liberation, who proved that if an individual made sufficient 'noise' he would be heard," but that in the opera, Susan B. recognizes her limited success in convincing others of the power of the individual (342, citing *Brewsie and Willie*, 89). Critics tend to concur that the opera expresses Stein's thoughts on her successes and failures at the end of her career (Brinnin, 399; Bridgman, 341–44). Stein—who began to feel some painful symptoms of her stomach cancer before she had finished the libretto (Bridgman, 341; Brinnin, 341)—may feel she has failed on the grand scale. At the same time, however, she asserts the primacy of individuality, and her own success in becoming and remaining an individual.

It is also important, as Robert K. Martin argues, to remember to read the opera as more than a simple autobiographical piece, for "to read the opera as a work about Stein herself, in which Anthony is simply 'equivalent to Gertrude Stein,' is to rob the text of its rich historical allusiveness and to diminish Stein's attempt at a commentary on American history" (210).[2] For example, Stein's history of America reiterates one sterling fact about the United States: we are a nation built on words—the Declaration of Independence, the Constitution, the law, and the verbal negotiations among individual interpretations of all these words. Anthony consistently challenged the standard readings of laws and constitutional amendments, going so far as to register to vote in 1871 based on a possible reading of the first article of the Fourteenth Amendment, which says all persons born or naturalized in the United States are citizens. The second article says it's a crime to deny *males* over age twenty-one the right to vote but, after her arrest, Anthony went on tour giving a lecture titled, "Is It a Crime for a Citizen of the United States to Vote?" (Dorr, 178, 254–55). Anthony did some writerly reading of her own, and words that are the foundation of the United States often beg for creative reading.

In Stein's opera, Martin points out, Stein highlights the difference between dead words and living words, contrasting "cant phrases repeated without meaning" against "their possible realization in the hands of a real democrat." Martin adds that Stein is calling "for a radical democracy that is true to its past, and that can be awakened by an undermining of the surfaces of an abused language" (214). All this goes to show that Stein is continuing her argument for self-determination, trying to persuade us to the same (but, of course, individualized) behaviors: to see and think and speak for ourselves, from our own perspectives, which involves making sure our language helps instead of hinders in these endeavors.

But *The Mother of Us All* also takes a turn toward disappointment or even resignation. The opera recalls a less sterling fact about the nation:

politicians are expedient, and committed political allies often prove unreliable. The opera is still playful, still a challenge, still sometimes funny,
and consistently, unpredictably Steinian. But what seems to be new in *The
Mother of Us All* is the unoriginal distinction Stein draws between the gen-
ders. She had never been blind to gender, but now she has come around to
clichés. As a young woman, Stein saw herself as male—a husband, a genius.
Martin notes a gradual shift throughout the thirties, as Stein's "early male
identification gives way" and "she finds her way out of the trap of associating
genius with masculinity and hence frees herself from adopting a 'mannish'
role" (217; and see Winston, 118).[3] She has asserted that the great literary
work of the twentieth century must be done by a woman—though she is
so clearly referring to herself that the gender commentary goes largely un-
noticed. In *Everybody's Autobiography*, Stein's gender assumptions show, as
when she says of Stalin, Mussolini, Roosevelt, Blum, Franco, and Hitler:
"There is too much fathering going on just now and there is no doubt about
it fathers are depressing. . . . England is the only country now that has not
got one and so they are more cheerful there than anywhere. It is a long
time now that they have not had any fathering and so their cheerfulness is
increasing" (133).

While *The Mother of Us All* continues Stein's "questioning of the entire
drive to power over others" (Martin, 217), there's a shift to straightforward,
clichéd complaints about men and to valorization of women: the opera's
male characters are privileged, selfish, and self-satisfied, and the female
characters tend to be insightful, or at least maturing, truly living beings.
Simply reading Dorr's biography of Anthony might leave one with this
strong impression, as at key moments in the struggle for universal suffrage,
the male players are unreliable or even turncoats.[4] Stein's sudden removal
from the airy world of writers and painters into one of war and poverty might
also have induced her to believe that men—the warmongers of these mas-
sive wars—were less than brilliant, and were certainly not enough focused
on the individual. And seeing how U.S. soldiers shared what she saw as
some of the worst failings of the Germans may have suggested a significant
masculine shortcoming.

Susan B. says, "Ladies there is no neutral position for us to assume,"
and Stein's libretto demonstrates her quick turn toward the nonneutral
position (*Mother*, 800). A friendly chat isn't going to work with the foes
who confront them. However neutral Stein may have been earlier in her
life on the question of the sexes, here males are directly criticized with
what start to look like second-wave feminist clichés. Susan B. says to Anne
(a character based on Anthony's partner of eighteen years but who plays

only a small role in Dorr's biography): "Men . . . are so conservative, so selfish, so boresome and . . . they are so ugly, . . . they are gullible, anybody can convince them" (789). She is disappointed in them for following her (although history shows that they did not when it mattered), but "they are men, and men, well of course they know that they cannot either see or hear unless I tell them so, poor things . . . I do not pity them. Poor things" (790). They cannot see or hear, they cannot notice and think for themselves, in her estimation, but their power probably prevents her from pitying them (though she seems a bit divided on this point, pitying them and not pitying them simultaneously). Another problem with men is that they cannot "be mixed," which I take to mean they cannot hold varying opinions at the same time: "How can anything be really mixed when men are conservative, dull, monotonous, deceived, stupid, unchanging and bullies, how said Susan B. how when men are men can they be mixed" (791).[5] Mixedness makes the French complicated and thoughtful in Stein's play *In Savoy*, and Stein advocates it to Americans in *Brewsie and Willie*. Mixedness also describes the way Americans were divided within themselves and their families during the American Revolutionary and Civil wars, when people fought for their beliefs and (sometimes also) loved the very people they were fighting.[6] With those kinds of complications and individual considerations, as well as the internal and personal search for beliefs, thoughtless crowd behavior is less likely. While championing mixedness, Stein offers a very unmixed summary of male characteristics.

Expressing the need to shut up loud pretentious voices is part of the serious work of Stein's opera (as opposed to most other operas). These voices prevent real conversation. Sometimes Stein includes parts of Daniel Webster's speeches (Winston, 122), and in this context they sound silly, as in: "When this debate sir was to be resumed on Thursday it so happened that it would have been convenient for me to be elsewhere" (*Mother*, 786); and in: "The harvest of neutrality had been great, but we had gathered it all" (787). He makes these grand rhetorical flourishes, regardless of what his interlocuter has said (not that Stein lets the famously straightforward Anthony, as Susan B., say anything that Webster would be able to make much sense of). Later, this famous orator is told he "needs an artichoke" to choke his artfulness (784). Thaddeus S.[tevens] harps on his pet causes: "I believe in public school education, I do not believe in free masons I believe in public school education, I do not believe that every one can do whatever he likes because (a pause) I have not always done what I liked" (791). John Adams thinks he is in love but, always aware of his class and position, he has to keep saying things like "if I had not been an Adams I would have kneeled at your feet" (792). Their love of their own voices and of their stubbornly held opinions, and their own limited (but grandiose) sense of self, keeps them from being able truly to interact.

The crowning example of these great men's self-love is the song that Andrew G., Thaddeus S. and Daniel Webster sing: "We are the chorus of the V.I.P. / Very important persons to every one who can hear and see, we are the chorus of the V.I.P." And: "We are the V.I.P. the very important persons, we have special rights, they ask us first and they wait for us last and wherever we are well there we are everybody knows we are there, we are the V.I.P. Very important persons for everybody to see" (*Mother*, 798, 799). These men get more than their share of attention, and they expect it. Adams says, "If you were silent I would speak" (796); he's used to people respectfully listening to him. One reason they get attention, as Susan B. explains, is that the rich get to talk and not listen; the poor have to listen (799). Stein's stage directions emphasize the problem with conversation: right after "Andrew J. and Thaddeus S. begin to quarrel violently," "Every-body [is] suddenly stricken dumb" (797). A slow chorus begins and ends: "Naughty men, they quarrel so" and "Naughty men naughty men, they are always quarreling" (793). There's no room for discussion and compromise, or even understanding, when the talkers never listen.

Stein also emphasizes that these men who get to do the talking share cookie-cutter thoughts and feelings. They are nothing like George Washington, who, she writes elsewhere, "was fairly famous because he wrote what he saw and he saw what he said" (*Four*, 168). One of the men in *The Mother of Us All* says about another: "they all listen to him, by him I mean me" (*Mother*, 798). These words could suggest a feeling of alienation from the self, but they also might suggest that the speaker agrees with whatever someone else says. Ulysses S. Grant likes only silence, but at least "he was not always quarreling" (804–5, 793). The silenced listeners, however, thoughtlessly agree with the speakers. Christ the Citizen says, "I always repeat everything I hear," and Jo the Loiterer responds (and this is funny), "You sure do" (802). These men talk, or don't, but none of them sees and then talks and listens at the same time. Men compromise with their own sensations, lives, experience: "Men want to be half slave half free. Women want to be all slave or all free, therefore men govern and women know" (803).

And in Stein's lexicon, to know is one of the best things a person can do. Knowledge comes from one's true self. Stein depicts Susan B. as attempting to get people to be themselves, to promote individualism, as well as individual rights—*and* as realizing that she has failed, that the only good that came from her work was incidental, beside the point, or completely personal. (The real Anthony was less self-flagellating, ending her final speech: "Failure is impossible" [qtd. in Dorr, 343]). In emphasizing gender distinctions, Stein seems to relinquish her ideas about individuality, but it is frustration on this very point that seems to lead her to this juncture. Her play's Susan B., too, keeps trying to get the other characters to take a more radical position on individuality. When Jo the Loiterer wants to come inside with a crowd of people, Susan B. says, "A crowd is never allowed but each one of you can come in" (*Mother*, 800). When everyone is on the stage, they say, "Now that we are all here there is nobody down there to hear." "They" seem to think that there are too many heads, too many bosses and talkers, but Susan B. seems to feel fine about talking to people who *aren't* below, who aren't waiting to listen, who are equals, who talk back (802).

For her, people *are* individuals, whether they know it or not. Susan B. reminds them that "even if they love them so, they are alone to live and die, they are alone to sink and swim they are alone to have what they own, to have no ideas but that they are here, to struggle and thirst to do everything first" (802).[7] No matter how loving and how loved, we are alone. Paradoxically however, Susan B. needs other people to validate her endeavors. She needs supporters to pass the laws that would enable women to be self-sufficient, but she is disappointed that people "will not do what they could do and I I will be left alone to die but they will not have done what I need to have done to make it right that I lived my life and fight" (807). Susan B. realizes that "they won't vote my laws, there is always a clause, there is always a pause, they won't vote my laws" (808). Knowing that women would never get the vote through popular referendum, Anthony worked on trying to get state and federal constitutional amendments passed. She came to rely on women activists and words, not male voters.[8]

All this is to say that by the end of her life, Stein was starting to believe that women might have a better chance than men at resisting the progressive death of language, and perhaps even that the female place outside the homogenizing public sphere allowed more, rather than less, of certain freedoms. Stein, after all, did gain freedom of action and thought by having her oldest brother, Michael, handle the money and Alice B. Toklas transact the pragmatic daily duties. It may have been easy for Stein to be patronizing about the way other people earned their livings. She has time to be creative and contemplative, and she can order her life as she pleases. But think of many of the young men Stein would have met: young journalists struggling to be writers, soldiers uncertain of their futures or their future livelihoods, even artists trying to figure out how to make a living at art.

Think of the sensitive young man you took Shakespeare with in college, who went into business: hotel management, a car rental agency, insurance, stocks, or journalism. More likely than not, his language has died, as would the language (and the creativity) of many of the young men Stein met. They speak (or write) in dead phrases: "the bottom line," "maximizing profit," "this isn't about you or me," and "the product sells itself." His words are deader even than those of Daniel Webster, who could revive them into being inspirational and meaningful if he meant to. But Webster is not listening to himself: he even inappropriately refers to Susan B. as a "gentleman," because that's the word he always uses to refer to his adversary in a debate (*Mother*, 788). As Martin says, and I concur: "Language must retain its full playful sense of itself so that it can never made over into [the] rhetoric" of "empty signs," and "language for Adams is power, and it is this kind of linguistic power that Stein's playfulness sets out to contest" (218). In short, "men have failed to fulfil the revolutionary potential of American history" (221). And if the founding fathers have ultimately failed, then it's time to look to the mothers. Stein didn't seem to recognize that mothers were already entering the workforce, too, and becoming conditioned in the same deadening ways.

Sublime Amalgamations

For Stein, mothers offer more, since Stein seems to understand the tendency toward less as masculine. The male characters in *The Mother of Us All* talk like stuck recordings, but even earlier Stein alludes to masculine deficiency. In *The Making of Americans*, she describes the communication between a father and daughter who take long walks together. After their conversation, always the same words on the same path, her father "would be looking at her with that sharp completed look that, always so full of his own understanding, could not leave it open any way to her to reach inside to him to let in any other kind of a meaning" (26). In *Ida*, Andrew also takes walks and talks, and he has a similar limitation: "He listened while he was listening but he did not hear unless he asked to have told what they were telling" (122). *Ida* offers strong evidence of Stein's belief that women are less daunted by "more," in this case the merging of identities. Andrew and Ida's merging in *Ida* makes "Ida more Ida" but "Andrew less Andrew" (90). And Susan B. can hold enough diverse ideas to say, "You are entirely right . . . only I disagree with you" (*Mother*, 789).

Earlier, I speculated that Stein's reading of William James may have convinced her that a change in language could effect change in thought.

I also argued that Stein was interested not only in written words but also in the sounds they produce and the spoken language they can approximately transcribe. I see parallels among those subtle meanings, those often un-noticed sounds, and the implicit relationships formed in the interval be-tween persons in conversation. The synergy of different voices produces a collective subjectivity separate from each speaker's and separate from the meanings of the words themselves.[9] But people's voices cannot converse or converge toward new knowings if they all say the same thing, if they don't have anything to say, or if they are too fearful to speak their ideas. If nothing else, Stein's writing is weird enough to give us something to talk about, and since we cannot contain it with our own words, the conversation continues. Stein's writing, so much of which is inspired by spoken comments, mediates and validates further conversations.

If we resist resisting it, reading Stein's writing can initiate a sublime experience. That which causes the sublime cannot be finally and categori-cally contained through language. Readers are never assured that they have done the organizing and containing "correctly," which leads us to wonder uncomfortably about whether the unknown phenomena have been prop-erly controlled or not. What has been called the feminine sublime exerts the same overwhelming force on a perceiver, but if the perceiver is "femi-nine enough," flexible enough about her idea of herself, then the usual reaction, sublime terror, is redirected into a melting together of what is usually (mis)perceived as self and other. The masculine tends to fear the multiple and the other, or, as Stein says in *The Mother of Us All*, men "fear women, fear each other, . . . fear their neighbor . . . fear other countries and then hearten themselves in their fear by crowding together and following each other . . . like animals who stampede" (811). But the feminine subject is said to experience an orgasmic merging, a return to being more, rather than the sublime anxiety or even terror that leads to the shutting down of possibilities.[10] Stein's writing advocates, and perhaps even coaxes and coaches us toward, this feminine subjectivity.

The sublime experience is coded male because of its five male Romantic writers, its Mont Blancs and Xanadus. One of the projects of the French feminists "is to reinvent the sublime as a feminine mode" (Yaeger, 192). Luce Irigaray writes that "we have so many voices to invent in order to express all of us everywhere, even in our gaps, that all the time there is will not be enough. We can never complete the circuit, explore our periphery: we have so many dimensions" (213). But this "horizontal sublime" (Yaeger, 202) can also be seen from a different perspective, or at a different time. Rather than spreading, it can be seen as coming up from interiorities that have become hidden (whether locked up or hiding out) within the confining structures of patriarchy:

> She will not say what she herself wants; moreover, she does not know, or no longer knows, what she wants. . . . One would have to dig down very deep indeed to discover beneath the traces of this civilization, of this history, the vestiges of a more archaic civilization that might give some clue to woman's sexuality. That extremely ancient civilization would undoubtedly have a different alphabet, a different language. . . . Woman's desire would not be expected to speak the same language as man's; woman's desire has doubtless been submerged by the logic that has dominated the West since the time of the Greeks. (Irigaray, 25)

Yaeger calls one type of female sublime (of course there would be many) "the pre-oedipal sublime—[which] offers the most striking revision of the 'oedipal' sublime" (204). Rather than resisting the self's secretly desired union with the (m)other, the subject of the pre-oedipal sublime welcomes the merger:

> We have learned that the subject is "infiltrated with the world" in such a way that "otherness is carried to the very heart of selfhood," and yet have not found a language to bring home the political and aesthetic consequences of this knowledge, to put this knowledge into praxis. I will suggest that the "feminine" sublime becomes an arena for discovering this language, it engenders a zone where self-empowerment and intersubjective bliss entertain one another in an atmosphere free of paranoia. (205)[11]

And I suggest that Stein has already discovered this language. First, Stein's exploration of voice in conversation has gone far toward expressing the essence of speech: motivating but invisible boundaries, subtle codes, patterns of equivocation. In a number of ways, Stein's writing expresses many of the amalgamations possible between the knower and the known or, perhaps more accurately, the knower and the to-be-known or even the potentially unknowable (who or which are often knowers, too). Perhaps Stein has moved past a feminine sublime to an epistemological sublime.

The primacy of conversation and amalgamation for Stein is perhaps why she seems so brutal about the atomic bomb. She says in "Reflection on the Atomic Bomb" that its ability to finalize all things makes it completely uninteresting to her. If the bomb destroys all things, then there is nothing left to be interested by; conversation ends. Her apolitical, even apathetic, stance becomes clearer when she posits that "really nobody else [besides "the people inventing the bomb or the people shooting it off"] can do anything about it so you have to just live along like always," but there is something commendably stubborn in her statement that "it's the living that are interesting not the way of killing them." In other words, you're immortal until you're dead.

On the other hand, if the bomb is "not as destructive as all that" then there will still be "lots left on this earth to be interested or to be interesting." Stein may appear to have lowered her valuation of single individuals (the dead ones, in this case) and raised that of the community (the masses who happen to survive). But she may also be expressing the recognition of how much there is in a single human being's experience. If the universe of one person's experience is infinite, it remains infinite even if it's shortened.

Stein willfully believes in what she feels she can effect, but this atomic bomb doesn't seem to budge when it's the subject of conversation, and so she must overlook it, ignore it, discount it, and insist that people use their "common sense" instead of listening to "so much [intractable?] informa-tion." It's such a big scary deal that she cannot turn her human nature's fear into the fertile topic of a masterpiece. The atomic bomb is a weapon she can't seem to defuse with her epistemological stance or her language games, so she wills its irrelevance. But she ends her short piece: "This is a nice story" (reminiscent of Hemingway's "Isn't it pretty to think so" at the end of *The Sun Also Rises*), which suggests she might be aware of the inadequacy of stubbornly willing herself not to believe in the bomb as a harbinger of the likely need for an even newer epistemological shift. Stein values fission rather than fusion, but the atomic bomb's fission models chaos instead of conversation.

Before she comes up against the atomic bomb, Stein uses language as a weapon against singularity and boundedness, and ingeniously rewires it, in work after work, style after style, to express multiplicity and integration. In *The Making of Americans*, Stein emphasizes the influences upon her characters from preestablished familial and national narratives, and in this way investigates the complex interaction between internal and exter-nal forces. The methods that reach toward multiplicity in *Tender Buttons* and *Geography and Plays* include developing unique interrelationships between words such that plural meanings are created in the conversation between them; writing from different I-positions in the same sentences or paragraphs; and actually (though not always obviously) writing about multiplicities—more options, more disagreement, more discussion, more growth, more associations. In *Ida*, Ida manifests herself in multiple ways, containing more than one voice or I-position and then dematerializing to the extent that she exists somewhere vaguely between the physical bodies of Ida and others. In *Brewsie and Willie*, Stein characterizes her ideal speaker as someone who can playfully and contrarily converse with oneself and others, change opinions in midsentence, and avoid adamant consistency or selfish "monologuing."

All this intersubjectivity, this sublime multiplicity, may make a reader wonder about one of my premises: that Stein advocates individuality. Perhaps it makes more sense to say that Stein valued individualities. Instead of letting her readers blindly and insincerely build coherent selves by lopping off whole parts of themselves, she induces many things that the "me" has considered "not-me" to come crowding back from the margins to petition for reacceptance (which is not quite the same as reassimilation). And she values our expressing those individualities so that they can communicate and play with one another. Her criticism of American society can be expressed as a critique of the ways people limit themselves and become alike. Stein believed society was becoming uniform; the multiple was merging into the single. The peril of corporate globalization was yet one more twenty-first-century controversy she anticipated. And Stein argues against this centripetal motion. But instead of advocating a reactionary centrifugal force in which each person spins out into space, she imagines an orderly but extremely complicated set of orbits that represent our complex but calculable mutual gravity—and levity.

NOTES

INTRODUCTION

1. By 1996, Marianne DeKoven had come to see Stein's writing as "a powerful utopian project" ("Introduction," 475).

2. Hereafter, Stein's works are cited parenthetically by short title in the text.

3. Clive Bush points out that Stein "was five times alienated from centrist American values. She was a woman, a lesbian, a Jew, an expatriate, and most important of all, an artist." He adds: "From such a vantage point she could offer a profound critique of the psychology produced by the 'normal' world of affairs" (360).

4. Clive Bush and Claudia Franken agree that it's time to risk looking for content in Stein's writing. Too much criticism has already been about whether or not to read her at all, and then whether or not readers should look for meaning.

5. In Hubly's presence, Haas said that Stein enabled the repetitive lyrics of popular contemporary music. Stein's words, as she says in *The Autobiography of Alice B. Toklas* (70), have also gotten "under [our] skin" enough to continually reappear in *Los Angeles Times* headlines: "A Rose Is a Rose, but Not Roseanne" (19 November 1994), "Will the Real Al Gore Please Sit Down: There's No There There within this Media Creature" (5 July 2002), "There's No There There" (19 November 2000), and "A Rose Is a Rose" (27 December 1992, 7 May 1987). "Rose Is a Rose Is a . . . Job?" (25 March 2000) and "For Translation Software, una rosa ist eine rose is a rose" (8 January 1995) are among Stein-inspired headlines that have appeared in the *New York Times*.

6. Putnam cites James, "Remarks," 15.

7. In Perloff, epigraph. This is Marjorie Perloff's own translation of the lines from Wittgenstein, *Culture and Value*, 24.

8. The idea, inspired by pragmatism, that "all intellectual discourse is subject to bias, partialities, and [the] values of its users" has inspired feminist thinkers and has allowed Stein into the feminist camp (Shuler and Tate, 212).

9. Linda Watts writes that "Stein embarks upon an exploration of language as itself an ideological instrument" (*Rapture*, 20). Watts quotes DeKoven's *A Different Language* (150): "If patriarchy is to be transformed at all, it must be transformed not only at its most visible levels (political, social, economic, cultural) but also at the fundamental or radical level of the structures of language which enable meaning." Watts goes on to say: "Language inscribes and serves the social order," and "Stein maintains that a writer's critiques are best targeted at language itself" (*Rapture*, 20).

10. Neil Postman and Charles Weingartner discuss the importance of "crap detecting" in their book *Teaching as a Subversive Activity*: "Those who *are* sensitive to the verbally built-in biases of their 'natural' environment seem 'subversive' to those who are not. There is probably nothing more dangerous to the prejudices of the latter than a man in the process of discovering that the language of his group is limited, misleading, or one-sided. Such a

man is dangerous because he is not easily enlisted on the side of one ideology or another, because he sees beyond the words to the processes which give an ideology its reality" (5).

11. "We" is not a single group with a tendency to say the same kinds of things based on what our identity politics might predict. Instead of political positions, Stein heard noises, sounds, turn taking, insistence, repetition, and copying; she heard what we don't usually hear ourselves, what we don't always know we're saying, what we might not intend anyone else to hear. One of the things we humans are proud of, one that makes us different from other animals, is that we have advanced language skills. "We" are human and "we" speak. If we can speak and hear, we can talk and listen, and most of us do. I don't think identity any more specific than that is relevant here. (I might add that "we" speak English—I am writing and you are reading in English—and different languages and cultures have different "rules" for conversation.) We might not agree on my "we," but we can talk about it, and—for my purposes in this book—that puts us in the same "we" group.

12. Critics have pointed to several other dialogic aspects of Stein's writing. Elizabeth Fifer concludes that "the domain of this discourse is the intimacy of the couple," which is further complicated by Stein's obfuscations in the face of a homophobic readership (131). Harriet Scott Chessman lists several kinds of dialogue in Stein's writing: between characters, between narrator and characters, between readers and words, among words themselves, between writer and words, and between words and "the objects they 'caress' but do not necessarily signify" (3). In spite of this promising list, Chessman expands only on the give-and-take relationship—the dance—into which Stein's writing invites the reader, rightly noting that readers become active in the creative process. Ellen E. Berry suggests another possible conversation when she writes that Stein's texts "wander intertextually" or speak to one another. Stein "grafts" pieces from one text to another, and she reworks themes over and over in different works, such that Berry claims every text is a "rewrite" (9). Berry also notes that A Novel of Thank You is interspersed with "snippets of realistic dialogue," which she assumes come from Stein's real experience, and which "highlight a strategy of saying and unsaying," "tantalizing us with the impulse to interpret the text autobiographically . . . and undercutting this impulse" (82). Stein's writing is also necessarily in dialogue with conventional forms of writing. Alison Rieke, in The Senses of Nonsense, claims that if writers stray too far from normal language their work will not be able to catch the attention of readers, who have to be able to recognize something familiar (9). Stein claimed her medium was the English language (Autobiography, 70, 76), and in keeping herself from straying too far from it, she enabled the conversation between the old and the new to continue.

13. Michael Hoffman, Lisa Ruddick, Steven Meyer, and Bush all discuss Stein in relation to William James, as do many earlier critics. Hoffman, helpfully making it "at least a bit clearer why Gertrude Stein wrote the way she did," points out Stein's emphasis on "verbal communication [as] a set of formalized habits to which no writer is beholden" ("Stein and James," 232–33, 231). Ruddick reminds us that Stein borrowed James's ideas of consciousness but, in leaving pragmatism behind, "used [them] in ways [James] would not have anticipated" ("William James," 63). In "Writing Psychology Over," Meyer discusses habit, but he comes to different conclusions than I do.

14. Quotations in the two previous sentences are from Donne, "The Canonization," line 32, and Jameson, Prison-House of Language.

CHAPTER 1

1. "Literally I count eight" is more difficult to interpret, and my own reading of it is too personal to warrant a place in the main text. Much later, Stein writes: "She had certain habits. . . . Living alone as she did counting was an occupation" (*Ida*, 624). When my daughter was born , I stopped doing intellectual work for a few months, and I found myself counting. I would not be aware of it, but suddenly I would discover myself at some ridiculously high number ("two hundred fifty-eight . . ."). During one confessional phone call, I warned my mother that something weird was happening to me, and she said: "Don't tell me. Let me guess. You're counting. I do too!" I think it's because our minds need work. They don't count for nothing.

2. Studs Terkel's *Working* proves her correct: a welder, a stone mason, an ad man, and others become philosophers when Terkel is listening. They reveal the truths of their own natures, as well as wax eloquent on larger truths.

3. Van Vechten cites Wright, review of *Wars*.

4. For example, although she stopped seeing her brother Leo in 1913, they inevitably stood in some relationship to each other. In 1931 Stein wrote "How she bowed to her brother," a short work that "break[s] up sentences into spoken units moving in pronounced irregular rhythms" that "lurch in uncomfortable, jerking, forward and backward movement 'like the flickers,' full of pauses and hesitations, stuttering in discomfort," and suggest the way a partly deaf person (such as Leo—and even herself later in life) might hear (Dydo, *Stein*, 564). Mimicking a difficult conversation, Stein's opaque work suggests that although she and Leo no longer interact, they still have a complex relationship, one understood differently by each of them. Her curt, almost imperceptible, and ambiguous bow to her brother is similar to the shallow bows Stein makes to her literary relations.

5. Wagner-Martin cites Aldrich, "Confessions," M-114.

6. Sources are Wilder, 187; Stein's letters to Sherwood Anderson (White, *Sherwood Anderson*, 26, 56, 95), Stein's college essays (reprinted in Miller); and *Lectures*, 241, 209. Available at Yale University's Beinecke Rare Book and Manuscript Library, the list of books in her library at her death includes more than two hundred authors from different periods on English literature. Stein owned multiple books by many authors, but her large collections of a few authors are most notable: twenty-three novels by James Fenimore Cooper, eleven novels by Charles Dickens, eight English translations of novels by Alexander Dumas, eight novels by William Dean Howells, six books by Washington Irving, eight titles by Rudyard Kipling, six novels by Frederick Marryat, all three of Samuel Richardson's novels, fifteen Shakespeare plays, ten of Robert Louis Stevenson's adventure novels, eighteen books of fiction (for adults and children) by Frank R. Stockton, five books by Trollope, seven works by Constance Fenimore Woolson, two several-volume sets of Flaubert's works, the twelve-volume *Complete Works* of George Eliot, a sixteen-volume set of *The Arabian Nights*, the *Complete Works* of Lewis Carroll, the eleven-volume *Works* by Samuel Johnson (plus his *Letters*), ten volumes of George Sand's work, the twenty-volume *Complete Works* of W. M. Thackeray, and twelve volumes of Jules Verne's *Works* in addition to twelve novels by Verne.

7. See *www.rootsweb.com~cenfiles/calsanfrancisco/1870/ed39/sanfrandisco/ward01/sanfrancisco-a23.txt*.

8. According to Katz, "*First Making,*" the manuscript of *The Making of Americans* identifies these families as Jewish.

9. *Annales* historians have recently emphasized that everything that happens is historical, although we tend to accept only certain things—those that involve the rich, powerful, or athletic—as "historical events." Many people try to be present when "history is made," but others prefer to make their own.

10. For example, between the turn of the century and World War I, my grandfather and his brothers formed a traveling vaudeville troupe, the Seven Cairns Brothers. Among the memorabilia, we have a picture of the extended family standing by their derailed train car. Thinking the great train robbery was a real event and not a movie, and then mistaking the great train robbery for the great train *wreck*, I long thought that this picture was of the great train wreck—and I thought my family had been involved in an important national disaster. Historical fact, fiction, family and national stories, and a lack of perspective get all mixed up in a child's head—and they may never quite be sorted out.

11. *Making*, 122, 128, 129, 124. This starting over was common in education, perhaps especially with well-off parents who were trying to expand their children's horizons toward Europe. Stein's father enrolled his children in several different schools, took them to several countries with different educational systems and languages of instruction, and hired a variety of tutors. William and Henry James's father did the same thing. After attending multiple schools, William James felt that he'd had a terribly haphazard education and thus felt like something of a fraud.

12. Linking David Hersland's life's progress to *The Arabian Nights*, Stein also points to the structure of her own novel. Her text seems to begin again and again, or it conceives its project over and over—a structure that accurately mimics many American lives. Priscilla Wald in *Reconstituting Americans* treats the first three paragraphs of *The Making of Americans* as three separate beginnings: of "a family narrative, a psychological narrative, and a culminating cultural narrative" (Wald, 254). Stein calls attention to her own recurrent beginnings by repeating phrases such as "now there is here a beginning" throughout her work (see *Making*, 176, 396–97, 692). Often her beginnings signal a new goal; sometimes they are just attempts to regroup, to reach an old goal again. Often she seems to be referring to all 925 pages of her writing as a beginning to some larger project that she will not be able to finish.

13. Reading *The Making of Americans* as a social novel makes it sound like *Main Street*. Stein and Lewis, however, did not recognize their shared interests, and they had no appreciation for each other's work. In *The Making of Americans*, Stein's line of identical fathers is sadly deterministic; sons tend to manifest versions of their fathers' limitations. She leaves little hope for succeeding generations to break free except through thoughtful inaction and death. Lewis places hope in the female line: Carol Kennicott sees her daughter as "a bomb to blow up smugness" and daydreams about "what that baby will see and meddle with before she dies" (432). Later in Stein's life, as I discuss in my conclusions to this book, Stein also seems to place her hope in the female. Although Lewis's novel ends with the birth of Carol's daughter, and Stein's novel ends with the death of the young David Hersland, Stein's unusual style seems to me to offer more hope for the surprising potential of the future.

14. While myth says the true innovators went west, and Mark Twain says the failures did, Stein assumes it was restless people who needed more elbow room—more freedom, more space. If these restless people are successful, if they build up the West to be much like the East and then stay there, they become tamed and conformist themselves. In Stein's view, their youthful conformity is worse than that in areas which have been settled longer (as teenagers tend to exert more peer pressure than adults); real eccentrics must leave the adolescent West for the Old

World: "it takes time to make queer people, and to have others know it, time a certainty of place and means. Custom, passion, and a feel for mother earth are needed to breed vital singularity in any man, and alas, how poor we are in all these three." This "singularity that is neither crazy, sporty, faddish, or a fashion, or low class with distinction" requires them to "flee before the disapproval of our cousins . . . [and] fly to the kindly comfort of an older world accustomed to take all manner of strange forms into its bosom." Stein's "Brother Singulars," born and bred in the newest part of the New World, have to escape to the Old World to find the freedom to develop themselves further, since (Stein asserts) only societies with solid traditions allow for eccentricity (*Making*, 21).

15. James reveals the importance he places on personal discovery and experience when he recommends that one "familiarize one's self with the mammalian brain. Get a sheep's head, a small saw, chisel, scalpel and forceps (all three can best be had from a surgical-instrument maker), and unravel its parts" with the aid of one of a couple of suggested books (*Principles*, 24n).

16. Stein's and Solomons's experiments in the Harvard Psychology Laboratory are described in two articles in the *Psychological Review* for September 1896 and May 1898. In the first article, titled "Normal Motor Automatism," Stein and Solomons discuss the "question of consciousness," and they analyze "attention" and the "habits of attention" at quite some length (Stein and Solomons, *Motor Automatism*, 9, 14, 13). The later article, of which Stein is sole author, was titled "Cultivated Motor Automatism: A Study of Character in Its Relation to Attention" (27).

B. F. Skinner, a notorious reductive mechanist of the human psyche, argued that Stein's early experiments prove that much of her later writing was just "automatic writing." Skinner's argument that Stein performs automatic writing is largely based on the fact that Stein and Solomons themselves were the only subjects of their first set of experiments, and he claims (but does not demonstrate, and I do not see) a similarity between texts such as *Tender Buttons* and the writing produced by distracted writers. According to Skinner, Stein was already developing her unintelligible style a decade before she decided to become an author. In his *Atlantic Monthly* article "Has Gertrude Stein a Secret?" Skinner writes that nobody "can fail to recognize a familiar note [between] these examples of automatic writing" and *Tender Buttons* (52). But not all repetition is alike, and not all nonsense "has very little to say" (56). Skinner concludes his article by saying that he does "not believe in the importance of the part of Miss Stein's writing that does not make sense" and that he kindly advises people "to enjoy the other and very great part [of Stein's work] without puzzlement" (57). He thus takes the mystery out of the mysterious, tries to make an end of the endlessly tantalizing questions that Stein's writing evokes in her readers, and throws away all the yeasty potential of Stein's most exciting writing.

17. Johns Hopkins Medical school opened in 1893 and immediately offered the best medical education in the nation. Admitting women and having the most difficult entrance requirements of any medical school went hand in hand. A group of women approached the trustees of the newly conceived college and promised $100,000 on the condition that women be admitted. The reluctant trustees agreed to admit women *only if* this group of benefactors would donate $500,000. (One cannot help but guess that the trustees thought *that* was the end of *that*.) Managing to raise an additional $100,000, the women's group was stumped—until one woman, Mary Garrett, donated the difference of $300,000. But she had her own conditions: admitted students must have a college degree, have taken premedical studies, and know French and German (Duffy, 277).

18. Ludmerer refers to Thayer's "Self-education under Guidance" (Thayer, *Osler*, 228–46) and quotes from Thayer, "Teaching and Practice," in *Osler*, 191.

19. Ludmerer cites Mall, 85. One student describes Osler's clinical amphitheater: "On these occasions he acted as a fellow student with us, guiding us in our examinations of the patient, causing us to see what we had not previously noted and making us realize that the Hippocratic dictum 'to see, to touch and to hear,' was not all in making a diagnosis, for Laennec introduced the words 'to auscult' and so revealed further facts. But he showed us that all of this went for naught if we did not follow what Louis, the great French clinician, had taught us 'to record.' He made us make careful notes of our findings" (qtd. in Harvey et al., 36; Harvey cites Chesney, 2:127).

20. Stein's grades dropped during her last two years of medical school, and it has been speculated that she was distracted by love, which was almost certainly one factor in her inattention. Wagner-Martin's view is that Stein "boycotted" classes taught by sexist professors (49): "Disguising the anger she felt at the sexism and racism evident during her years at medical school, Gertrude pretended to be apathetic" (50).

21. Early biographers somewhat apologetically acknowledge Stein's apparent acceptance of sexist policies that encouraged female students to do the "mechanic" work of drawing brain tracts (Hobhouse, 24–25; Brinnin, 36). Brinnin even writes that Stein "knew it was absurd to make models of brain tracts" (36; information attributed to Stein's brother Leo). I'm not sure why it would be absurd to diagram processes in which one is interested. (Women used to do most computer programming, too, until someone figured out the great potential in the field.)

22. Barker himself describes the fibers as "concerned in the conduction of sensory impulses toward the somoaesthetic area of the cortex, . . . [but] not at all well understood." Further, "if the fasciculus longitudinalis medialis is to be regarded as one of the paths mediating sensory impulses on their way to the cerebral cortex, this path is almost certainly interrupted in the hypothalamus or thalamus" (*Nervous System*, 726).

CHAPTER 2

1. James asserts that experience can only be what we attend to, and there is plenty we miss. His assertion applies to noticing what's happening around us, but it also applies to our language environment. James gives the example of how we tend to read: because language is written in such habitual phrases, reading becomes almost a "*reflex action*" instead of a "*psychic act*" (*Principles*, 97; his italics). But if we attended more carefully to language—or if we were forced to have the language experience become a psychic act because of the unusual nature of the language confronting us—then the words would inspire our "latent excitement" (89) or "expectant attention" (97), we'd be truly experiencing language, and our minds would continue to be formed.

James also employs an example from language experience when he distinguishes "sensorial blindness" (the physical inability to see) and "psychic blindness" (the mental inability to assign meaning to what one sees): "psychic blindness is inability to recognize the *meaning* of the optical impressions, as when we see a page of Chinese print but it suggests nothing to us" (52; his italics). Psychic blindness is a "*loss of associations* between optical sensations and what they signify," James continues (59). He cannot discuss the ways that attention to experience develops the mind (or fails to develop the mind) without resorting to a discussion of the way signification—necessitating if not exactly equivalent to language—is the medium by which this modification takes place.

James asserted the constant remodification of the brain (227): "We believe the brain to be an organ whose internal equilibrium is always in a state of change"; he compares the brain to a "kaleidoscope" in which "the figures are always rearranging themselves" (239). Different qualities of these "figures" he calls "images," "sensations," "percepts," "concepts," "thoughts," "transitive states," and "feelings of relation"—at least a few of which tend to rise to our consciousness through words, phrases, and sentences.

James also employs examples from language use and experience to demonstrate habitual acts such as repeating the alphabet and saying one's prayers (121), and even the more complex "movements of our tongues and pens" (136), sensitivity to bad grammar, a dog's noticing its name being called, and a young child's recognition of a few words (395).

In short, language is one form of experience, and experience tends to be stored away in our minds as language.

2. James's textbook takes this approach (49–51, 70); so does the 1993 textbook *Contemporary Linguistics* (O'Grady, chap. 9).

3. O'Grady gives an example of a conversation with a Wernicke's patient, a set of utterances that might remind the reader of Stein's short plays.

How are you today, Mrs. A?
Yes.
Have I ever tested you before?
No. I mean I haven't.
Can you tell me what your name is?
No, I don't I . . . right I'm right now here.
What is your address?
I [could] if I can help these this like you know . . . to make it. We are seeing for him. That is my father. (351)

Sometimes, severely impaired speakers borrow phonemes and intonation instead of whole words to create something that sounds like English, and this disease is called "jargonaphasia" (O'Grady, 352). Redefined, jargonaphasia could be what Stein is fighting against: prefabricated jargon as our main means of communication, one that doesn't allow us to mean what we want and need to mean.

During Stein's U.S. tour, Morris Fishbein, the editor of the *Journal of the American Medical Association*, compared Stein's writing to the speech of patients with palilalia, palilogia, perseveration, or verbigeration—all speech disorders that involve repetition. A person with palilalia "repeats many times a word, a phrase or a sentence which he has just uttered"; one with palilogia repeats in order to emphasize herself; perseveration occurs because "the original idea persist[s] in the speaker's mind for an undue length of time, keeping fresh ideas from entering"; and verbigeration causes one to repeat "the same sentence over and over" (Meyer, *Irresistible*, 50.). In the interests of full disclosure, I should add that palilalia is said to be brought on by encephalitis—a serious illness I had as a child. Could this be why Stein is so appealing to me? I think, however, that Meyer is right to call Fishbein's idea "absurd" (*Irresistible*, 53).

4. In 1914, Van Vechten records that "some [readers] say that the 'fringe of thought,' so frequently referred to by [William James], may dominate [Stein's] working consciousness" ("How to Read," 155). I haven't found any early reviews to confirm his point.

Bain, to whom James alludes quite often in his *Principles of Pyschology*, similarly describes the effect of a sum of several mild stimuli:

> It might admit of a doubt whether four faint links of contiguous adhesion would be equal to one strong, but it would be against our whole experience of the workings of similarity, to doubt the utility of multiplying faint resemblances, when there was no one sufficiently powerful to effect the revival [of a word or memory]. . . . By raising some single feature almost up to the point of identity, we should do more good than could be done by scattering faint and detached likenesses over the picture. This, however, is not always in our power; and we are glad to find that, when the similarity, in any one particular, is too feeble to suggest the resembling past, the existence of a plurality of weak resemblances will be the equivalent of a single stronger one. (586)

5. Bain in 1855 alludes to the "well-known fact that objects do, on many occasions, bring before the mind their contraries" (599).

6. Steven Meyer reads Stein as disliking habit *and* association, but I see her using her knowledge of mental association to fight against habit ("Writing," 151–52). In other words, habits are pitted against each other. Timothy V. Kaufman-Osborn makes the argument that if we shed all habit, we would shed all means by which to think (190–91). He goes on to say (in his enigmatic way): "Deliberation, elicited from the dialectic between unreflective habit and the habit of reflecting, is one moment within the more comprehensive form of conduct that is 'art'" (194).

7. Linda S. Watts writes: "A reader's uncertainties are no longer regarded as sites of failures but rather as liminal ground, where new possibilities take shape" (*Gertrude Stein*, 10). She also nicely describes "the underlying principles at work in Stein's writing" as creating works that "explore rather than explain" and "complicate rather than enumerate" (25). Living a life in two cultures may also produce this intellectual life; another culture's habits can certainly make one hesitate and doubt one's own, and all, habits.

8. Ruddick then "unravel[s]" this very theory by further analysis of Stein's words, but her choice to argue for Stein's revision of the crucifixion story seems a less convincing—although fascinating—alternative.

9. I hesitate to draw "information" from a novel, but Steward's novels are not the worst place to try to get an idea of Stein's daily life and conversation. Steward seems mainly to write from fact, as most of the description and episodes in his novels correspond to real places and actual happenings. His descriptions of the gardens and terrain around Belignin correspond exactly to those I saw there in 2000, when the current owner was kind enough to invite my family into the gardens and tell us about her childhood luncheons with Stein. Even the far-fetched plot of Steward's *Parisian Lives*, in which a man has a love affair with his own illegitimate son, seems to have been based on the experience of Francis Rose (*Chapters*, 69).

10. My readings are tendentious, some more than others, but readers should not be so overwhelmed by multiplicity as to refuse to see anything at all. Michael J. Hoffman asserts that Stein revitalized the English language, but he is more interested in how Stein upsets generic conventions than in how she chooses words. In *Gertrude Stein*, he argues that it is not necessary or productive to read Stein's words too closely. After describing only two ways to understand the opening lines of Stein's "Kristians Tonny," he suggests that

we leave ourselves open to a polysemous situation in which a sentence can have an infinite number of meanings. . . . It is easy to see into what a linguistic slough of despond we would fall if we troubled ourselves too much with the *sense* of the lines. In treating language so cavalierly, Stein runs the danger of a maddening polysemy; but, in return for taking this chance, she achieves the great pleasure of showing that language can be turned into a plastic instrument stripped of meaning by any writer or speaker who is willing to tamper with its traditional linguistic structures. Stein, more than Joyce or any other writer I can think of, can show us just what ambiguous possibilities are inherent in language. (64–65)

I agree that Stein successfully demonstrates the polysemy of the word, but I do not think that showing there are two meanings has ever proved there are an infinite number of meanings. Instead of finding oneself in a "linguistic slough of despond"—although sloughs and swamps are organic and rich—I would hope that readers would discover themselves in a linguistic realm of opportunity, a glorious web of words full of panoramic prospects and unfolding secrets.

Hoffman cites sections of *Tender Buttons* and ask questions about them, but he argues that his tendency to question is just "further proof of the suggestive power of words and of the inability of even the most self-conscious author to divest them completely of their associative powers" (*Abstractionism*, 183–84). His assumption that Stein was naively attempting to treat words as if they did not have any meaning leads to the conclusion that she has failed. But what if he, and other critics who have made similar arguments, are wrong in their assumption? If we look at the works in Stein's *Geography and Plays* that were written around the same time as *Tender Buttons*, we see not only similarities of structure, but also similarities of word choice. There seem to be certain words—piece, change, single, slice, cousin, whole, disorder, spreading, difference and different, center, more, circle, surface, colors, tending, order, resembling, tender, and silence—that have importance for Stein. These are the words she has come to know.

In the end, Hoffman can conclude only that "*Tender Buttons* is a series of black symbols on a white page" and that all we can do as readers is "admire . . . the wonders of creation" (*Gertrude Stein*, 68). This is not enough of a claim for Stein's art. It is certainly not enough of an accomplishment to support Hoffman's assertion that Stein "is a major writer historically and intrinsically and that she has written some of the finest and most complex books of our time" (9). Hoffman admits that "it is possible to give anything—even a telephone book—a dramatic reading" (73); I would claim that "even a telephone book" can let us notice "black symbols on a white page" and that, if Hoffman is right about Stein's meaninglessness, a thick telephone book might be even more likely to inspire admiration at "the wonders of creation."

Lisa Ruddick, writing since Hoffman's book of essays was published, strikes a healthy balance between vague appreciation of words as sensation and the search for meaning. She reads Stein for the pleasure of the sound and the feel of the words on her tongue, as well as for a hidden meaning. It seems reasonable to think that Stein would disrupt the binarism between these two different kinds of reading as much as she would reject other binarisms. Of *Tender Buttons*, Ruddick writes:

Within poems, moreover, there are invariably words that do not contribute to any continuous idea and whose importance is either in their sheer soundplay or in their ability to dislodge other, more logically embedded words in the vicinity from unitary meanings by stimulating alternative associations. Stein constructs a text that invites the reader to find coherent themes but that also makes him or her choose a point beyond which to stop piecing things together. My readings are not meant to substitute for this experience of uncertainty and mobility.(203)

And neither are mine.

11. Booth is writing about literature that people assume they understand: nursery rhymes, the Gettysburg Address, Ben Jonson poems, a Shakespeare play. He writes: "Great works of art are daredevils . . . always on the point of one or another kind of incoherence" (*Precious*, 35). Stein's *Tender Buttons* teeters the other way, on the edge of coherence.

12. This time, that reminder is accurate etymologically, but it is not always: pronunciation shifts and spelling anomalies often make words remind readers of other words and meanings that are *not* etymological relatives. Allegra Stewart often uses etymology as a key to Stein's writing. In interpreting this paragraph, Stewart traces "quintal" through Egyptian and Arabic to the meaning "pertaining to the fifth," which she in turn links to "the quintessential element, that invisible fire worshiped by the ancient Chaldeans and Egyptians as the principle of creativity," then to a variety of other religious rituals, and finally to Stein's own "religious ritual" of writing (133). Compared to this reading, mine makes the jump from religion to rhetoric much more directly, by listening to the words in their order on the page.

13. It may appear that I'm willfully deciding what all this means, but "to decide" is from the root "caedere," which means "to cut off." I am trying to understand meaning by including rather than cutting off or excluding.

14. Randolph Bourne, writing in 1913, sees a similar role for irony: "Irony was Greek, with all the free, happy play of the Greek spirit about it, letting in fresh air and light into others' minds and our own. It was to the Greek an incomparable method of intercourse, the rub of mind against mind . . . without committing one's self. . . . this pleasant challenging of the world, this insistent judging of experience, this sense of vivid contrasts and incongruities, of comic juxtapositions, of flaring brilliances, and no less heartbreaking impossibilities, of all the little parts of one's world being constantly set off against each other, and made intelligible only by being translated into and defined in each other's terms" (135). He later writes that the ironist's "life is expressed in the social intercourse of ourselves with others. The daily fabric of the life of irony is woven out of our critical communings with ourselves and the personalities of our friends, and the people with whom we come into contact" (137). And finally, like Stein's ideal, Bourne's ironist tries to live and think through true experience, distinguishing it from the secondhand: "We are born into a world that is an inexhaustible store of ready-made ideas, stored up in tradition, in books, and in every medium of communication between our minds and others. All we have to do is accept this predigested nourishment, and ask no questions. We could live a whole life without ever making a really individual response, without providing ourselves out of our own experience with any of the material that our mind works on" (139). Like Stein, "the ironist forces his friends to move their rusty limbs and unhinge the creaking doors of their minds" (145).

15. "The winner loses" is quoted from Stein, "The winner loses: A Picture of Occupied France," *Atlantic*, November 1940, 571–83.

CHAPTER 3

1. Kadlec quotes from James, *Principles*, 238.

2. The definition of conversation in this paragraph is based on the ideas of many thinkers in the fields of conversation and discourse analysis: Sacks, *Lectures*; Schegloff, introduction; Moerman, *Talking*; several of Deborah Tannen's academic and popular books; and Clark and Clark, "Discourse."

3. Picasso's collage is reproduced in Stendhal, 75.

4. I refer the reader to Bowers's careful and perceptive examination of the play *Can You See the Name* (112–17). In the course of this analysis, Bowers points out that "our attention is focused on phonology and orthography, not on meaning," when we notice the way Stein has used homophones (116). I would add, of course, that phonology and orthography themselves point toward meaning.

Betsy Alayne Ryan also asserts that Stein breaks dramatic conventions: "Gertrude Stein's disruption of the alternate reality—or fiction—of the traditional theatre is the unifying principle of all her plays, regardless of period" (67). It shouldn't be surprising to anyone familiar with any of Stein's various styles of writing that she makes us rethink our generic expectations in her drama, too.

5. Probably most full-length plays get around to mentioning food somewhere, but Stein's plays in *Geography and Plays* are short. Half of them are less than five pages long. Six more are between six and twelve pages long. Even these numbers are sometimes misleading: In *Counting Her Dresses* (eleven pages long), the longest act has three lines; the longest speech is two sentences; in short, there is much blank space on those eleven pages (but not many empty stomachs).

6. *Bonne Annee* might remind one of Stein's "The Good Anna," from *Three Lives*, and the words in its one and a half pages often recall that good woman.

7. And my French friend Françoise Tillard, in a discussion of what the 2003 strikers were defending—a way of life, daily pleasures without the impingement of possible future stresses, and not just a couple years more of retirement—tells the truth when she says that when the French eat a leisurely meal together, they talk about the food. Meanwhile, the coffee shop owner was outside bringing a bowl of water and feeding cookies to my dog. Food is love, and an appreciation of the present moment of bodily presence.

8. Cheepen cites Bronislow Malinowski, "Phatic Communion," reprinted in J. Laver and S. Hutcheson, eds., *Communication in Face to Face Interaction* (Middlesex, Eng.: Penguin, 1972), 149.

9. Tannen cites Scollon and Scollon, "Cooking."

10. According to Stein: "They [Gertrude and Leo] certainly are not at all alike. One of them is hearing himself and is having then sound come out of him. One of them is hearing some one and is then having sound come out of her" ("Two," 3). Biographical information concurs that Leo was a bad listener—at least partly caused by his loss of hearing—and that Gertrude was "'a terrific talker, but an elegant listener too'" (Wagner-Martin, 31).

11. Gertrude Stein was called "baby" by her family (Wagner-Martin, 23). This nickname seemed to reemerge on her lecture tour, when she was called "baby" by Toklas and Van Vechten (Burns, 434, 435). She refers to herself as a baby in these letters and as a husband in some of her other writings. For example, she implies it by noting that *The Autobiography of Alice B. Toklas* was almost titled "Wives of Geniuses I Have Sat With" (*Autobiography*, 251).

12. Janet Malcolm might disagree, at least to the extent of arguing that Stein let her position as youngest child influence her behavior quite considerably. She cites Stein's description of being "the baby of the family," which meant that "'nobody can do anything but take care of you'" (Malcolm, 62; the Stein quotes are from *Autobiography*). Malcolm also denies that Stein was staunch or even very vulnerable in Vichy France because Faÿ was watching out for her safety and comfort, but I believe this protection was probably something that evolved, not something Stein was depending on when she decided to stay in France for the war. As the conductor of the couple's transactions, Toklas may have had some dealings with Faÿ on the subject of ration cards and deportation lists, but perhaps Stein did not. And finally, youngest children are often protected, but we (yes, me too) also tend to be careful observers of the social dynamics around us.

13. Bush quotes from a Stein notebook: "Activity is a cheap commodity." He adds: "Like Hannah Arendt [Stein] recognized that the contemplative life was more difficult, and more energy-consuming, than a life of pragmatic action" (346, with a short citation from Stein, Notebook [small grey], 2, note d [Stein papers, Beinecke]).

14. In another lecture, Stein repeated this idea: "Seeing a person in the act of doing something is not interesting, but it is interesting when they are doing nothing for the person is not distracted from being something by doing something. In Paris two American doughboys standing on the corner doing nothing for some time are more interesting than when one of them says let's go home and they move off" (Meyers).

15. Inspired by Stein's *Lectures in America*, a reviewer writes: "Listen, consciously listen the next time a person tells you a story—not to what they are telling you but the way they are telling it. 'And then I sez to him, I sez, sez I, when he asks me what I thinks of it, I sez to him, I sez . . .' Just watch—I mean listen" (Winter, 82).

16. After some staring and pondering and some counting, one might notice that each character speaks the number of paragraphs that corresponds with his name—except in two instances—so we could say that those exceptions are the two exciting scenes, but I think that unlikely. A listener would not know how many paragraphs had been spoken, and just the surprise and excitement generated by the surprising words themselves is going to overshadow any emotion one might feel about discovering this pattern with the number of paragraphs.

17. William James writes: "The stream of our thought is like a river. On the whole easy simple flowing predominates in it, the drift of things is with the pull of gravity, and effortless attention is the rule. But at intervals an obstruction, a set-back, a log-jam occurs, stops the current, creates an eddy, and makes things temporarily move the other way. If a real river could feel, it would feel these eddies and set-backs as places of effort" (*Principles*, 427). There are paragraphs in *Tender Buttons* that have this flowing, pausing, eddying, and then speeding momentum to them, as does, for example, the third paragraph of "Roast Beef" at the beginning of "Food."

18. Stein's distinctions between knowing and understanding may remind readers of those made by Coleridge and Emerson. "Not any nuisance is depressing" looks forward to "A Life" by Howard Nemerov: "Innocence? / In a sense. / In no sense!" (in *The Blue Swallows* [Chicago: U of Chicago P, 1967], 13).

19. But is "use" all words *do* have? Rorty makes the case that language "provides tools for coping with objects rather than representations of objects" (*Philosophy*, 65). One way of using language may be more useful than another, and the more useful, the better, he says, while Stein writes: "do not say that words have a use." But when Rorty tells us "to stop thinking of words as representations and to start thinking of them as nodes in the causal

network which binds the organism together with its environment" (xxiii), his thought seems to parallel Stein's valuation of wordy interaction and mutual causation much more closely. For Rorty, the "goal of inquiry" is the "coordination of behavior" ("to achieve agreement . . . about what to do"). He makes an exception for "simply wordplay" (whatever that means to him), but it is probably something like this wordplay that Stein seems to hold out as the last great hope for creative solutions (xxv).

20. What Marxists claim about economics should remind us of Stein on words: Human beings "become alienated from [products] and . . . increasingly fail to recognize them as products of their labor, thus forgetting their history" (Winders, 488). Stein tries to reacquaint people with their verbal production and rescues words from being alienated from their histories.

Of course, words are never quite clear signals. We just pretend they are. Stein says that people can communicate clearly about "mechanics" but "about every other thing nobody is of the same opinion nobody means the same thing by what they say as the other one means and only the one who is talking thinks he means what he is saying even though he knows very well that that is not what he is saying" (*Everybody's*, 290).

21. Similarly, in "Unharvested"—in which there is a "there there"—Robert Frost seems to be discussing poetic beauty when he appreciates the "scent of ripeness from over a wall" and entreats: "May something go always unharvested! / May much stay out of our stated plan, / Apples or something forgotten and left, / So smelling their sweetness would be no theft" (305, ll. 8, 1, 11–14). Stein's words are so arranged that something must always go unharvested in spite of attempts to do a thorough picking.

To move away from gardening, one might also notice the scent of a hunt in this third paragraph. At a hunt there is "blessing and chasing"; the dogs are "mixed strangely"; the prey is "surrounded" and then sometimes escapes through a "vegetable window"; and if the hunt is "complete" then the kill is "exchange[d] in parts" among the hunters. I imagine a fox hunt, but the "simple melancholy clearly precious and on the surface" might remind some readers of the hunted deer, who was purported to go to the water and weep.

22. This paragraph from *What Happened* most resembles National Book Award nominee Harryette Mullen's poetry in *Trimmings*, published by Tender Buttons Press. Mullen offers vivid social commentary about women's lives, employing punning echoes of common phrases. Musing on Stein, Mullen writes:

> Girt, a good old girl got hipped. They thrive with wives, broad beams. Most worthy girth, providing firm. Foundations in midriff. Across (between) girdled loins, tender girders. Gartered, perhaps, struts. Stretching, a snap crotch. (26)

23. According to Sandra M. Gilbert and Susan Gubar, Stein's giving life to words would be a feminist project. They assert that a representative male author both "generates and imprisons his fictive characters, he silences them by depriving them of autonomy. . . . He silences them and . . . embedding them in the marble of his art—kills them" (14). Gilbert and Gubar describe this tendency as masculine, but both men and women have masculine tendencies—which fact may allow Stein to see her project as epistemologically universal, rather than alternatively feminist. By the end of her life, however, Stein may be coming over to Gilbert and Gubar's feminist conviction (see "Feminine Endings" in the conclusions of this book).

24. Silverman quotes from Sacks, *Lectures*, 2:169.

25. This repetition of "goodbye" means two very different things to me: "I adore you," and

"Would you please just leave already?" There seems to be strife and disagreement in *Do Let Us Go Away,* so it probably means the latter in this case. On the other hand, I think it also is a play on "good buy," since the play just mentioned "100 dollars." (It could *also* mean "I adore you," if the speaker regrets leaving her money with somebody else.) Other parts of the play suggest dissatisfaction with a rental agreement: The landlord hates the dog's barking, the renters hate the loud servants' voices and their impoliteness, the neighbors are annoying, and so forth. *Do Let Us Go Away* is probably a serious conversational proposition, too, addressed either to a partner or to the landlord to release them from the lease.

26. I have assumed that two speakers take turns speaking the lines in these examples. In only a few cases is it at all likely that the same speaker voices subsequent lines, as in the case of "Yes I agree with you. / Yes." Although the lines I have chosen may seem arbitrary, I have selected only what I interpret as entire conversations. One can easily go through the text of this play and draw lines between separate conversations, although there are a few statements that seem to stand alone.

27. That readers do not know how many people are participating in each conversation, or even whether each line is spoken by a different person than spoke the previous line, is another source of ambiguity. To limit this discussion to a manageable size, I again assume that there are two speakers in each conversation, and that subsequent lines are usually spoken by different people.

28. Phillips here misquotes Stein's *Ladies' Voices,* in *Geography and Plays,* 204; the correct words are "made no difference."

29. In her excellent introduction to the 1993 reprint of *Geography and Plays,* Pondrom classifies "Susie Asado" as a "transitional piece" between the style of *Tender Buttons* and that of early plays. As she points out, her classifications are similar to but not identical with those of DeKoven (Pondrom, lvii).

30. Of "Susie Asado" and "Preciosilla," Van Vechten comments that "there is reason to believe these two poems paint a portrait and make an attempt to recapture the rhythm of the same flamenco dancer" (*Selected,* 548). I can hear that possibility, but I am also looking for more. Why *these* words in *this* order? There does not seem to be any question that "Susie Asado" is a portrait of the flamenco dancer La Argentina, but Wagner-Martin goes so far as to say that "Susie" is "a reference to sexual effluvia" (107).

31. Stein's writing is full of these lovely rhymes. Reviewing *Four Saints in Three Acts,* Stark Young writes that the stream of words will not "trouble people who have always known by instinct or cultivation that Mother Goose is better poetry than Longfellow—'Hickory, dickory, dock,' for example, which at least lives in the ear, as compared to 'Be not like dumb, driven cattle,' which is born dead" (72).

32. Cheepen discusses how scapegoating allows conversants to repair interactional trouble (*Predictability,* chapter 5).

33. Janet Flanner reports that Stein's "Shakespeare consisted of leftovers from all sorts of editions of him with omissions of absent volumes which she had lent. She thought that when borrowers did not return a volume it was proof they must be reading it still. Her Shakespeare was mostly limp leather editions or paperbacks held together by elastic bands and she carried them in her pocket and read them when she walked Basket the poodle along the quais" (xv).

34. *Macbeth,* 4.1.10–11, 20–21, 35–36. Numbers in parentheses for Shakespeare's plays cited in the text represent act, scene, and lines.

35. Soap is "an essential ingredient in this private world that Stein's plain language

champions," Koestenbaum imagines. "The little we know we're also happy to rinse off. It's possible to think of Stein's work as one long rinsing or cleaning operation: The sentences that remain are the suds, or the dirt that gathers in the sink basin, traces of a past ablution" (304). Koestenbaum refers to Lady Macbeth, then continues: "The dialectic of progress/stasis that informs all of Stein's compositions (we're getting somewhere, we're getting nowhere) obeys soap's laws: Soap only serves its function in the process of disappearing; you must rub and unmake soap in order to enjoy its cleansing properties; using soap corrects and recapitulates the act of primary autoeroticism" (305).

CHAPTER 4

1. See appendix 1, "Gertrude Stein's American lecture Tour," in Burns and Dydo, 333–51, for the most complete itinerary of her lecture tour: the places she stayed, with whom she ate and where, and to whom she lectured.

2. Blackmer cites Van Vechten, *Peter Whiffle*, 123.

3. Buchalter seems to have caught Stein when she was being as contrary as possible, maybe because the room was too cold, and maybe because she wanted to bait a "zealot" who was present. She said she doesn't "take from" causes, which Buchalter interprets as her not being able to "get excited about formulas for saving the world." She seems just as disgusted with one theory as the next ("the Russians," "the Nazis," humanitarian causes). Disgust with hypocrisy is the primary cause, as she says that the people "who talk and worry about the poor being hungry ought to stay hungry themselves." (Elsewhere, she says that "she had no use for people who lived in comfort and luxury and then advocated Communism" ["A Snub"].) Knowing my own tendency to disagree with certain people, or only on certain days, I think Stein was having one of those days. She was mean about her brother, complained about the cold, threw out other random one-liners on painting and the military, and ("with a sly grin") stated a preference for Baltimore to Buchalter, a reporter for a Washington, D.C., newspaper.

4. W. G. Rogers wrote for the *Springfield Daily Republican*, so he may have written this glowing story; this was the only paper I found that printed a portion of her written lecture "through the courtesy of Miss Stein."

5. Actually, Stein describes several ways of writing, but I've lumped some of them together: "what you intend to write," "what you intended to write," "what has always been intended, by any one, to be written," and "what some one [else?] has intended to write," all seem to be related by intention and planning, as opposed to spontaneity (*Four in America*, 124). Stein seems to do the same lumping when she says, "There are then really there are then two different ways of writing," which have to do with how the "words next to each other make a sound" (124–25).

6. Stein continues to discuss these two kinds of writing in ibid., 125, 129, 131, 135.

7. In a 1924 letter to Sherwood Anderson, Stein praises his *Story Teller's Story* by comparing it to Borrow's *Lavengro*. Fifteen years later, Stein wrote a short essay titled "My Debt to Books" in which she mentions *Lavengro* and Borrow's *Romany Rye* by title in a list with Shakespeare, Trollope, and Edgar Wallace. She continues: "But which have I read the most often, of the novelists, Walter Scott and Anthony Trollope, of the playwriters Shakespeare, of the poets Coleridge, Poe and Wordsworth, at least they stick most to my mind, of miscellaneous George Borrow." Stein would not let anyone borrow her Borrow, "which she had in many kinds of editions because they were too hard to come by" (Flanner, xvi).

Affinities between Stein and Borrow abound. First, they both love and write about Daniel Defoe's *Robinson Crusoe*. Second, their texts often share the hybrid genre of autobiography and novel. Third, Borrow and Stein directly address their readers, as when Borrow commands certain "crotchet[y]" readers to "fling down my book, I do not wish ye to walk any farther in my company" (*Lavengro*, 369). Fourth, they express antiauthoritarian views within the puns and other byways of their prose. For example, in attempting to teach a friend Armenian, Lavengro asks her to decline the Armenian noun "Master"; she "neither likes the word nor the sound," does not want to pluralize masters, and wants to decline them all. Fifth, like Belle, who continually misunderstands Lavengro's Armenian words as English, Stein writes in one of her plays: "Many words spoken to me have seemed English" (*Ladies' Voices*, in *Geography and Plays*, 204). Sixth, Lavengro says that superstition is the soul of poetry (458), and Stein discusses how important superstition is to creativity. Seventh, Lavengro meets an author who credits "a single word in conversation, or some simple accident in a street, or on a road" for "some of the happiest portions" of his writing, and whole works by Stein are indebted to the same kinds of accidents. For example, in *Wars I Have Seen*, she describes what she has overheard in conversation or things that she heard, said, witnessed, or did during her almost daily walk of twelve kilometers to the nearest bakery. Eighth, this same author in Borrow's novel names a painting as his "principal source of inspiration," as Stein credits Cezanne's painting with influencing her creation of *Three Lives* (*Autobiography*, 34). But while this author says, "My neighbors are of opinion that I am a great reader, and so I am, but only of those features—my real library is that picture" (359–60), and while many of Stein's critics have discussed Stein solely in relation to paintings she collected, Stein loved books at least as much. Ninth, Lavengro's extensive discussion of the differences between British English and Scots English parallels Stein's interest in the difference between British English and American English (see *Lectures*, 49–54).

The eighteenth-century English novel is a productive place to look for interesting parallels with Stein's work. William Carlos Williams believed that Stein was anticipated by Laurence Sterne's *Life and Opinions of Tristram Shandy* (Meyer explores some of these connections in *Irresistible Dictation*), and I think there are some interesting parallels between Richardson's *Clarissa* and Stein's *The Making of Americans* (W. Williams, 41–42; and see D. Watson, 220–21). When Toklas published Stein's *How to Write*, the two women were careful to make the book "look like an eighteenth-century copy of a novel by Laurence Sterne [that Alice] had found in London" (Souhami, 176). In *Irresistible Dictation*, Meyer not only explores the connection between Stein and Sterne, but also finds fertile discussion of Stein's possible literary conversation with William Wordsworth, Ralph Waldo Emerson, George Eliot, and Walter Pater—just to list the more literary connections he draws. Meyer writes of his "conviction that texts exist in relation to other texts or they do not exist at all" (xvii).

8. In fact, "divine" and "devil" are *not* etymologically related. "Devil" is derived from a Greek word that means "slanderer," while the oldest relative of "divine" is a Latin word that means "god" or "one inspired by gods." While "divine" maintained the v sound, the v in "devil" evolved from f (*déofol*) *and* b (*diabolus*). Shakespeare might draw on this similarity when Othello speaks of "the divine Desdemona," but probably not (*Othello* 2.1.73).

9. Stein writes in *Autobiography*: "From her eighth year when she absorbed Shakespeare to her fifteenth year when she read Clarissa Harlowe, Fielding, Smollett etcetera and used to worry lest in a few years more she would have read everything and there would be nothing unread to read, she lived continuously with the english language" (74).

Smollett's novel is interesting in its epistolary style, which is quite conversational, and his character types—the overbearing manager of others' lives and the passively good-natured subservient female—are the kind one sees in Stein's early prose, *Three Lives* and *The Making of Americans*. Stein's early writings are full of uneducated, subordinated women who (sometimes) manage to gain some power through language. The "good Anna" needs to work for people who "freely let her do it all" (*Three Lives*, 77) and the "patient, gentle" Lena very much likes being a servant (239) and "was so still and docile, she would never want to do things her own way" (245). In *The Making of Americans*, Stein detours away from the Hersland family's story to tell about the succession of governesses and seamstresses that trooped through their lives.

10. Bramble and Jenkins write in simple and silly malapropisms, which must be the evidence upon which Sandra M. Gilbert and Susan Gubar base their assessment of Smollett. They group him with Sheridan and Fielding, who "construct[ed] cartoon figures" of women and "implied that language itself was almost literally alien to the female tongue" (30–31). But later in their analysis, Gilbert and Gubar recognize the potential of these characters' voices; they describe Jane Austen's characters as "taking on the persona of Mrs. Slipshop or Mrs. Malaprop (that wonderful 'queen of the dictionary') or Tabitha Bramble." In their view: "Austen was indisputably fascinated by double-talk, by conversations that imply the opposite of what they intend, narrative statements that can only confuse, and descriptions that are linguistically sound, but indecipherable or tautological" (127).

11. Other substitutions of near homophones also act as social commentary. To get her housekeeper to behave in her absence, Tabitha reminds her that she "must render accunt, not only to your earthly master, but also to him that is above" (Smollett, 156). It's more likely that her words are meant to remind us more of her attempt to catch a husband than to make any statement about sexuality and submission, but we can note both. The same joke is repeated when she tells her housekeeper and her assistant to "get your accunts ready for inspection" because she and her new husband are on their way home. Smollett does not pass up any opportunity to emphasize Tabitha's sexual obsessions, having her also write: "let Roger search into, and make a general clearance of the slit holes which the maids have in secret" (274); in the same letter, she hopes that when they arrive home, Humphry Clinker's preaching "may have power given to penetrate and instill his goodness, even into your most inward parts" (275).

But when Winifred Jenkins describes the marriage of Tabitha Bramble and Lismahago, who seems to marry her for her money, as "the holy bands of mattermoney," we certainly can't help noticing the comment on this marriage and other marriages of convenience (Smollett, 352). Humphry Clinker successfully converts Winifred to pious (usually spelled "pyehouse" [261]) devotion to Methodism and to "improv[e] in grease and godliness" (262). When Winifred marries Humphry Clinker, Tabitha's long lost illegitimate nephew, Winifred expresses a great truth in the sentiments of her last letter. She hopes that she and Tabitha, her former employer, will be able to adjust to their new social relationship: "I hope she and I will live upon dissent terms of civility—Being, by God's blessing, removed to a higher spear" (353). Her spelling errors—caused again by the near homophones—suggest the likelihood that these two women will not be able to adjust peaceably to their new situation, and even that their disputes will be more rancorous now that their social stations—their "spear[s]" or weapons—are more nearly equal.

The dissidence expressed through mistakes of diction, spelling, grammar, and pronunciation demonstrate the possibilities for the female voice to speak in a male society and with a language taught to educated men but (fortunately) disruptable by uneducated—or even some resistant educated—women. These women can see and understand differently, and make us see differently, because their minds have not been infiltrated by the male point of view. Judith Fetterley in *The Resisting Reader* argues that education makes women masculine, giving them a masculine point of view and masculine values (xx). Tabitha Bramble and Winifred Jenkins have escaped this supposedly masculinizing education and can teach us something, if we refuse to acquiesce to the criticism those characters, especially Tabitha, receive in Smollett's novel.

12. The human mind cannot be right about human nature because human nature is stuck in time and the timeless human mind cannot conceive of that:

> Human nature is not natural it is what anybody does and what anybody does is not natural and therefore it is not interesting.
> There is no doubt that human nature is not interesting although the human mind has always tried to be busy about this thing that human nature is interesting and the human mind has made so many efforts always it is doing this thing trying to make it be to itself that human nature is interesting but it is not and so the master-pieces always flatten it out, flatten human nature out so that there is no beginning and middle and ending. (*Geographical History*, 186)

13. Stein's understanding of and appreciation for the history of and relationships between words is important and too often overlooked in Stein criticism. For example, Randa Dubnick observes that Stein "uses words as if they were new and had no history" and that *this* constitutes her "innovative use of language" (xiv). Perhaps this disagreement stems from different definitions of "history." For Dubnick, a word's history may arise from etymology, normal context, and usage—the assumptions that people have come to about the meaning of a word. For me, history is what is carried in the word, which includes etymology (both true and false) but tends to allow us to understand the word anew. Readers must escape history, but words carry their own complex histories (and stories). In addition, individual readers and individual words build their own histories together.

CHAPTER 5

1. Postman is more interested in advertising and big media sources (in news, television shows, and radio) than in privately tendered language. The language Postman discusses, when he's not discussing the images that have replaced it, comes at us like a strong wind to which we bend. It is difficult to reply to, or even to think about (and internalize or reject), much of the fast, loud, often irrational language input we get these days. But I like to imagine that in Stein's day—and I think this is particularly likely in France—give-and-take conversation formed a higher percentage of language experience. Advertising was just starting to take on its current characteristics (Stein was struck by the slogans when she visited the United States in 1934–35). Postman observes that "in the eighteenth and nineteenth centuries those with products to sell . . . assumed that potential buyers were literate, rational, analytical" (*Amusing*, 58). The change to "the nonpropositional use of language" such as "slogans" and "jingles" started in the last decade of the nineteenth century, only a decade before Stein left for France—where, at the beginning of the twenty-first century, advertising is still less smoothly manipulative, still involves less "depth psychology," than in the United States (60).

2. At the outset of *Principles of Psychology*, William James distinguishes two main ways of approaching "the Science of Mental Life." One is "the orthodox 'spiritualistic' theory" and the other is the "'associationist'" school, or *"psychology without a soul."* Stein's theories fall under the second category, about which James writes: "Another and a less obvious way of unifying the chaos is to seek common elements *in* the divers mental facts rather than a common agent behind them, and to explain them constructively by the various forms of arrangement of these elements, as one explains houses by stones and bricks. . . . The very Self or *ego* of the individual comes in this way to be viewed no longer as the pre-existing source of the representations, but rather as their last and most complicated fruit" (15–16). His metaphor of humans and houses emphasizes the common materials we are made up of, rather than any particular qualities of individuality.

3. Hermans and Kempen also cite V. M. Colapietro ("The Vanishing Subject of Contemporary Discourse: A Pragmatic Response," *Journal of Philosophy* 87:11 [November 1990] 644–55) for his analysis of Dewey.

4. Hermans and Kempen credit Michael Holquist, *Dialogism: Bakhtin and His World* (London: Routledge, 1990) for this analysis.

5. The possibility that there is no such thing as "one" may remind the reader of Luce Irigaray's speculations in *The Sex Which Is Not One.* My feeling has long been that Stein is exploring the multiple selves of anyone, not just women, but Stein suggests (and later reaffirms) her belief that multiplicity is a more natural or comfortable state for women than for men.

6. By dyeing her hair to create this beautiful twin, Ida subsumes her plainer self, committing partial suicide by choosing to be "a suicide blond." Ida predicts that she will murder her twin, and Stein critic Ellen Berry (164) asks the thought-provoking question: "If Ida eradicates Winnie, is it an act of suicide or murder or neither or both?"

7. It is also possible to understand the two women in the car as the beauty queen and a companion, and the lost Ida in the road as the original. Later, the walking Ida sees the two women in the car and her dog, Love, is with them. Love is carrying a package that was last in the walking Ida's possession. In a letter to her twin, Ida writes: "the day you won, I saw a funny thing, I saw my dog Love belonging to some one. He did not belong to me he did belong to them. That made me feel very funny, but really it is not true he is here he belongs to me and you and now I will call you Winnie because you are winning everything and I am so happy that you are my twin. Your twin, Ida-Ida" (*Ida*, 621). The letter writer remembers that when a part of her was elected beauty queen she felt distant enough from this twin that it felt like Love belonged to somebody else. While writing, she feels close enough to the twin that they can own the dog together. But her feelings double back, and she gives her famous twin a name different from her own. This passage is further complicated by her mixing singular and plural pronouns ("some one" and "them") and the possibility that the passage could be jointly authored by Ida, Winnie, and the lost Ida. Notice that she signs the letter "Ida-Ida," which was the twin's earlier name. For a different reading of this same episode that emphasizes the dreamlike quality of *Ida*, see Berry, 163–64.

8. In *Ida*, Stein explores the topic of "publicity saints." She told a friend: "I want to write a novel about publicity, a novel where a person is so publicized that there isn't any personality left. I want to write about the effect on people of the Hollywood cinema kind of publicity that takes away all identity" (W. Rogers, 168).

9. Stein also anticipates DeLillo in recognizing the materialist's cure for death: "Another one had it in him to be completely certain in all his acting and his feeling and his living that

to be dead is to be a dead one and so this one must keep on being a live one and must have everything he can be seizing to keep by him" (*Making*, 525). In DeLillo's *White Noise*, Murray says, "Here we don't die, we shop" (38).

10. One way the body influences our ways of knowing results from our standing upright. We tend "to employ an up-down orientation in picking out meaningful structures of our experience," which also influences the metaphors through which we come to know the world—for instance, "more is up" for "no intrinsic reason" except the "structure of [our] bodily interactions" (Hermans and Kempen, 9).

11. Copeland argues that the reason Ida's marriages fail is that she does not know her husbands' true identities when she marries them (154). This hypothesis assumes that the uniforms represent the men's whole, or at least most important, self, which I think has to be incorrect.

12. How people react to our appearance changes with location, culture, and climate. Perhaps this is one reason Ida keeps moving. She may not want to be able to predict how people will react to her any more than she wants to have predictable reactions to their given identities.

13. Stein's obituary in the *Saturday Review* says that "there was an earthy, peasant quality about her and at the same time a spiritual force that was somewhat bewildering to those who expected to find in her the essence of mockery" (Smith).

14. The writer and the cuckoo incident recalls a related moment in Sammy Steward's novel *Parisian Lives*, in which Stein is a character. On a walk, Stein hears a cuckoo and gets "very excited," digs into her pockets for money, and says: "Don't you know the old superstition, if you have money in your pocket when you hear the first cuckoo of the year then you'll have money in your pocket for the next twelve months." She goes on: "Superstitions are my new passion. Take spiders for instance, not in the morning but only in the evening when they are lucky, not at noon when they bring care and worry. . . . But I am a lot more interested in money than in spiders or cuckoos, and now we will have money all year round because the cuckoo said so" (33). In the novel, however, Stein's money is immediately stolen.

15. Posnock quotes Connolly, 371.

16. Posnock cites Pitkin, 301, 300.

17. Stein's own poodle was named Basket (because she tried and failed to teach him to carry one [Wagner-Martin, 190]), and when she got a second dog she named him Basket II. Stein appreciated the fact that when he wasn't trimmed like a poodle, Basket looked like a sheep.

CHAPTER 6

1. "Pith," like "pit," means "the single, central kernel" or "essence," but it also refers to deadly extraction; "doubt" means "to waver" or "to vibrate"—as life does.

2. *Mrs. Reynolds* was written during World War II, although it is not known when Stein completed it. Bridgman reports: "The Yale editors have dated *Mrs. Reynolds* 1940–42, but the eleventh section refers to 23 December 1942, and the twelfth and thirteenth sections were almost certainly written more than a year later" (324). He is correct that the novel contains "references . . . to the springing up of the Resistance, the German debacle in Russia, rumors of the Nazis weakening, and the comforting hum of bombers on their way to Italy" (324), although all these references are so oblique that they could be wishful thinking. Assuming *Mrs. Reynolds* was completed even earlier, Ellen E. Berry describes Stein's "imaginative resistance . . . to the power of fascism, prophetically announcing in 1940 the certainty of Harper's/Hitler's demise" (125). I believe that most of the novel was written

between 1940 and the end of 1942, but that Stein probably added the thirteenth section (pp. 314–330), or even the last few pages, significantly later, after Allied airplanes could be heard overhead.

Wishful thinking and a faith in her book of prophecies encouraged Stein's optimism even before there was any basis for it. Predicting that news of the war's end would be announced in huge typescript, that she and Alice would celebrate the end of the war with cake (which they eventually do), and (incorrectly) that Angel Harper would die before he was fifty-five (Hitler had turned fifty-six ten days before killing himself) are all easy inventions. *Mrs. Reynolds* has a character who "conspires" and is a "deserter," but "the first units of the *maquis* were established in the last two to three months of 1942 . . . and composed of refugees or Jews sought by the authorities, deserters from Vichy youth camps, and workers escaping the *Relève*" (Kedward, *Resistance*, 233). It's less likely she foresaw Mr. and Mrs. Reynolds' joy in response to the sound of planes flying overhead (*Mrs. Reynolds*, 328), but since this is five paragraphs from the end of the novel, it could have been tacked on long after the bulk of the novel was written.

John Whittier-Ferguson convincingly argues that *Mrs. Reynolds* represents the struggle of trying to live as a human mind in time, especially a time of war: "The human mind may seem liberating" when we are reading *The Geographical History of America*, for example, but *Mrs. Reynolds* reveals "a state of mind that is historical in spite of itself" (Whittier-Ferguson, 129). While Whittier-Ferguson offers a convincing and impressive reading of *Mrs. Reynolds*, he ignores the pervasive conversations, only mentioning one in which Mrs. Reynolds is talking to herself (128). In another perceptive reading of *Mrs. Reynolds*, Phoebe Stein Davis emphasizes narrative storytelling over interaction when she alludes to conversation.

3. Stein's letter to Francis Rose in 1946 (qtd. in Bridgman, 335), as well recent criticism (Van Dusen), refers to Stein's life in "occupied" France, but Stein and Toklas spent the war in Bilignin and Culoz, which are in southeastern France and not part of the zone originally officially occupied by the Germans. Considering the nature of the Vichy government, that this part of France was occupied by the Italians in 1942, and that all France was occupied after November 1942, most writers still refer to this area as "occupied France" (Jones, 272; Kedward, *Resistance*, v). Nazi soldiers did crowd Belley after the May 1940 blitzkrieg, but once the armistice was signed in late June, people again began showing lights in the evening and French conscripts came home from their eight months in the trenches at the Maginot Line (Jones, 205, 264; Brinnin, 368–69). In Vichy France, the authorities required that all residents be listed—the mayor of Belley kept Stein and Toklas off that list, ostensibly because they were "obviously too old for life in a concentration camp" (Sevareid, 459) and perhaps because Faÿ told the prefect to keep them safe—curfews were enforced, and at least once, at the very end of the war, German soldiers quartered themselves in Stein and Toklas's home and the women hid upstairs for fear their American accents would be recognized (Stein, *Wars*, 211). A Resistance newspaper describes life in the "free zone" as of January 1942 (and uses the characteristic "they" to describe the enemy): "Here they have not dared to use fire and sword. Here they destroy underhandedly, by means of cold, sickness, and privations." The paper reports that the prisons are crowded with veterans, workers, intellectuals, girls who get caught distributing leaflets, and so on (see Liebling, 192).

4. Whittier-Ferguson explains the false positive connotations of the name as one of Stein's most audacious experiments with the possibility of disconnecting words and things, language and history. To change "Adolf" to "Angel" is not simply to make a semantic

equation but, as we experience a dissonance in the rechristening, to expose our presuppositions about how names should fit the world. That is, Stein presents "Adolf" and "Angel," without commentary, as different, though similar, collections of letters. Our desire for a semantic order that corresponds to an ethical one causes us to read the substitution as a grotesque and deliberate mismatching, an affront to our deepest sense of order.

Whittier-Ferguson perceptively adds, however: "But then, nothing adds up with Angel Harper" (126).

5. The pronoun referring to Mr. Reynolds is not usually capitalized. This capitalization is probably a misprint, and I have not interpreted it as a purposeful choice of Stein's.

6. Or are the two women laughing because they have together just quoted a familiar radio refrain? "well well, as the Englishman who does the propaganda in English from Berlin always says, well well" (Stein, *Wars*, 226). Here I emphasize that silence can communicate and even resist authority, but silence can also be considered "the real crime against humanity," which is what Nadezhda Mandelstam calls it in *Hope against Hope* (43). Writing of her experiences in Stalinist Russia, Mandelstam recalls: "After 1937 people stopped meeting each other altogether, and the secret police were thus well on the way to achieving their ultimate objective. Apart from assuring a constant flow of information, they had isolated people from each other" (34). Several of Stein's readers—Thornton Wilder and Janet Malcolm among them—see Stein's silence in this light. They think that she should have been more up-front about being Jewish, and that she should have confronted Faÿ on his Nazi collaboration and anti-Semitism. But no one reading *Mrs. Reynolds* sensibly can doubt Stein's detestation of the Nazi regime.

7. For a different reading, see Davis, who argues that "Stein undercuts the notion that the battlefields are the only sites of death during war" (583).

8. This statement is in third person, but it imitates Mr. Reynolds's speech patterns. Here Stein emulates Jane Austen's technique of indirect discourse, and she imitates Austen's (related) tendency to write dialogue that is "an exercise in noncommunication" (Brown, 169). Stein suggested to Ernest Hemingway that he read Austen to learn how to represent conversation in writing (Wagner-Martin, 170–71), and he best demonstrates what he learned about subtlety and miscommunication in "Hills Like White Elephants."

9. Stein's regular twelve-kilometer walk "gave her opportunities both to barter for food and to exchange news" (Wagner-Martin, 239). Later in the war, barricades made the walk seventeen kilometers. See Wagner-Martin, 242–43, for more on food shortages.

10. Stein loves questions, but people who see themselves as authorities avoid them. Mandelstam notes similar resistance to polite social forms by the policemen in Stalinist Russia (40, 53).

11. Bridgman (316–18) and Wagner-Martin (246–47) each discuss Stein's interest in Pétain. Bridgman describes Stein's introduction to Pétain's speeches but says it was Toklas who loved Pétain. Wagner-Martin says that the introduction is "vapid," that Stein was commissioned to do it, that Stein saw Pétain as her personal savior, and that Pétain really did help keep the worst from happening in France, multiple claims that seem to work against each other. The best extended argument against Van Dusen is Whittier-Ferguson's, which deals specifically with Stein's interest in Pétain's speeches (118–21), more generally with the difficulty of understanding an author "at odds" with our contemporary scholarly interests and categories (144), and even more generally with the problem of "foreshadowed history"—our tendency to assume that Stein knew what we know now (141). Here, Whittier-Ferguson is alluding to Michael André Bernstein, "Foregone Conclusions: Narrating the Fate of Austro-German-Jewry," *Modernism/Modernity* 1.1 [1994]: 57–79.

12. H. R. Kedward, author of two volumes on the French Resistance, writes that his sources are mainly "memoirs, the Resistance Press, and oral testimony from Resisters themselves." He adds that "there are few, if any, 'official' documents to underpin a study of this kind. In fact, there are very few documents for any kind of history of French Resistance," because "it was clearly in the nature of Resistance activity to avoid all paper records which might fall into the wrong hands" (*Resistance*, vi).

13. For the historical version of maquis techniques and the July 1944 German attack on the maquis in Stein's area of Ain, see Kedward, *In Search of*, 50, 178–79.

14. Stein comments:

> It is funny the different nations begin their broadcasting I wish I knew more languages so that I could know how each one of them does it. The English always begin with here is London, or the B. B. C. home service, or the over seas service, always part of a pleasant home life, of supreme importance to any Englishman or any Englishwoman. The Americans say with poetry and fire, this is the voice of America, and then with modesty and good neighborliness, one of the United Nations, it is the voice of America speaking to you across the Atlantic. Then the Frenchman, say *Frenchmen speaking to Frenchmen*, they always begin like that, and the Belgians are simple and direct, they just announce, radio Belge, and the national anthem, and the Frenchman also say, Honor and Country, and the Swiss so politely say, the studio of Geneva, at the instant of the broadcasting station of Berne will give you the latest news, and Italy says live Mussolini live Italy, and they make a bird noise and then they start, and Germany starts like this, *Germany calling, Germany calling*, in the last war, I said that the camouflage was the distinctive characteristic of each country, each nation stamped itself upon its camouflage, but in this war it is the heading of the broadcast that makes national life so complete and determined. (*Wars*, 155–56; my italics).

Notice that the French radio announcer alludes to speaker and listener, while the German radio announcement leaves out the listener and mentions the speaker (or speaking nation) twice.

15. In his book *Propaganda*, Jacques Ellul writes: "Propaganda must be total" (9). "It furnishes [people] with a complete system for explaining the world"; "it must produce quasi-unanimity, and the opposing faction must become negligible, or in any case cease to be vocal" (11). Competing propaganda on stations that all come from the same radio set precludes its effectiveness.

Mandelstam describes the effects of total propaganda: "Propaganda for historical determinism had deprived us of our will and the power to make our own judgments. We laughed in the faces of the doubters, and ourselves furthered the work of the daily press by repeating its sacramental phrases, by spreading rumors about each new round of arrests ('that's what passive resistance leads to!') and finding excuses for the existing state of affairs" (44).

16. The National Endowment for the Humanities sponsored "A National Conversation on American Pluralism and Identity" from 1994 to 1997. The NEH funded 135 grants totaling $6.26 million to enable forums, conversations, and writing projects, as well as research projects and exhibitions (Hackney, *One America*, 131–62). The goals of the conversations included "transform[ing] into a productive discussion [on American identity] what had already become an ill-tempered argument among scholars" in "drive-by debates" (4), and one participant said: "Too many of our public spaces—think of shopping malls—bring us

together only as consumers, not as citizens" (7). Stein's suggestion is earlier, more open, and much less expensive, and its informality makes it impossible for participants to lose sight of the ultimate goal: "deliberat[ing] with each other," as Amy Gutman puts it (in ibid., 184, 183) "because no single person's point of view contains all the insights on these issues." Clearly, conversation promises no complete solutions, but, as Ellis Close writes, it is important to "keep the conversation going" (qtd. in Hackney, 6, from *Color Blind: Seeing beyond Race in a Race-Obsessed World* [New York: HarperCollins, 1997], 240).

Sheldon Hackney, then chair of the National Endowment for the Humanities and former president of the University of Pennsylvania, writes:

> The challenge of our time is to revitalize our civic life in order to realize a new birth of freedom. All of our people . . . have a responsibility to examine and discuss what unites us as a country, what we share as common American values in a nation composed of so many divergent groups and beliefs. . . .
>
> The conversation that I envision will not be easy. [As Cornel West writes:] ". . . Even the very art of public conversation—the precious activity of communicating with fellow citizens in a spirit of mutual respect and civility—appears to fade amid the backdrop of name-calling and finger-pointing in flat sound bites."
>
> . . . What I envision is a national conversation open to all Americans, a conversation in which all voices need to be heard . . . .
>
> This will be a risky enterprise, because the NEH comes only with questions—not answers. The outcome is therefore unpredictable, contingent as it is on the course of the discussion and on what we learn from each other as we talk. ("National Conversation")

17. Gabriel Tarde argued that "personal relationships" might at least "temp[er] the effects of broader structural modifications" (T. Clark, 57).

18. "Absolute Powerpoint" in the *New Yorker* (28 May 2001) reminds us that this problem is still with us and has grown. "Before there were presentations, there were conversations," and not only did people get to know each other in well-lighted rooms, they also got to ad lib when they had a sudden fresh idea (Parker, 76, 87). As language and experience may limit our perceptions, PowerPoint software seems to limit our ideas and expression. One Stanford professor admitted that he removed a book from his syllabus because he "'couldn't figure out how to PowerPoint it'" (87). Relatedly, a journalist at one of Stein's lectures reports that she "defied our system of note-taking" (Winsten).

19. Jacques Ellul discusses the power of facts in *Propaganda*: "Modern man worships 'facts'—that is, he accepts 'facts' as the ultimate reality. . . . He believes that facts in themselves provide evidence and proof" (xv). Herbert Marcuse also laments our faith in facts: "The range of judgment is confined within a context of facts which excludes judging the context in which the facts are made, man-made, and in which their meaning, function, and development are determined" (115–16).

20. Stein uses the now recognized to be highly objectionable term "niggers." As a result, Donald Paul's statement sounds like an alarmist call for change: If white Americans don't get their act together and prevent what seems the inevitable downfall of all industrial nations, then black Americans will rule. But Stein may have meant it differently. Elsewhere, the GIs agree that it's a relief to be in Europe, where they don't feel called upon to assert their white privilege. They praise the agricultural economy of the South because it would have nicely

balanced the industrialism of the North, if only the slaveholders had peacefully accepted the end of slavery with a buyout instead of fighting the Civil War. And in this book that promotes pioneering, one character says, possibly admiringly, "the only pioneering there is in America these days is done by the Negroes" (*Brewsie*, 65).

21. For a discussion of Stein's understanding of "fathering" in *Mrs. Reynolds*, see Berry, chapter 5.

22. The kind of conformity Stein writes against was certainly evident much earlier than World War II, but she may see her opportunity to do something about it in 1946, now that more people have noticed the way individual rights were given up in order to fight Fascism in that war. Martha Banta's *Taylored Lives* discusses the push for uniformity in all aspects of life between the mid-nineteenth century and the 1930s, tracing the relationship between the efficiency of assembly-line production and human conformity. Julie Abraham makes the point that Stein has long seen herself as one of the "Brother Singulars," the "queer people" who have "vital singularity," and that anyone tracing Stein's idea of an American must take into account her experience as a lesbian (Abraham, 511, quoting phrases from *Making of Americans*, 21).

23. Americans now get weekends off (or did, until overtime became the way to save on worker training and benefits costs), many Americans get substantial vacations, and early retirement is common. What we buy through the "installment plan" and other credit (the products, as well as their accompanying desires and accumulations), however, has also cut into the time we spend thinking. If we have to have a motocross bike, an all-terrain vehicle, and a boat, then we have to spend time caring for those "recreational" vehicles and driving the six hours each way to trails or a desert or a lake just to use them. Ownership, the requisite desire in a "healthy" capitalist industrial society, itself takes time away from our thinking. The very popularity of these activities demonstrates our loss of individualism. That we have to buy things in order to ride them also contrasts with the pastime of making things that can serve as expressions of our individuality—meals, quilts, furniture, clothing, even cars (my dad built his first one).

24. World War I "exposed the political naivete at the heart of pragmatism's tough-minded rhetoric" to radical essayist Randolph Bourne, who "contended that [it was necessary to] . . . reconstruct pragmatism on a new basis—one that accepts 'inexorable' capitalist efficiency rather than free will and choice as the fundamental given of modernity" (qtd. in Posnock, 257, citing Bourne, 322). Bourne makes the case that pragmatist thinkers (liberal realists) are wrong in believing that any war could be "democratic and antiseptic" or controlled to reach only toward ideal outcomes. He concludes: "The pacifists opposed the war because they knew this was an illusion, and because of the myriad hurts they knew war would do the promise of democracy at home. For once the babes and sucklings seem to have been wiser than the children of light" (324). Stein did not see capitalism as the end of pragmatism—possibly because for most of her life she is interested in individualism more for the sake of the individual than for its effects on the larger society—but neither do Marcuse or Rorty or any of the later philosophers who understand human will as an important agent in change. As I suggest at the very end of this book, however, Stein may have seen the atomic bomb as a snag to some of her views.

25. For a very different opinion on Stein's relationship to mass production, see Ann Douglas's *Terrible Honesty*; for example: "Stein loved the effortlessness and abundance created by the new technology of consumer-oriented mass production and saw her own art as its ally and analogue" (127).

26. The Germans were taught to follow orders without thinking: "'We must distrust the intelligence and the conscience,' Hitler counseled, 'and must place our trust in our instincts. We have to regain a new simplicity,'" John Wesley Young reports (68). When defining Hitler's "ideal Nazi," Young writes "that Hitler neglected mentioning mental dexterity as an indispensable trait," and "it is fair to say, and amply borne out by the record, that he preferred followers unaccustomed to doing their own thinking" (67). To get people to react to orders instinctively, the Nazis "form a language of assent and domination [yes and no] whose essential characteristic is its univocacy: for every politically significant word, one meaning" (31). Young cites George Orwell's essay on *Gulliver's Travels*: "One of the aims of totalitarianism is not merely to make sure that people will think the right thoughts, but actually to make them *less conscious*" (30; Orwell, "Politics vs. Literature: An Examination of *Gulliver's Travels*," 291).

Stein is not wrong to see a resemblance to business practices of the time. Banta, citing J. David Houser's 1927 report *What the Employer Thinks: Executives' Attitudes Toward Employees*, writes: "Businessmen shaving the line between workaday brutality and lofty social reforms catch at phrases that are 'clearly substitutes for thought'—phrases 'charged with so much emotion that they resemble shibboleths.'" Houser cites phrases such as "management's responsibility," "the desire to be fair," "employees' ingratitude," "decent treatment," and "it pays in dollars and cents" as examples of how "business uses [words] to fight 'free from any intellectual process'" (Banta, 82–83).

27. Herbert Marcuse says something similar in *One-Dimensional Man*. He criticizes polls for the limited range of acceptable response: Republican, Democrat, and (this poll allowed a third choice) "ambivalent." He writes: "The established parties themselves, their policies, and their machinations are not questioned, nor is the actual difference between them questioned as far as the vital issues are concerned (those of atomic policy and total preparedness), questions which seem essential for the assessment of the democratic processes, unless the analysis operates with a concept of democracy which merely assembles the features of the *established form* of democracy" (118; his italics).

28. Stein criticized Hemingway as being a bit "Rotarian," and Banta reads this as a comment on Hemingway's "tales of male bonding in times of war," which, like "business fiction narratives," emphasized "team-work" and "the 'old spirit' of 'solidarity'" (Banta, 13).

29. Joseph Lane's speech is described very differently from Angel Harper's: "Joseph Lane was leading a regular life"; "he just said how do you do and very well I thank you and led an ordinary life just like that." Angel Harper says, "leave it to me" (*Mrs. Reynolds*, 309).

30. In this sense, "it *is* doubtful whether he was ever a boy." What Stein describes of Angel Harper's childhood does not suggest that he was ever a comfortable entity or creatively imaginative. Stein's descriptions of moments in Angel Harper's life "combine to produce a remarkably complex and vivid impression of a fearful, isolated, and vulnerable child behind the facade of the powerful dictator" (Berry, 130).

31. This suggestion of mass action may also be provoked by the success of women's protests in Vichy France from winter 1941 through spring 1942. Several demonstrations by "housewives" and mothers, particularly one held on *la Fête des méres* (Mother's Day), succeeded in improving food rations—an extra three eggs and three hundred grams of dried vegetables for every ration card (Kedward, *Resistance*, 221–23). With all the fathering going on in centers of power, these demonstrations might have emphasized the differences between mothering and fathering in Stein's mind.

32. Environmentalist Murray Bookchin also asks for a different kind of answer. He argues for an ecological position that does not "tak[e] the present social order for granted"; "it is the prevailing order that sets the terms of any 'compromise' or 'trade-off,' just like the rules of a chess game and the grid of a chess board determine in advance what the players can do—not the dictates of reason and morality." Further: "To 'play by the rules' of the environmental game means that the natural world, including oppressed people, always loses something piece by piece until everything is lost in the end." He argues that capitalism and socialism both "devour the natural world," only one is more "systematic" than the other (15). A woman Stein spoke with during World War II expressed a similar sentiment about adapting to the status quo: "well now as we have all made all our arrangements to live in a state of war I suppose the war will go on" (Stein, *Wars*, 140).

33. Mike LeFevre, a steelworker interviewed by Studs Terkel in the late sixties or early seventies, asks: "What do you think would happen in this country if, for one year, they experimented and gave everybody a twenty-hour week? How do they know that the guy who digs [George] Wallace today doesn't try to resurrect Hitler tomorrow? Or the guy who is mildly disturbed at pollution doesn't decide to go to General Motors and shit on the guy's desk? You can become a fanatic if you had the time. The whole thing is time. . . . Time, that's the important thing" (Terkel, xxxiv).

34. As Roland Barthes writes: "Denotation is not the first meaning, but pretends to be so; under this illusion, it is ultimately no more than the *last* of the connotations (the one which seems both to establish and to close the reading)" (9).

35. This anarchic isolationism that I describe is a straw man, but one that gets propped up quite often in American political arguments. Democrats want the government to imitate and sustain interpersonal relations; Republicans are afraid the government might replace and thereby undermine interpersonal relations. Both want to prevent anarchy, and each sees the other side as promoting or at least enabling it.

36. Marcuse cites Bridgeman, 31. In *Halfway to Revolution: Investigation and Crisis in the Work of Henry Adams, William James, and Gertrude Stein*, Bush denounces this operationalism in literary criticism. "Anglo-American critics tend to market 'continental' philosophers in such a way as to neutralize their efforts by turning their thought into sets of techniques" (5). Stein criticizes a kind of operationalism when she discusses newspaper writing: "The yellow press [has] become stereotyped having become a way of doing a machinery that all the schools of journalism teach and as soon as anybody can teach it it is a way of doing a thing and is not the thing itself and it begins to move backward" ("American Newspapers," 93).

37. DeKoven, who in *Different Language* quotes part of this passage from Barthes, also cites it in reference to Stein's writing, her point being that Stein's insistent writing is a success when, as Stein puts it in *The Making of Americans* (540), the words have "'many meanings many ways of being used to make different meanings to every one'":

> Stein's responsibility is to make this core of meaning capable of evoking and support-
> ing private layers of association. . . . The writing in this style fails precisely when it has
> no underpinning or core meaning, when it gives itself up completely to repetition of
> words that have "really existing being" only for Stein. Such writing would deny the
> reader not only the possibility of active, imaginative participation in the creation of
> the text, but of reading it at all. (DeKoven, *Different Language*, 57)

I mostly agree with DeKoven. But my understanding of the situation leaves less room for Stein's failure and more room for failure on her readers' side of the interaction. If we learn to be writerly, we will understand greater meaning in our reading of Stein, as well as in the orally and visually transmitted texts of everyday life, no matter how personal or functional their intent.

38. Present-day computerized hypertexts present themselves as "writerly" in that the reader (of the screen) is making choices: "readers choose among pathways within plots that form a mosaic" (Swerdlow, 9). But these choices are limited. A *National Geographic* article reports that "information technologies, for all the attention they receive, lag far behind the power of the human brain. Researchers estimate that the normal brain has a quadrillion connections between its nerve cells, more than all the phone calls made in the U.S. in the past decade," and that "no hypertext novel can achieve what the brain does naturally. . . . Readers react to . . . [a passage from Dostoyevsky] in different ways, creating their own combinations of texture, mood, detail, and emotion" (Swerdlow, 9). In short, our brains can turn any text into a hypertext more effectively than can computer programs—and without the limitations of technology and other people's imaginations. Neural connections, like footnotes, are a hypertext technology that far predates computers.

39. Adamant adherents of a political party may be so offensive that they train their brethren to join the opposing party. In "How Nazis are Made," Ingo Hasselback tells the story of how his childhood in Communist East Berlin prepared him to become a neo-Nazi. His parents' work "to establish the first German 'anti-Fascist' state . . . created . . . a state in which there was nothing to strive for but conformity" (39). His hatred of anti-Fascism led him straight to Fascism; later, seeing himself "rattling on about the Jews," *saying things he didn't know from his own experience,* he realized he "needed to explore some hard questions" and *come up with answers to them on his own* (53). To borrow from "Won't Get Fooled Again," by The Who's Pete Townshend, Hasselback's "new boss" (neo-Nazism) was just like his "old boss" (Communism), and he finally became an entrepreneur, thinking his own thoughts

40. Stein had long been interested in saying and seeing, and even in rephrasing this line from "The Star-Spangled Banner." Melanctha's father "tried to make her say a thing she did not know" (*Three Lives*, 95), and later Melanctha says to Jeff: "I can't say as I see just what you mean," and "I certainly don't just see what you mean by what you say" (120). F. Scott Fitzgerald seems to draw on the distinction between real experience and abstractions in *Tender is the Night*, when he writes of a girl who waves her underwear at some sailors: "Oh, say can you see the tender color of remembered flesh?—while at the stern of the battleship arose in rivalry the Star-Spangled Banner" (297).

CONCLUSIONS

1. See Winston, 117; Van Vechten, "How Many Acts," xii; and Bridgman, 341–45. Toklas, however, insisted to Van Vechten that Stein "didn't at all feel [Susan B.] was she herself," although Stein had respected Anthony for her "heroi[sm]" (Van Vechten, "How Many Acts," xiin5).

2. Martin cites Sutherland, 167n57.

3. Winston understands the character Indiana Elliot as a "less obvious" "alter-ego" for Stein, one "who, in the course of the opera, moves from a young ingenue awed by male authority to assertive (albeit disillusioned) married woman, committed to the suffragist cause" (118). Winston makes a convincing but complicated claim for the relationship between

"Indiana Elliot" and Stein's mentors George Eliot (Marian Evans), Currer Bell (Charlotte Brontë), and George Sand (Aurore Dupin).

4. The passage in 1866 of the Fourteenth Amendment, which extended suffrage to all men, was the biggest blow. The very men who had been allies with women's suffrage—men such as Frederick Douglass, Horace Greeley, Wendell Phillips, George W. Curtis, Henry Ward Beecher, Theodore Tilton, Aaron Powell, and Gerrit Smith (Dorr, 198)—jumped ship, told women to be patient, and got the word "male" put in the Constitution for the first time (185–99). Stein's Susan B. can't get over the way her most powerful efforts went so wrong.

5. Dorr gives a great example of one man who could easily have reacted with mixedness if he hadn't so reactively retreated to a conservative, antisuffrage position. As editor of the *New York Tribune*, Horace Greeley was an early supporter of Anthony, but when he was chair of the committee on suffrage at the New York Constitutional Convention, he was antagonistic to the cause. He is said to have "drawled" in his "acid voice" that "the ballot and the bullet go together. If you vote are you also prepared to fight?" "Certainly, Mr. Greeley," Anthony answered, "Just as you fought in the late war—at the point of a goose-quill." Greeley, an old friend of Anthony, insisted "that the best women he knew did not want to vote"; at that, a suffrage advocate pointed out that he had a petition attesting to the contrary signed by Mrs. Horace Greeley. His pride hurt, Greeley then remained "a life enemy of the women" (189–90). He could have been divided—by personal attachments, by changing circumstances, et cetera—but he retreated to the safe position.

6. Van Vechten, "How Many Acts," xvn9, citing Stein's notes for the program of the Pasadena production of *In Savoy*. There Stein writes of "the divided families, the bitterness, the quarrels and sometimes the denunciations, and yet the natural necessity of their all continuing to live their daily life together, because after all that was all the life they had, besides they were after all the same family or their neighbors, and in the country neighbors are neighbors." She wanted the audience "to realize that French families were divided as our American families were divided in our Civil War and even in our Revolutionary War, and it is complicated and simple, and I hope it will make you feel the French as they really were during the long years of the occupation" (qtd in Van Vechten, xvn9). But this complexity makes Stein look bad in the eyes of her critics. For example, maintaining her friendships with neighbors who were collaborators, and especially with Bernard Faÿ, suggests an unbecoming passivity during World War II. Zofia P. Lesinska asserts that "Stein's dramatization of the complexity of the actual is unparalleled," but that "it is difficult to condone Stein's decision to live comfortably in the South of France under the auspices of Fäy, a Vichyite and a resolute anti-Semite" (40, 25). In short, Lesinska can "defend Stein's war autobiographies as historically and artistically compelling," but like Stein's "early critics and like Van Dusen," she finds "Stein's wartime personal and political choices to be quite objectionable" (24–25). Stein might appreciate the very dividedness of this evaluation, although Lesinka's taking friendship, cordiality, the desire to survive, and the continuation of one's "daily life" (as much as that was possible) as "loyalty to the collaborationist government" is going too far (26). (And trying to survive the winters in the foothills of the Alps is much different from enjoying the war along the Riviera, which is what "the South of France" implies.)

7. Winston (125) points out that Elizabeth Cady Stanton spoke words very similar to these in "The Solitude of Self," her 1892 farewell address to the National Woman Suffrage Association.

8. Of course, constitutional amendments require votes in Congress, and the federal

amendment wasn't passed until 1919, thirteen years after Anthony's death and seventy-two years after the Seneca Falls Convention (Dorr, 339–43, 358).

9. Borrowing from a somewhat different field—R. Keith Sawyer's study of improvisational drama, in which Sawyer uses methods of conversation analysis (which describes "how bottom-up processes lead to emergent macro-structure") augmented by a greater interest in "the 'top-down' processes of social causation" (62)—I note that another investigator has seen conversations grow their own attributes. Sawyer writes that "an analytically distinct entity emerges from collective action and then has causal power over individual action" (57), but he calls this thing that arises from his "theory of collaborative emergence" the "frame" for the conversation rather than a separate causal subjectivity (45). Sawyer also posits that "a properly theorized conceptualization" of "the realm of the emergent intersubjective frame as social fact" might allow us "empirically to investigate—to 'see'—creativity" in process (viii). It might be important to note that in improvisational drama, the participants must quickly negotiate a frame for their interaction (Are we children? Are you a storekeeper and am I a customer? etc.). That's one kind of creativity, but another kind occurs in "real" interactional conversations.

10. See Yaeger, Irigaray, and Kristeva. Elizabeth Gross's chapter "The Body of Signification" also helped me think about the relationship between abjection and the feminine sublime.

11. Yaeger here quotes McCarthy, viii.

BIBLIOGRAPHY

PRIMARY WORKS

Stein, Gertrude. "An American and France." In *What Are Masterpieces*, 59–70. 1940. New York: Pitman, 1970.

———. "American Newspapers." 1935. In *How Writing Is Written*, ed. Robert Bartlett Haas, 89–93. Santa Barbara: Black Sparrow, 1977.

———. "And Now." 1934. In *How Writing Is Written*, ed. Robert Bartlett Haas, 63–66. Santa Barbara: Black Sparrow, 1977.

———. *The Autobiography of Alice B. Toklas*. 1933. New York: Vintage, 1961.

———. *Bee Time Vine and Other Pieces*. Preface and notes by Virgil Thomson. New Haven: Yale UP, 1953.

———. *The Blue Swallows*. Chicago: U of Chicago P; 1967, 13.

———. *Brewsie and Willie*. 1946. London: Brilliance, 1988.

———. "The Capital and Capitals of the United States of America." 1935. In *How Writing Is Written*, ed. Robert Bartlett Haas, 73–76. Santa Barbara: Black Sparrow, 1977.

———. "A Circular Play/A Play in Circles." In *A Stein Reader*, ed. Ulla E. Dydo, 326–42. Evanston, Ill.: Northwestern UP, 1993.

———. "Composition as Explanation." 1926. In *Selected Writings of Gertrude Stein*. Edited by Carl Van Vechten, 511–23. New York: Vintage Books, 1952

———. *Everybody's Autobiography*. 1937. New York: Cooper Square, 1971.

———. *Four in America*. Introduction by Thornton Wilder. New Haven: Yale, 1947.

———. *The Geographical History of America, or The Relation of Human Nature to the Human Mind*. 1936. Introduction by William H. Gass. Baltimore: Johns Hopkins UP, 1995.

———. *Geography and Plays*. 1922. Intro. Cyrena N. Pondrom. Madison: U of Wisconsin P, 1993.

———. "I Came and Here I Am." 1936. In *How Writing Is Written*, ed. Robert Bartlett Haas, 67–72. Los Angeles: Black Sparrow, 1977.

———. *Ida*. 1941. In *Gertrude Stein: Writings, 1932–1946*, 609–704. New York: Library of America, 1998.

———. *In Savoy, or "Yes" Is for Yes for a Very Young Man*. London: Pushkin, 1946.

———. *Last Operas and Plays*. Edited by Carl Van Vechten. New York: Rinehart, 1949.

———. *Lectures in America*. 1935. Boston: Beacon, 1957.

———. "Lifting Belly." In Stein, *Bee Time Vine*, 61–115.

———. "A Long Gay Book." In *Matisse Picasso and Gertrude Stein*. Barton: Something Else, 1972.

———. *The Making of Americans Being a History of a Family's Progress*. 1925. New York: Something Else, 1966.

———. "Matisse." 1912. In *Gertrude Stein: Writings, 1903–1932*, 278–81. New York: Library of America, 1998.

———. *The Mother of Us All.* 1949. In *Gertrude Stein: Writings, 1932–1946*, 779–819. New York: Library of America, 1998.

———. *Mrs. Reynolds.* 1952. Los Angeles: Sun and Moon, 1980.

———. "My Debt to Books." *Books Abroad: An International Quarterly of Comment on Foreign Books* 13.3 (summer 1939): 307–8.

———. *Narration: Four Lectures by Gertrude Stein.* Introduction by Thornton Wilder. Chicago: U of Chicago P, 1935.

———. *A Novel of Thank You.* 1958. Introduction by Steven Meyer. Normal, Ill.: Dalkey, 1994.

———. "Off We All Went to See Germany." In *How Writing Is Written*, ed. Robert Bartlett Haas, 135–41. Santa Barbara: Black Sparrow, 1977. Originally published in *Life*, August 6, 1945.

———. *Paris France.* 1940. New York: Liveright, 1970.

———. *Painted Lace and Other Pieces [1914–1937].* New Haven: Yale UP, 1955.

———. "Picasso." 1938. In *Gertrude Stein: Writings, 1932–1946*, 495–533. New York: Library of America, 1998.

———. "Portraits and Repetition." 1930. In *Gertrude Stein: Writings and Lectures, 1909–1945*, ed. Patricia Meyerowitz, 99–124. Baltimore: Penguin, 1974.

———. "Q.E.D." In *Gertrude Stein: Writings, 1903–1932*, 1–63. New York: Library of America, 1998.

———. "Reflection on the Atomic Bomb." 1947. In *Gertrude Stein: Writings, 1932–1946*, ed. Catharine R. Stimpson and Harriet Chessman, 823. New York: Library of America, 1998.

———. *A Stein Reader.* Edited by Ulla Dydo. Evanston, Ill.: Northwestern UP, 1993.

———. *Tender Buttons.* 1914. Los Angeles: Sun and Moon, n.d.

———. *Three Lives.* 1909. New York: Vintage, 1936.

———. "Two: Gertrude Stein and Her Brother (1910–1912)." In *Two: Gertrude Stein and Her Brother and Other Early Portraits (1908–1912)*, 1–142. Foreword by Janet Flanner. New Haven: Yale UP, 1951.

———. *A Village Are You Ready Not Yet: A Play in Four Acts.* Paris: Galerie Simon, 1928.

———. *Wars I Have Seen.* New York: Random House, 1945.

———. "What Are Master-pieces and Why Are There So Few of Them." 1940. In *Gertrude Stein: Writings and Lectures, 1911–1945*, ed. Patricia Meyerowitz, 148–56. Baltimore: Penguin, 1974.

———. "The Winner Loses: A Picture of Occupied France," *Atlantic*, November 1940, 571–83.

Stein, Gertrude, and Leon M. Solomons. *Motor Automatism.* New York: Phoenix Book Shop, 1969. Originally published as "Normal Motor Automatism" and "Cultivated Motor Automatism: A Study of Character in Its Relation to Attention," *Psychological Review*, September 1896 and May 1898.

SECONDARY WORKS

Books and Journal Articles

Abraham, Julie. "'We are Americans': Gertrude, *Brewsie and Willie*." *Modern Fiction Studies* 42.3 (fall 1996): 508–27.

Adams, Henry. *The Education of Henry Adams.* 1918. Edited by Ernest Samuels. Boston: Houghton, 1973.

Aiken, Conrad. "We Ask for Bread." Review of *The Making of Americans,* by Gertrude Stein. In Curnutt, 37–40. Originally published in *New Republic,* 4 April 1934.

Aldrich, Mildred. "Confessions of a Breadwinner." Microfilm. Radcliffe College Archive, Schlesinger Library, Radcliffe Institute, Cambridge, Mass.

Alpers, Benjamin L. *Dictators, Democracy, and American Public Culture: Envisioning the Totalitarian Enemy, 1920s-1950s.* Chapel Hill: U of North Carolina P, 2003.

Auden, W. H. "In Memory of W. B. Yeats." In *The Norton Anthology of Modern Poetry,* ed. Richard Ellman and Robert O'Clair, 741–43. New York: Norton, 1973.

Bain, Alexander. *The Senses and the Intellect.* 1855. 4th ed. New York: D. Appleton, 1902.

Banta, Martha. *Taylored Lives: Narrative Productions in the Age of Taylor, Veblen, and Ford.* Chicago: U of Chicago P, 1993.

Barker, Lewellys F. *The Nervous System and Its Constituent Neurones.* New York: Appleton, 1899.

———. *Time and the Physician: The Autobiography of Lewellys F. Barker.* New York: Putnam, 1942.

Barthes, Roland. *S/Z.* Translated by Richard Miller. New York: Noonday, 1988.

Becker, Mary Lamberton. "Books for Young People." Review of *The World Is Round,* by Gertrude Stein. In Curnutt, 114–15. Originally published in *New York Herald-Tribune Books,* 24 September 1939.

Bellah, Robert N., Richard Madsen, William M. Sullivan, Ann Swidler, and Steven M. Tipton. *Habits of the Heart: Individualism and Commitment in American Life.* Berkeley: U of California P, 1996.

Berry, Ellen E. *Curved Thought and Textual Wandering: Gertrude Stein's Postmodernism.* Ann Arbor: U of Michigan P, 1992.

Blackmer, Corrine E. "Selling Taboo Subjects: The Literary Commerce of Gertrude Stein and Carl Van Vechten." In *Marketing Modernisms: Self-Promotion, Canonization, and Rereading,* ed. Kevin J. H. Dettmar and Stephen Watt. Ann Arbor: U of Michigan P, 1996.

Bloom, Harold. *The Anxiety of Influence: A Theory of Poetry.* London: Oxford UP, 1975.

Bookchin, Murray. *Remaking Society: Pathways to a Green Future.* Boston: South End, 1990.

Booth, Stephen. *King Lear, Macbeth, Indefinition, and Tragedy.* New Haven: Yale UP, 1983.

———. *Precious Nonsense:* The Gettysburg Address, *Ben Jonson's* Epitaphs on His Children, *and* Twelfth Night. Berkeley: U of California P, 1998.

Borrow, George. *Lavengro: The Scholar, the Gypsy, the Priest.* Oxford: Oxford UP, 1982.

Bourne, Randolph. *The Radical Will: Selected Writings, 1911–1918.* Compiled and edited by Olaf Hansen. New York: Urizen Books, 1977.

Bowers, Jane Palatini. *Gertrude Stein.* New York: St. Martin's, 1993.

Bridgeman, P. W. *The Logic of Modern Physics.* New York: Macmillan, 1928.

Bridgman, Richard. *Gertrude Stein in Pieces.* New York: Oxford UP, 1970.

Brinnin, John Malcolm. *The Third Rose: Gertrude Stein and Her World.* 1959. Reprint, Reading, Mass.: Addison-Wesley, 1987.

Bromfield, Louis. "Gertrude Stein, Experimenter with Words." Review of *The Autobiography of Alice B. Toklas,* by Gertrude Stein. In Curnutt. 63–66. Originally published in *New York Herald-Tribune Books,* 3 September 1933.

Brooks, Van Wyck. *America's Coming-of-Age.* 1915. Reprint, New York: Octagon Books, 1975.

Brown, Lloyd W. *Bits of Ivory: Narrative Techniques in Jane Austen's Fiction.* Baton Rouge: Louisiana State UP, 1973.

Burke, Kenneth. "The Impartial Essence." In *Gertrude Stein Advanced: An Anthology of Criticism,* ed. Richard Kostelanetz, 187–89. Jefferson, N.C.: McFarland, 1990.

———. "Two Brands of Piety." Review of *Four Saints in Three Acts,* by Gertrude Stein. In Curnutt, 70–73. Originally published in *The Nation,* 28 February 1934.

Burns, Edward, ed. *The Letters of Gertrude Stein and Carl Van Vechten, 1913–1946.* 2 vols. New York: Columbia UP, 1986.

Burns, Edward M. and Villa E. Dydo, eds. with William Rice. *The Letters of Gertrude Stein and Thorton Wilder.* New Haven: Yale UP, 1996.

Bush, Clive. *Halfway to Revolution: Investigation and Crisis in the Work of Henry Adams, William James, and Gertrude Stein.* New Haven: Yale UP, 1991.

Camus, Albert. "Toward Dialogue" (30 November 1946). In *Between Hell and Reason: Essays from the Resistance Newspaper Combat, 1944–1947.* Selected and translated by Alexandre de Gramont, 137–40. Hanover: Wesleyan UP, 1991.

Canby, Henry Seidel. "Cheating at Solitaire." Review of *Portraits and Prayers,* by Gertrude Stein. In Curnutt, 79–82. Originally published in *Saturday Review of Literature,* 17 November 1934.

Cheepen, Christine. *The Predictability of Informal Conversation.* London: Pinter, 1988.

Chesney, Alan M. *The Johns Hopkins Hospital and the Johns Hopkins University School of Medicine.* 3 vols. Baltimore: Johns Hopkins UP, 1943.

Chessman, Harriet Scott. *The Public Is Invited to Dance: Representation, the Body, and Dialogue in Gertrude Stein.* Stanford: Stanford UP, 1989.

Clark, Herbert H., and Eve V. Clark. "Discourse Plans." In *Psychology and Language: An Introduction to Psycholinguistics,* 227–37. New York: Harcourt Brace Jovanovich, 1977.

Clark, Terry N. Introduction to *On Communication and Social Influence,* by Gabriel Tarde. Edited by Clark, 1–69. Chicago: U of Chicago P, 1969.

Connolly, William. "Taylor, Foucault, and Otherness." *Political Theory* 13 (August 1985).

Copeland, Carolyn Faunce. *Language and Time and Gertrude Stein.* Iowa City: U of Iowa P, 1975.

Cordasco, Francesco. *Dictionary of American Immigration History.* Metuchen, N.J.: Scarecrow, 1990.

Cowley, Malcolm. "Gertrude Stein, Writer or Word Scientist?" Review of *Selected Writings of Gertrude Stein,* by Gertrude Stein. In Curnutt, 147–50. Originally published in *New York Herald-Tribune Weekly Book Review,* 24 November 1946.

Crawford, John W. "Incitement to Riot." Review of *Geography and Plays,* by Gertrude Stein. In Curnutt, 26–27. Originally published in *New York Call,* 19 August 1923.

"Curious Fiction Study." Review of *Three Lives,* by Gertrude Stein. In Curnutt, 11–12. Originally published in *Chicago Record Herald,* 22 January 1910.

Curnutt, Kirk, ed. *The Critical Response to Gertrude Stein.* Westport, Conn.: Greenwood, 2000.

Davis, Phoebe Stein. "'Even Cake Gets to Have Another Meaning': History, Narrative, and 'Daily Living' in Gertrude Stein's World War II Writings." *Modern Fiction Studies* 44.3 (1998): 568–607.

de Beaugrande, Robert. "Discourse Analysis." In *The Johns Hopkins Guide to Literary Theory and Criticism*, ed. Michael Groden and Martin Kreiswirth, 207–10. Baltimore: Johns Hopkins UP, 1994.

DeKoven, Marianne. *A Different Language: Gertrude Stein's Experimental Writing*. Madison: U of Wisconsin P, 1983.

———. "Introduction: Transformations of Gertrude Stein." *Modern Fiction Studies* 42.3 (fall 1996): 469–83.

———. *Rich and Strange: Gender, History, Modernism*. Princeton: Princeton UP, 1991.

DeLillo, Don. *White Noise*. New York: Penguin, 1986.

Dewey, John. *Democracy and Education: An Introduction to the Philosophy of Education*. New York: Macmillan, 1916.

———. *Experience and Nature*. 1929. Reprint, New York: Dover, 1958.

Dodge, Mabel. "Speculations, or Post-Impressionism in Prose." In Curnutt, 151–54. Originally published in *Art and Decoration*, March 1913.

Dodge Luhan, Mabel, and Gertrude Stein. *A History of Having a Great Many Times Not Continued to Be Friends: Mabel Dodge and Gertrude Stein, 1911–1934*. Edited by Patricia R. Everett. Albuquerque: U of New Mexico P, 1996

Donne, John. "The Canonization." In *The Complete English Poems*, 47–48. London: Penguin, 1971.

Dorr, Rheta Childe. *Susan B. Anthony: The Woman Who Changed the Mind of a Nation*. New York: Frederick A. Stokes, 1928.

Dos Passos, John. *U.S.A.* New York: Modern Library, 1937.

Douglas, Ann. *Terrible Honesty: Mongrel Manhattan in the 1920s*. New York: Farrar, 1995.

Dryden, John. *Selected Poetry and Prose of John Dryden*. Edited by Earl Miner. New York: Modern Library, 1985.

Dubnick, Randa. *The Structure of Obscurity: Gertrude Stein, Language, and Cubism*. Urbana: U of Illinois P, 1984.

Duffy, John. *The Healers: The Rise of the Medical Establishment*. New York: McGraw-Hill, 1976.

Dydo, Ulla E., ed. *"Stanzas in Meditation*: The Other Biography." *Chicago Review* 35. 2 (1985): 4–20.

———. *A Stein Reader*. Evanston, Ill.: Northwestern UP, 1993.

Eagleson, Harvey. "Gertrude Stein: Method in Madness." *Sewanee Review Quarterly* 44.2 (April–June 1936): 164–77.

Eliot, T. S. "Charleston, Hey! Hey!" *Nation and Athenaeum* 29 (January 1927): 595.

———. "Tradition and the Individual Talent." In *Selected Prose of T. S. Eliot*. Edited by Frank Kermode. New York: Harcourt Brace Jovanovich, 1975.

Ellul, Jacques. *Propaganda: The Formation of Men's Attitudes*. Translated by Konrad Kellen and Jean Lerner. New York: Knopf, 1968.

Elson, Ruth Miller. *Guardians of Tradition: American Schoolbooks of the Nineteenth Century*. Lincoln: U of Nebraska P, 1964.

Faÿ, Bernard. "A Rose Is a Rose." Review of *The Autobiography of Alice B. Toklas*, by Gertrude Stein. In Curnutt, 55–63. Originally published in *Saturday Review of Literature*, 2 September 1933.

Fetterley, Judith. *The Resisting Reader: A Feminist Approach to American Fiction*. Bloomington: Indiana UP, 1978.

Fifer, Elizabeth. *Rescued Readings: A Reconstruction of Gertrude Stein's Difficult Texts.* Detroit: Wayne State UP, 1992.

Fitzgerald, F. Scott. *Tender Is the Night.* 1934. New York: Scribner's, 1995.

Flanner, Janet. "Frame for Some Portraits." Foreword to *Two: Gertrude Stein and Her Brother and Other Early Portraits, 1908–1912,* ix-xvii. New Haven: Yale UP, 1951.

Foucault, Michel. *The Order of Things: An Archaeology of the Human Sciences.* New York: Vintage, 1994.

Franken, Claudia. *Gertrude Stein: Writer and Thinker.* Münster: Lit. Verlag, 2000.

Frankenberg, Lloyd. "On First Meeting *Mrs. Reynolds.*" In *Mrs. Reynolds and Five Earlier Novelettes,* by Gertrude Stein, v-xii. New Haven: Yale UP, 1952.

Frieling, Kenneth. "The Becoming of Gertrude Stein's *The Making of Americans.*" In *The Twenties: Fiction, Poetry, Drama,* ed. Warren French, 157–70. DeLand, Fla: Everett/Edwards, 1975.

Frost, Robert. *The Poetry of Robert Frost.* Edited by Edward Connery Lathem. New York: Holt, Rinehart and Winston, 1969.

"A Futurist Novel." Review of *Three Lives,* by Gertrude Stein. In Curnutt, 12–13. Originally published in *Philadelphia Public Ledger,* 10 April 1915.

"Gertrude Stein in Critical French Eyes." In Curnutt, 32–34. Originally published in *Literary Digest,* 6 February 1926.

Gilbert, Sandra M., and Susan Gubar. *The Madwoman in the Attic: The Woman Writer and the Nineteenth-Century Literary Imagination.* New Haven: Yale UP, 1984.

Goody, Jack. "Alternative Paths to Knowledge in Oral and Literate Cultures." In *Spoken and Written Language: Exploring Orality and Literacy,* ed. Deborah Tannen, 201–15. Norwood, N.J.: Ablex, 1982.

Gopnick, Adam. "Orange and White," Talk of the Town, *New Yorker,* 3 March 2003, 31.

Gordon, Bertram M., ed. *Historical Dictionary of World War II France: The Occupation, Vichy, and the Resistance, 1938–1946.* Westport, Conn.: Greenwood, 1998.

Gross, Elizabeth. "The Body of Signification." In *Abjection, Melancholia, and Love: The Work of Julia Kristeva,* ed. John Fletcher and Andrew Benjamin, 80–103. London: Routledge, 1990.

Hackney, Sheldon. *One America Indivisible: A National Conversation on American Pluralism and Identity.* National Endowment for the Humanities, n.d. (between 1997 and 2000).

———. "Toward a National Conversation." *Responsive Community* 4.3 (summer 1994): 9.

Harvey, A. McGehee, Gert H. Brieger, Susan L. Abrams, and Victor A. McKusick. *A Model of Its Kind: A Centennial History of Medicine at Johns Hopkins.* Baltimore: Johns Hopkins UP, 1989.

Hasselback, Ingo, and Tom Reiss. "How Nazis Are Made." *New Yorker,* 8 January 1996, 36–57.

Hemingway, Ernest. *The Sun Also Rises.* 1926. New York: Scribner's, 1970.

Heritage, John. *Garfinkel and Ethnomethodology.* Cambridge: Polity, 1984.

Hermans, Hubert J. M., and Harry J. G. Kempen. *The Dialogical Self: Meaning as Movement.* San Diego: Academic, 1993.

Hobhouse, Janet. *Everybody Who Was Anybody: A Biography of Gertrude Stein.* New York: Doubleday, 1975.

Hoffman, Michael J. *Critical Essays on Gertrude Stein.* Boston: Hall, 1986.

———. *The Development of Abstractionism in the Writings of Gertrude Stein.* Philadelphia: U of Pennsylvania P, 1965.

———. *Gertrude Stein.* Boston: Twayne, 1976.

———. "Gertrude Stein and William James." *The Personalist: An International Review of Philosophy, Religion, and Literature* 47.2 (spring 1966): 226–33.

Hubly, Erlene. "Gertrude Stein: "When this you see, remember me . . ."" *North American Review,* September 1986, 65–74.

Irigaray, Luce. *This Sex Which Is Not One.* Translated by Catherine Porter. Ithaca, N.Y.: Cornell UP, 1985.

James, Henry. *The Portrait of a Lady.* 1881. New York: Signet, 1979.

James, William. "The Hidden Self." In *A William James Reader,* ed. Gay Wilson Allen, 90–108. Boston: Houghton, 1971.

———. *Pragmatism and Other Essays.* 1907, 1909, 1896. Reprint, New York: Washington Square, 1968.

———. *The Principles of Psychology.* 1890. 3 vols. Edited by Frederick H. Burkhardt. Cambridge: Harvard UP, 1981.

———. "Remarks on Spencer's Definition of Mind as Correspondent." In *A William James Reader,* ed. Gay Wilson Allen, 3–15. Boston: Houghton, 1971.

Jameson, Fredric. *Prison-house of Language: A Critical Account of Structuralism and Russian Formalism.* Princeton: Princeton UP, 1972.

Jay, Martin. *The Dialectical Imagination: A History of the Frankfurt School and the Institute of Social Research, 1923–1950.* Boston: Little, Brown, 1973.

Jones, Colin. *The Cambridge Illustrated History of France.* Cambridge: Cambridge UP, 1994.

Jonson, Ben. "Epigrams." In *Poems,* ed. Ian Donaldson, 1–84. London: Oxford UP, 1975.

Kadlec, David. *Mosaic Modernism: Anarchism, Pragmatism, Culture.* Baltimore: Johns Hopkins UP, 2000.

Kahnweiler, Daniel-Henry. Introduction to *Painted Lace and Other Pieces [1914–1937],* by Gertrude Stein, ix–xviii. New Haven: Yale, 1955.

Kammen, Michael. *Mystic Chords of Memory: The Transformation of Tradition in American Culture.* New York: Vintage Books, 1993.

Katz, Leon. "The First Making of *The Making of Americans*: A Study Based on Her Notebooks and Early Versions of Her Novel (1902–1908)." Ph.D. diss., Columbia U, 1963.

———. "Weininger and *The Making of Americans.*" *Twentieth Century Literature* 24.1 (spring 1978): 8–26.

Kaufman-Osborn, Timothy V. *Politics/Sense/Experience: A Pragmatic Inquiry into the Promise of Democracy.* Ithaca, N.Y.: Cornell UP, 1991.

Kedward, H. R. *In Search of the Maquis: Rural Resistance in Southern France, 1942–1944.* Oxford: Clarendon, 1993.

———. *Resistance in Vichy France: A Study of Ideas and Motivations in the Southern Zone, 1940–1942.* Oxford: Oxford UP, 1978.

Kennedy, Alan. *The Psychology of Reading.* London: Methuen, 1984.

Keyser, Antoine. "Introduction to Carl Wernicke." In *Reader in the History of Aphasia: From Gall to Geschwind,* ed. Paul Eling, 63–68. Amsterdam: John Benjamins, 1994.

Koestenbaum, Wayne. "Stein Is Nice." *Parnassus: Poetry in Review* 20.1–2 (1995): 297–319.

Kristeva, Julia. *Powers of Horror: An Essay on Abjection.* Translated by Leon S. Roudiez. New York: Columbia UP, 1982.

Krutch, Joseph Wood. "A Prepare for Saints." Review of *Four Saints in Three Acts,* by Gertrude Stein. In Curnutt, 74–76. Originally published in *The Nation,* 4 April 1934.

Lehman, David. *Signs of the Times: Deconstruction and the Fall of Paul de Man.* New York: Poseidon, 1992.

Leonhirth, William J. "William James and the Uncertain Universe." In *American Pragmatism and Communication Research,* ed. David K. Perry, 89–110. Mahwah, N.J.: Lawrence Erlbaum Associates, 2001.

Lerman, Leo. "A Wonderchild for 72 Years." Review of *Selected Writings of Gertrude Stein,* by Gertrude Stein. In Curnutt, 143–46. Originally published in *Saturday Review,* 2 November 1946.

Lesinska, Zofia P. *Perspectives of Four Women Writers on the Second World War: Gertrude Stein, Janet Flanner, Kay Boyle, and Rebecca West.* New York: Peter Lang, 2002.

Lewis, Sinclair. *Main Street.* New York: Harcourt, 1980.

Liebling, A. J., ed. *The Republic of Silence.* New York: Harcourt, 1947.

Loy, Mina. *The Lost Lunar Baedeker.* Edited by Roger L. Conover. New York: Noonday, 1996.

Ludmerer, Kenneth M. *Learning to Heal: The Development of American Medical Education.* New York: Basic Books, 1985.

Lynd, Robert S., and Helen Merrell Lynd. *Middletown: A Study in Modern American Culture.* 1929. Reprint, San Diego: Harcourt, 1957.

Malcolm, Janet. "Gertrude Stein's War: The Years in Occupied France." *New Yorker,* 2 June 2003, 58–81.

Mall, Franklin Paine. "The Anatomical Course and Laboratory of the Johns Hopkins University." *Bulletin of the Johns Hopkins Hospital* 7 (1896).

Mandelstam, Nadezhda. *Hope against Hope: A Memoir.* Translated by Max Hayward. New York: Atheneum, 1970.

Marcuse, Herbert. *One-Dimensional Man: Studies in the Ideology of Advanced Industrial Society.* 1964. Reprint, with an introduction by Douglas Kellner. Boston: Beacon, 1991.

Martin, Robert K. "*The Mother of Us All* and American History." In *Gertrude Stein and the Making of Literature,* ed. Shirley Neuman, 210–22. Houndmills, Eng.: Macmillan, 1988.

McCarthy, Thomas. Introduction to *The Theory of Communicative Action,* by Jurgen Habermas, vol. 1, *Reason and the Rationalization of Society.* Boston: Beacon, 1981.

McLuhan, Marshall. *The Gutenberg Galaxy: The Making of Typographic Man.* Toronto: U of Toronto P, 1962.

Mead, George Herbert. "The Social Self." 1913. In *Selected Writings,* ed. Andrew J. Reck, 142–49. Indianapolis: Bobbs-Merrill, 1964.

———. *Mind, Self, and Society from the Standpoint of a Social Behaviorist.* 1934. Edited by Charles W. Morris. Chicago: U of Chicago P, 1962.

Mellow, James R. *Charmed Circle: Gertrude Stein and Company.* New York: Avon, 1975.

Menand, Louis. "The Devil's Disciples." Review of *Dictators, Democracy, and American Public Culture,* by Benjamin Alpers. *New Yorker,* 28 July 2003, 83–87.

———. *The Metaphysical Club.* New York: Farrar, Straus and Giroux, 2001.

Mencken, H. L. "A Cubist Treatise." Review of *Tender Buttons,* by Gertrude Stein. In Curnutt, 14–15. Originally published in *Baltimore Sun,* 6 June 1914.

Meyer, Steven. *Irresistible Dictation: Gertrude Stein and the Correlations of Writing and Science.* Stanford, Calif.: Stanford UP, 2001.

———. "Writing Psychology Over: Gertrude Stein and William James." *Yale Journal of Criticism* 8 (1995): 133–63.

Miller, Rosalind S. *Gertrude Stein: Form and Intelligibility.* New York: Exposition, 1949.

Moerman, Michael. *Talking Culture: Ethnography and Conversation Analysis.* Philadelphia: U of Pennsylvania P, 1988.

Moore, George B. *Gertrude Stein's* The Making of Americans: *Repetition and the Emergence of Modernism.* New York: Peter Lang, 1998.

Moore, Marianne. *The Complete Poems of Marianne Moore.* New York: Macmillan, 1986.

Morrow, Elizabeth. *"All Gaul Is Divided": Letters from Occupied France.* New York: Greystone, 1941.

Morson, Gary Saul, and Caryl Emerson. "M. M. Bakhtin." In *The Johns Hopkins Guide to Literary Theory and Criticism,* ed. Michael Groden and Martin Kreiswirth, 63–68. Baltimore: Johns Hopkins UP, 1994.

Mullen, Harryette. *Trimmings.* New York: Tender Buttons, 1991.

O'Grady, William, Michael Dobrovolsky, and Mark Aronoff. *Contemporary Linguistics: An Introduction.* 2d edition. New York: St. Martin's, 1993.

Ong, Walter J. *Orality and Literacy: The Technologizing of the Word.* London: Methuen, 1982.

Orwell, George. "Politics and the English Language" In *The Orwell Reader: Fiction, Essays, and Reportage by George Orwell,* 355–66. New York: Harcourt, 1956.

———. "Politics vs. Literature: An Examination of *Gulliver's Travels.*" In *The Orwell Reader: Fiction, Essays, and Reportage by George Orwell,* 283–300. New York: Harcourt, 1956.

———. "The Prevention of Literature." In *The Orwell Reader: Fiction, Essays, and Reportage by George Orwell,* 367–79. New York: Harcourt, 1956.

Parker, Ian. "Absolute Powerpoint: Can a Software Package Edit Our Thoughts?" *New Yorker.* 28 May 2001, 76–87.

Pepys, Samuel. Excerpts from *The Diary of Samuel Pepys.* In *Eighteenth-Century English Literature,* ed. Geoffrey Tillotson, Paul Fussell, Jr., and Marshall Waingrow. San Diego: Harcourt Brace Jovanovich, 1969.

Perloff, Marjorie. *Wittgenstein's Ladder: Poetic Language and the Strangeness of the Ordinary.* Chicago: U of Chicago P, 1996.

Phillips, K. J. "Ladies' Voices in Donald Barthelme's *The Dead Father* and Gertrude Stein's Dialogues." *International Fiction Review* 12.1 (winter 1985): 34–37.

Pitkin, Hannah. *Fortune Is a Woman.* Berkeley: U of California P, 1984.

Pondrom, Cyrena N. "An Introduction to the Achievement of Gertrude Stein." In *Geography and Plays,* by Gertrude Stein, vii–lv. Madison: U of Wisconsin P, 1993.

Posnock, Ross. *The Trial of Curiosity: Henry James, William James, and the Challenge of Modernity.* New York: Oxford UP, 1991.

Postman, Neil. *Amusing Ourselves to Death: Public Discourse in the Age of Show Business.* New York: Penguin, 1986.

———. *Conscientious Objections: Stirring Up Trouble about Language, Technology, and Education.* New York: Knopf, 1988.

———. *Technopoly: The Surrender of Culture to Technology.* New York: Vintage, 1993.

Postman, Neil, and Charles Weingartner. *Teaching as a Subversive Activity.* New York: Delacorte, 1969.

Preminger, Alex, ed. *Princeton Encyclopedia of Poetry and Poetics.* Princeton: Princeton UP, 1974.

Preston, John Hyde. "A Conversation with Gertrude Stein." In *Gertrude Stein Remembered,* ed. Linda Simon, 153–65. Lincoln: U of Nebraska P, 1994.

Putnam, Hillary. "The Permanence of William James." In *Pragmatism: An Open Question,* 5–26. Oxford: Blackwell, 1995.

———. "Was Wittgenstein a Pragmatist?" In *Pragmatism,* 27–56. Oxford: Blackwell, 1995.

Pychon, Thomas. *The Crying of Lot 49.* 1965. Reprint, New York: Perennial Classics, 1999.

Quintilian. *Quintilian on the Teaching of Speaking and Writing: Translations from Books One, Two, and Ten of the Institutio Oratoria.* Edited by James J. Murphy. Translated by John Selby Watson. Carbondale: Southern Illinois UP, 1987.

Rabaté, Jean-Michel. "Roland Barthes." In *The Johns Hopkins Guide to Literary Theory and Criticism,* ed. Michael Groden and Martin Kreiswirth, 68–73. Baltimore: Johns Hopkins UP, 1994.

Richardson, John. *A Life of Picasso: Volume 1, 1881–1906.* New York: Random House, 1991.

Rieke, Alison. *The Senses of Nonsense.* Iowa City: U of Iowa P, 1992.

Rogers, Robert Emons. "New Outbreaks of Futurism: *Tender Buttons,* Curious Experiment of Gertrude Stein in Literary Anarchy." Review of *Tender Buttons,* by Gertrude Stein. In Curnutt, 18–21. Originally published in *Boston Evening Transcript,* 11 July 1914.

Rogers, W. G. *When This You See Remember Me: Gertrude Stein in Person.* New York: Rinehart, 1948.

Rorty, Richard. *Contingency, Irony, and Solidarity.* Cambridge: Cambridge UP, 1989.

———. *Philosophy and Social Hope.* London: Penguin, 1999.

Rothstein, William G. *American Medical Schools and the Practice of Medicine: A History.* New York: Oxford UP, 1987.

Ruddick, Lisa. *Reading Gertrude Stein: Body, Text, Gnosis.* Ithaca, N.Y.: Cornell UP, 1990.

———. "William James and the Modernism of Gertrude Stein." In *Modernism Reconsidered,* ed. Robert Kiely, 47–63. Cambridge: Harvard UP, 1983.

Ryan, Betsy Alayne. *Gertrude Stein's Theatre of the Absolute.* Ann Arbor, Mich.: UMI Research P, 1984.

Sacks, Harvey. *Lectures on Conversation.* 2 vols. Edited by Gail Jefferson. Oxford: Blackwell, 1992.

Sartre, Jean-Paul. "The Republic of Silence." In *The Republic of Silence,* 498–500. Edited by A. J. Liebling. Translated by Ramon Guthrie. New York: Harcourt, 1947.

Sawyer, R. Keith. *Improvised Dialogues: Emergence and Creativity in Conversation.* Westport, Conn.: Ablex, 2003.

Schegloff, Emanuel A. Introduction to *Lectures on Conversation,* by Harvey Sacks, ed. Gail Jefferson, ix–lxii. Oxford: Blackwell, 1992.

Scollon, Ron, and Suzanne B. K. Scollon. "Cooking It Up and Boiling It Down: Abstracts in Athabaskan Children's Story Retellings." In *Coherence in Spoken and Written Discourse,* ed. Deborah Tannen, 173–97. Norwood, N.J.: Ablex, 1984.

Sevareid, Eric. *Not So Wild a Dream.* New York: Atheneum, 1976.

Shakespeare, William. *Hamlet, Prince of Denmark.* Edited by Philip Edwards. Cambridge: Cambridge UP, 1995.

———. *Macbeth.* Edited by David Bevington. New York: Bantam, 1988.

"The Shape of Things." *Nation,* 10 August 1946, 142–43.

Shepherd, Gregory J. "Pragmatism and Tragedy, Communication and Hope: A Summary Story." In *American Pragmatism and Communication Research,* ed. David K. Perry, 241–54. Mahwah, N.J.: Lawrence Erlbaum Associates, 2001.

Shuler, Sherianne, and Melissa Tate. "Intersections of Feminism and Pragmatism: Possibilities for Communication Theory and Research." In *American Pragmatism and Communication Research*, ed. David K. Perry, 209–24. Mahwah, N.J.: Lawrence Erlbaum Associates, 2001.

Silverman, David. *Harvey Sacks: Social Science and Conversation Analysis*. New York: Oxford UP, 1998.

Simon, Linda. Introduction to *Gertrude Stein Remembered*, ed. Simon, ix–xv. Lincoln: U of Nebraska P, 1994.

Simonson, Peter. "Varieties of Pragmatism and Communication: Visions and Revisions from Peirce to Peters." In *American Pragmatism and Communication Research*, ed. David K. Perry, 1–26. Mahwah, N.J.: Lawrence Erlbaum Associates, 2001.

Sitwell, Edith. "Miss Stein's Stories." Review of *Geography and Plays*, by Gertrude Stein. In Curnutt, 25–26. Originally published in *The Nation and the Anthenœum*, 14 July 1923.

Skinner, B. F. "Has Gertrude Stein a Secret?" *Atlantic*, January 1934, 50–57.

Smith, Harrison. "A Rose for Remembrance." *Saturday Review of Literature*, 10 August 1946, 11.

Smollett, Tobias. *The Expedition of Humphry Clinker*. Oxford: Oxford UP, 1991.

Souhami, Diana. *Gertrude and Alice*. London: Pandora, 1991.

Spenser, Edmund. "The Faerie Queene." In *Edmund Spenser's Poetry*, ed. Hugh Maclean, 1–398. New York: Norton, 1968.

Steiner, Wendy. "Mother." *London Review of Books*. 19 October 1995, 23–24.

"Stein's Way." *Time*. 11 September 1933, 57–60.

Stendhal, Renate. *Gertrude Stein in Words and Pictures: A Photobiography*. Chapel Hill: Algonquin, 1994.

Steward, Samuel M. *Chapters from an Autobiography*. San Francisco: Grey Fox, 1981.

———. *Murder is Murder is Murder*. Boston: Alyson Publications, 1985.

———. *Parisian Lives*. New York: St. Martin's, 1984.

Stewart, Allegra. *Gertrude Stein and the Present*. Cambridge: Harvard UP, 1967.

Sutherland, Donald. *Gertrude Stein: A Biography of Her Work*. New Haven: Yale UP, 1951.

Swerdlow, Joel L. "Information Revolution." *National Geographic*, October 1995, 5–37.

Tannen, Deborah. *The Argument Culture: Stopping America's War of Words*. New York: Ballantine Books, 1999.

———. "The Oral/Literate Continuum in Discourse." In *Spoken and Written Language: Exploring Orality and Literacy*, ed. Deborah Tannen, 1–16. Norwood, N.J.: Ablex, 1982.

Tarde, Gabriel. "Opinion and Conversation." 1898. In *On Communication and Social Influence*, ed. Terry N. Clark, 297–318. Chicago: U of Chicago P, 1969.

———. "The Public and the Crowd." 1901. In *On Communication and Social Influence*, ed. Terry N. Clark, 277–94. Chicago: U of Chicago P, 1969.

Terkel, Studs. *Working: People Talk about What They Do All Day and How They Feel about What They Do*. 1972. Reprint, New York: Pantheon Books, 1974.

Thayer, William Sydney. *Osler and Other Papers*. Baltimore: Johns Hopkins UP, 1931.

Toklas, Alice B. *The Alice B. Toklas Cookbook*. New York: Harper, 1954.

———. *What Is Remembered*. New York: Holt, Rinehart and Winston, 1963.

Tomiche, Anne. "Repetition: Memory and Oblivion. Freud, Duras, and Stein." *Revue de Littérature Comparée* 65.3 (July–September 1991): 261–76.

Townshend, Pete. "Won't Get Fooled Again." on *Who's Next*, 1971.

U.S. Bureau of the Census. *Historical Statistics of the United States: Colonial Times to 1970, Bicentennial Edition, Part 1*. Washington D.C., 1975.

Van Dusen, Wanda. "Portrait of a National Fetish: Gertrude Stein's 'Introduction to the Speeches of Marechal Pétain' (1942)." *Modernism/Modernity* 3.3 (September 1996): 69–92.

Van Vechten, Carl, "How Many Acts Are There in It?" Introduction to *Last Operas and Plays*, by Gertrude Stein, vii–xix. New York: Rinehart, 1949.

———. "How To Read Gertrude Stein." In Curnutt, 154–58. Originally published in *Trend*, August 1914.

———. *Peter Whiffle: His Life and Works*. New York: Knopf, 1922.

———, ed. *Selected Writings of Gertrude Stein*. 1945. Reprint, New York: Vintage, 1962.

Wagner-Martin, Linda. *"Favored Strangers": Gertrude Stein and Her Family*. Totowa, N.J.: Rutgers UP, 1995.

Wald, Priscilla. *Constituting Americans: Cultural Anxiety and Narrative Form*. Durham, N.C.: Duke UP, 1995.

Walker, Jayne L. "History as Repetition: *The Making of Americans*." In *Gertrude Stein*, ed. Harold Bloom, 177–99. New York: Chelsea, 1986.

Watson, Dana Cairns. "'Oh Say What You See': The Conversational Structures and Liberating Senses in Gertrude Stein's Poetry, Plays, and Prose." Ph.D. diss., UCLA, 1996. UMI # 9711582.

Watson, Steven. *Prepare for Saints: Gertrude Stein, Virgil Thomson, and the Mainstreaming of American Modernism*. New York: Random House, 1998.

Watts, Linda S. *Gertrude Stein: A Study of the Short Fiction*. New York: Twayne, 1999.

———. *Rapture Untold: Gender, Mysticism, and the "Moment of Recognition" in Works by Gertrude Stein*. New York: Peter Lang, 1996.

Wernicke, Carl. "The Aphasia Symptom-Complex: A Psychological Study on an Anatomical Basis." 1874. In *Reader in the History of Aphasia: From Gall to Geschwind*, ed. Paul Eling, 69–98. Amsterdam: John Benjamins, 1994.

White, Ray Lewis. *Gertrude Stein and Alice B. Toklas: A Reference Guide*. Boston: G. K. Hall, 1984.

———, ed. *Sherwood Anderson / Gertrude Stein: Correspondence and Personal Essays*. Chapel Hill: U of North Carolina P, 1972.

Whittier-Ferguson, John. "Stein in Time: History, Manuscripts, and Memory." *Modernism/Modernity* 6.1 (1999): 115–51.

Wilder, Thornton. "Gertrude Stein's *The Geographical History of America*." In *American Characteristics and Other Essays*, by Thornton Wilder, 187–92. Edited by Donald Gallup. New York: Harper and Row, 1979.

Williams, William Carlos. "Asphodel, That Greeny Flower: Book 1." In *The William Carlos Williams Reader*, ed. M. L. Rosenthal. New York: New Directions, 1966.

———. "The Work of Gertrude Stein." *Pagany* 1.1 (January–March 1930): 41–45.

Wilson, Edmund. "Gertrude Stein." In Hoffman, *Critical Essays*, 58–62. Excerpt from *Axel's Castle*, by Wilson, originally published New York: Charles Scribner's Sons, 1931.

Winders, James A. "Karl Marx and Friedrich Engels." In *The Johns Hopkins Guide to Literary Theory and Criticism*, ed. Michael Groden and Martin Kreiswirth, 486–91. Baltimore: Johns Hopkins UP, 1994.

Wineapple, Brenda. *Sister Brother: Gertrude and Leo Stein.* New York: Putnam, 1996.

Winston, Elizabeth. "Making History in 'The Mother of Us All.'" *Mosaic* (Winnipeg, Man.) 20.4 (fall 1987): 117–29.

Winter, Ella. "Gertrude Stein Comma." Review of *Lectures in America,* by Gertrude Stein. In Curnutt, 82–85. Originally published in *Pacific Weekly,* 12 April 1935.

Wittgenstein, Ludwig. *Culture and Value.* Edited by G. H. von Wright in collaboration with Heikki Nyman. Translated by Peter Winch. Chicago: U of Chicago P, 1980.

Wittke, Carl F. *We Who Built America: The Saga of the Immigrant.* Ann Arbor, Mich.: P of Western Reserve U, 1939.

Wright, Richard. Review of *Wars I Have Seen. PM,* 11 March 1945.

Yaeger, Patricia. "Toward a Feminine Sublime." In *Gender and Theory: Dialogues on Feminist Criticism,* ed. Linda Kauffman, 191–211. New York: Blackwell, 1989.

Young, John Wesley. *Totalitarian Language: Orwell's Newspeak and Its Nazi and Communist Antecedents.* Charlottesville: UP of Virginia, 1991.

Young, Stark. "One Moment Alit." Review of *Four Saints in Three Acts,* by Gertrude Stein. In Hoffman, *Critical Essays,* 71–73. Originally published in *New Republic,* 3 July 1934.

Zurif, Edgar. "Language and the Brain." In *Language: An Invitation to Cognitive Psychology.* Vol. 1, ed. Daniel N. Osherson and Howard Lasnik. Cambridge: MIT P, 1990.

NEWS ARTICLES RELEVANT TO STEIN'S
1934–1935 LECTURE TOUR

"4 Saints in 3 Acts 1 of Many." *New York Sun,* 16 November 1934.

"About Gertrude Stein." Editorial. *Cleveland Press,* 21 December 1934.

Allen, Lester. "Miss Stein Likes Things Cubical." *Boston Post,* 20 November 1934.

Alsop, Joseph W., Jr. "Gertrude Stein Likes to Look at Paintings." *New York Herald Tribune,* 2 November 1934.

———. "Gertrude Stein Says Children Understand Her." *New York Herald Tribune,* 3 November 1934.

Beck, Clyde. "Gertrude Stein Explains Theory of 'Seeing Things.'" *Detroit News,* 13 December 1934.

Boardman, Frances. "Few Lucidities Found Hiding in Stein Lecture." *St. Paul* (Minn.) *Pioneer Press,* 9 December 1934.

Bower, Helen C. "Miss Stein Tells Everything: Detroit Seems to Understand." *Detroit Free Press,* 13 December 1934.

Brickell, Herschel. "Books on Our Table." *New York Post,* 22 November 1934.

Buchalter, Helen. "Gertrude Stein Doesn't 'Take from' Causes, She Tells an Ardent Reformist." *Washington Daily News,* 31 December 1934.

"But a Stein Is a Stein Is a Stein." Review of *Portraits and Prayers. New York Times,* 18 November 1934.

Butcher, Fanny. "English Letters to Flower Next in U.S.: Gertrude Stein." *Chicago Daily Tribune,* 26 November 1934.

Chamberlain, John. "Books of the Times." *New York Times,* 7 November 1934, 19.

Davidson, Grace. "Radcliffe Laughs." *Boston Post,* 20 November 1934.

Deene, Dian. Letter to the editor. *New York Sun,* 22 November 1934.

"The Devoted Band." Editorial. *New York Times,* 3 November 1934.

The Dowager. "Gertrude Stein Makes Address at the Arts Club." *Chicago Herald and Examiner*, 26 November 1934.

Dush, Sarah L. "Gertrude Stein Is Here Is Here Here Is." *Ohio State Journal*, 18 December 1934.

"Einstein 'Explains' Theories to Reporters." *Washington, D.C., Sunday Star*, 30 December 1934.

"Elite Fete Fete Elite Miss Stein." *New York Evening Journal*, 17 November 1934.

Evans, A. Judson. "Gertrude Tells All about All but Audience Just Can't Take It." *Richmond Times Dispatch*, 7 February 1935.

"Fancy Writing: Fine If You Like It." Editorial. *New York Evening Journal*, 30 October 1934.

Fessenden, Donald. "Gertrude Stein Too Much for Harvard and Radcliffe; She Wonders If It Is Necessary to Stand Still to Live." *Boston Herald*, 20 November 1934.

Flutterbye, Mme. "Gertrude Stein Attracts Fashionables." *New York Evening Journal*, 17 November 1934.

Frey, Virginia. Letter to the editor, *Chicago Daily Tribune*, 14 March 1935.

"Frying Pan into Palalia." Editorial. *New York Times*, 1 December 1934.

Gannett, Lewis. "Books and Things." *New York Herald Tribune*, 7 November 1934.

Genauer, Emily. "Gertrude Stein, It Seems, Likes to Look at Pictures." *New York World-Telegram*, 2 November 1934.

"Gertrude Stein Arrives and Baffles Reporters by Making Herself Clear." *New York Times*, 25 October 1934.

"Gertrude Stein Baffles Radcliffe; Harvard Understands Informal Talk." *Boston Evening Press*, 20 November 1934.

"Gertrude Stein Discusses Art." *New York Sun*, 2 November 1934.

"Gertrude Stein Explains Work." *Birmingham News*, 17 February 1935.

"Gertrude Stein Home, Upholds Her Simplicity." *New York Herald Tribune*, 25 October 1934.

"Gertrude Stein in Greenwich." *New York Times*, 3 November 1934, sec. 2.

"Gertrude Stein, Noted Writer, Speaks Here Today." *Virginia Gazette*, 8 February 1935.

"Gertrude Stein Speaks on Art to D.C. Guests." *Washington Post*, 30 December 1934.

"Gertrude Stein Talks before College Group." *Virginia Gazette*, 15 February 1935.

"Gertrude Stein Tells Paris She Is 'Wed to America.'" *New York Times*, 13 May 1935.

"Gertrude Stein, Visitor in City, Explores Archives at Foster Hall." *Indianapolis News*, 17 December 1934.

"Gertrude Stein Will Speak on Paintings before Chicago Women's Club." *Chicago Herald and Examiner*, 25 November 1934.

Gilbreth, Frank B. "Gertrude Stein Talks on Nouns." *Charleston News and Courier*, 14 February 1935.

Grey, James C. "Books This Week." *New York Sun*, 2 November 1934.

Guest, Edgar. "Love and a Passing Fancy." *New York Evening Journal*, 30 October 1934.

Hansen, Harry. "The First Reader." *New York World-Telegram*, 5 November 1934.

———. "No Stein Song by First Reader." *New York World-Telegram*, 8 November 1934.

Henry, Thomas R. "Brows of Great Minds Pucker as Einstein Proves His Theory." *Washington, D.C., Evening Star*, 29 December 1934.

Jackson, Joseph Henry. "A Bookman's Notebook." Editorial. *San Francisco Chronicle*, 13 April 1935.

Jewell, Edward Alden. "The Realm of Art: Sounds of Firing on Many Fronts." *New York Times*, 3 March 1935.

Jones, Melissa. "Gertrude Stein Speaks of 'Poetry and Grammar' at Lecture Wednesday." *Columbus Evening Dispatch*, 18 December 1934.

Kennedy, Kenneth R., and Morris H. Rubin. "It Took Two Hardy Men to Do This, Reader; You'd Better Call for Help." *Wisconsin State Journal*, 7 December 1934.

Kennedy, Paul. "Gertrude Stein and Boxing Show in One Evening Leave Reporter Punch Drunk." *Toledo News-Bee*, 20 December 1934.

Kirnon, Hodge. Letter to the editor. *New York Times*, 2 November 1934.

Knoblock, K. T. "'Oils on Flat Surfaces' Are Pleasing to Gertrude Stein." *New Orleans Item*, 20 February 1935.

Laird, Donald A. "Science Explains Gertrude Stein's Word Puzzles." *Washington Herald's American Weekly*, 30 December 1934.

Laurie, Annie. "Sound and Fury—La Stein Speaks." *San Francisco Examiner*, 13 April 1935.

Lawner, Rhoda. Letter to the editor. *New York Sun*, 26 November 1934.

L.B.W. Letter to the Editor. *New York Sun*, 3 December 1934.

Liebling, A. J. "Gertrude Stein Interprets as Poetry is Wed to Music." *New York World-Telegram*, 16 November 1934.

"Literary Enigma in Truth Proves Real Friendly." *Boston Daily Globe*, 20 November 1934.

"Literary Snobbery." Editorial. *New York Times*, 6 February 1935.

"Made Herself Understood." Editorial. *New York Times*, 26 October 1934.

Marer, Helene. Letter to the editor. *New York Sun*, 19 November 1934.

Marlow, James. "Gertrude Stein Doesn't Stammer, Reporter Simply Hears Poorly." *New Orleans Times Picayune*, 19 February 1935.

Marx, Carolyn. "Book Marks for Today." *New York World-Telegram*, 25 October 1934.

———. "Book Marks for Today." *New York World-Telegram*, 26 October 1934.

McClain, John. "On the Sun Deck." *New York Sun*, 25 October 1934.

McDermott, William F. "McDermott on Gertrude." *Cleveland Plain Dealer*, 21 December 1934.

Meyers, Lorene. "Miss Gertrude Stein Sinks Society Writer at Lecture without a Solitary Trace." *Dallas Morning News*, 19 March 1935.

"Miss Stein a Wow." *New York Sun*, 1 November 1934.

"Miss Stein Lets in Some Fresh Air." Editorial. *Chicago Daily Tribune*, 12 March 1935.

"Miss Stein Makes It All Very Clear." *Philadelphia Evening Bulletin*, 16 November 1934.

"Miss Stein Puzzle to Psychiatrists." *New York Times*, 29 November 1934.

"Miss Stein to Talk for Xmas Fund." *New York Evening Journal*, 8 November 1934.

"Miss Stein Speaks to Bewildered 500." *New York Times*, 2 November 1934.

"Miss Stein Uses Saints as Scenery." *New York Times*, 17 November 1934.

"Miss Stein Visits City: No More Words to Conquer." *Cleveland Press*, 22 December 1934.

M.L.K. Letter to the editor. *New York Times*, 8 November 1934.

"Multitude Greets Highbrow Thinking She's Movie Idol." *Dallas Morning News*, 18 March 1935.

Murray, Marian. "Gertrude Stein Lecture Given with Sincerity." *Hartford Daily Times*, 19 January 1935.

O'Connell, Grattan. "Miss Stein Speaks with Meaning Here." *Hartford Courant*, 19 January 1935.

O'Hara, Kenneth. "Greeted Greeted at Airport: Oh Gertrude Oh Stein Here to Here to Talk." *Los Angeles Times*, 30 March 1935.

"A Painting Is a Painting Is a Gertrude Stein Axiom on Art." *Richmond Times Dispatch*, 8 February 1935.

"Paris Aroused over Reply to Gertrude Stein." *Chicago Daily Tribune*, 9 March 1935.

"Passion in Literature." Editorial. *New York Times*, 25 August 1935.

Pereda, Prudencio de. Letter to the editor. *New York Sun*, 23 November 1934.

"Perfecting Language." Editorial. *New York Times*, 19 November 1934.

"Princeton Dazed by Gertrude Stein." *New York Times*, 6 November 1934.

"Radcliffe Giggles It Does Giggle at Her Style." *Boston Daily Globe*, 20 November 1934.

"Recalls Early Endeavors." *Washington, D.C., Evening Star*, 29 December 1934.

[Rogers, W. G.?] "Gertrude Stein Gives Talk before Century Club Here." *Springfield Daily Republican*. 8 January 1935.

———. "Stein Gives Talk at Classical High; About 250 Attend." *Springfield Daily Republican*, 25 January 1935.

"Says Writers Are Confused." *Indianapolis Sunday Star*, 16 December 1934.

Schriftgiesser, Karl. "Gertrude Stein Traces Course of Writing—Chaucer to Stein!" *Washington Post*, 31 December 1934.

"Science Understands." *Evening Star*, 29 December 1934.

"Scientists' Meeting Hears Demand for New Mode of Thinking." *Washington Daily News*, 28 December 1934.

Seeley, Evelyn. "Stein, the Bohemian, Doesn't See Our Life." *New York World-Telegram*, 13 November 1934.

"A Snub, a Snub, a Snub." *San Francisco Examiner*, 8 April 1935.

"Someone Called Stein Sails with Alice B. Toklas." *New York Herald Tribune*, 5 May 1935.

Stafford, Jane. "Science Tells How Gertrude Stein Gets That Way." *Times Picayune Everyweek Magazine*, 17 February 1935.

"Stein Likes Stein Opera." *New York Times*, 9 November 1934.

"Stein Opera Sung by All-Negro Cast." *New York Times*, 9 February 1934.

"Topics of the Times: Made Herself Understood." *New York Times*, 26 October 1934.

"Two Steins." Editorial. *New York Times*, 1 January 1934.

Warren, Lansing. "Gertrude Stein Views Life and Politics." *New York Times Magazine*, 6 May 1934.

Weiss, Helene. Letter to the editor. *New York Sun*, 30 November 1934.

Welshimer, Helen. "I Know I Shall Be Lonely." *New York World-Telegram*, 26 October 1934.

"What Is an Oil Painting?—Gertrude Stein Lets It Out." *Baltimore Sun*, 29 December 1934.

Williams, Edgar. "Policeman in Phone Booth Misses Gertrude Stein Talk." *Baltimore News and Baltimore Post*, 29 December 1934.

Winsten, Archer. "In the Wake of the News." *New York Post*, 6 November 1934.

"Youth Understands, Says Gertrude Stein." *New York Times*, 5 May 1935.

INDEX

Chesney, Alan M., 120n19
Chessman, Harriet Scott, 9, 43, 206n12
Chicago, University of, 92, 101, 191
Chomsky, Noam, 1–2, 77
Civil War, American, 18, 169, 196, 228n20, 233n6
Clark, Eve and Herbert, 215n2
Clark, Terry N., 169, 182, 228n17
Close, Ellis, 227n16
Colapietro, V.M., 223n3
Coleridge, Samuel Taylor, 102, 216n18, 219n7
collage, 59–61, 215n3
Colony Club, 92
Columbia University, 92, 101
Combat, 191
Comte, Auguste, 169
Confluences, 163
Connolly, William, 224n15

conversation
    amiable disagreement, 79–83, 156, 159–160
    argument, 55
    avoiding, 154–61
    with books, 18–20
    chat, 63, 65, 110
    collaborative thought, 54–5, 175
    conversation analysis, 62, 75–79, 84–85
        definition of, 75
    definition, 59, 108, 215n2
    dialogic aspects of Stein's writing, additional, 206n12
    dramatic dialogue, 61–62
    experimental, 174–75
    interactional, 63–65, 83, 120, 131–32
    interactive trouble, 85, 218n32
    internal, 12, 122–25, 180–81
    NEH National Conversation, 227–28n16
    pleasantries, 157, 161–62
    and politics, mutual influence of, 13–14, 149–92 (and see Stein, utopian project)
    rituals or habits of, rules or patterns of, 1, 18, 61, 120–21, 156, 160–62
    speech-in-action, 83
    subjectivity, related to, 120–26
    transactional, 63–65, 132

Copeland, Carolyn Faunce, 224n11
copying, repetition, and insistence, 11, 22–26, 101, 105, 121
Cordasco, Francesco, 26
Cowley, Malcolm, 3

Crawford, John W., 76–77
Cronkite, Walter, 91
cubism, 57, 59–60
Curie, Marie, 100–101
Curtis, George W., 233n4

Darwin, Charles, 20, 57
Davidson, Donald, 36
Davidson, Grace, 29
Davis, Phoebe Stein, 224n2, 226n7
death, 144–47
de Beaugrande, Robert, 75
Declaration of Independence, 194
DeKoven, Marianne, 44, 67, 150, 205n1, 205n9, 218n29, 231n37
DeLillo, Don, 129–30, 223n9
Depression, the, 27–28, 175
Descartes, René, 123, 126, 131
Derrida, Jacques, 46, 117
Dewey, John, 4–6, 36, 104, 126
Dodge Luhan, Mabel, 2, 30, 86, 92
Donne, John, 206n14
Dorr, Rheta Childe, 193, 195, 198, 233n4–5, 233n8
Dos Passos, John, 18, 29
Douglas, Ann, 229n25
Douglass, Frederick, 233n4
Dreiser, Theodore, 2, 27
Dreyfus, Alfred, 169
Dryden, John, 82
Dubnick, Randa, 222n13
Durkheim, Emile, 169
Dush, Sarah L., 98
Dydo, Ulla, 90, 93, 207n4, 219n1
Dylan, Bob, 95

Eagleson, Harvey, 17–18
ecriture feminine, l' or feminine writing, 37, 116
Edison, Thomas, 100
Einstein, Albert, 98–101
Eliot, George, 20, 219n7, 232n3
Eliot, T.S., 19, 88
Ellul, Jacques, 169, 227n15, 228n19
Emerson, Caryl, 21
Emerson, Ralph Waldo, 43, 216n18, 219n7
entity and identity, 22–27, 106, 107, 121, 131, 142
etymology, 43, 47–49, 66–67, 74–75, 110–11, 214n12, 220n8, 222n13, 224n1
Evans, A. Judson, 65, 100, 102–3

fame, 119–21, 127–30, 132–34, 137–38, 141–42, 145–47, 149
fascism, 1, 10, 149–50, 176, 224n2, 229n22, 232n39
Faÿ, Bernard, 2–3, 150, 216n12, 226n6, 233n6
feminism, 13, 49, 195, 200–1, 205n8, 217n23
Fessenden, Donald, 100
Fetterley, Judith, 221n11
Fielding, Henry, 19, 220n8, 221n10
Fifer, Elizabeth, 206n12
Fishbein, Morris, 211n3
Fitzgerald, F. Scott, 20, 232n40
Flanner, Janet, 218n33, 219n7
Flutterbye, Mme., 102
food, 1, 62–3, 65–66, 83–85, 121, 161, 164–65, 188, 215n5, 215n7, 226n9, 230n31
Fourteenth Amendment to the U.S. Constitution, 194, 233n4
Franco, Francisco, 195
Franken, Claudia, 205n4
Frankenberg, Lloyd, 33, 155
Frankfurt Institute, 31
frontier, 11, 28–29
Frost, Robert, 217n21

Gable, Clark, 91
Gallup polls, 179, 186
Gannett, Lewis, 95
Garrett, Mary, 209n17
gender, 195–200, 217n23, 223n5
genius, 2, 12, 41, 103–5, 110, 142–43, 195
German language, 117
Gide, André, 2
Gilbert, Sandra M., 217n23, 219n10
Gopnick, Adam, 18
Greeley, Horace, 233n4–5
Green, Nicholas St. John, 4
Gross, Elizabeth, 234n10
Gubar, Susan, 217n23, 219n10
Guest, Edgar, 98
Gutman, Amy, 227n16

Haas, Robert, 4, 205n5
habit, 4, 6–7, 9, 11, 13, 24, 27–28, 35–37, 39–43, 45–49, 55–56, 104, 112–13, 156, 159–60, 181, 183, 190, 206n13, 207n1, 209n16, 212n6–7
Hackney, Sheldon, 227n16
Hansen, Harry, 95
Harvard Psychology Laboratory, 32–3
Harvey, A. McGehee, 210n19
Hasselback, Ingo, 232n39

Hearst, Mrs. William Randolph, 101
Hemingway, Ernest, 20, 202, 226n8, 230n28
Henry, Thomas R., 99–100
Heraclitus, 39
Heritage, John, ix, 77–78, 123
Hermans, Hubert J.M., 126, 131, 223n3–4, 224n10
Hitler, Adolf, 93, 150, 155–56, 162, 176–77, 184, 188, 195, 225n4, 230n26
Hobhouse, Janet, 210n21
Hoffman, Michael J., 170–71, 178, 206n13, 212n10
Holquist, Michael, 223n4
Houser, J. David, 230n26
Hubly, Erlene, 4, 165, 205n5
Hughes, Langston, 18
human nature and human mind, 103, 105–7, 109–10, 113–15, 202, 222n12, 224n2
Hutcheson, Sandy, 215n8
Hutchins, Robert, 191
hypertexts, 232n38

identity, see entity
immigrants, 25–6
individualism, 1, 11, 13, 25, 27–8, 149–51, 170, 184, 187, 193–94, 198, 203, 229n23–4
industrialism, 10, 28, 153, 177–80, 186–87
insistence, see copying
Internet, 18
Ionesco, Eugene, 61
Irigaray, Luce, 200–1, 223n5, 234n10
irony, 214n14

James, Henry, 19, 139–141, 208n11, 216n17
James, William, 4–6, 11, 13, 33, 36–42, 44–46, 50, 54–57, 61, 77, 126, 139 40, 148, 172, 199, 205n6, 206n13, 208n11, 209n15, 210n1, 211n2, 211n4, 215n1, 223n2
    association, 37, 39, 40, 46
        attention, 46, 54
        consciousness, 40, 56
        fringe, 40, 50
        genius, 41
        grammar, 57
        habit, 39–41, 46
        language as a form of experience, 36
        memory, 37
        mental modification, 38–39
        psychic blindness, 55
        thought, 37, 39
        unclassifiable facts, 54
Jameson, Fredric, 206n14

Index   253

Parker, Dorothy, 18
Parker, Ian, 228n18
patriarchy, 205n9
Peirce, Charles Sanders, 4
Pepys, Samuel, 154
Perloff, Marjorie, 44, 205n7
Pétain, Maréchal, 163, 226n11
Phillips, K.J., 82, 218n28
Phillips, Wendell, 233n4
Picabia, Francis, 92
Picasso, Pablo, 57, 59–60, 215n3
pioneering, 11, 25, 27, 29, 76–77, 99, 172, 177–79, 182, 228n20
Pitkin, Hannah, 140, 224n16
Pondrom, Cyrena N., 218n29
Porter, Cole, 101
portraits, 90, 103, 105
Posnock, Ross, 140, 224n15–16
Postman, Neil, 8–9, 52, 115, 123, 205n10, 222n1
postmodernism, 27, 147
Powell, Aaron, 233n4
Powerpoint presentations, 228n18
pragmatism, 4–7, 36, 57, 126, 205n8, 206n13, 229n24
proletarian writers, 102
propaganda, 4, 92, 153–54, 160, 167–69, 171, 226n6, 227n14–15, 228n19
Putnam, Hillary, 4–5, 205n6
Pynchon, Thomas, 18, 61

Quine, William, 36, 46
Quintilian, 47

race, 16–17, 131, 175–76
radio, 162, 167–68, 227n14–15
Random House, 89, 163
reading, theory of, 8, 70–71
realism, 59, 62
repetition, see copying
"resisting," see "attacking"
Revolutionary War, American, 196, 233n5
rhetoric, 11–12, 44, 47, 49, 51, 107–108
Richardson, John, 59
Richardson, Samuel, 15, 19, 219n7, 220n9
Rieke, Alison, 61, 206n12
Riis, Jacob, 27
Rodgers, Daniel T., 150
Rogers, Robert Emons, 7, 42, 60
Rogers, W.G., 96, 150, 219n4, 223n8
Roosevelt, Eleanor, 91
Roosevelt, Franklin D., 103, 150, 195

Rorty, Richard, 5–6, 20, 25, 36, 54–55, 67, 148, 171, 216n19, 229n24
Rose, Francis, 212n9, 225n3
Rothstein, William G., 34
Royce, Josiah, 42
Ruddick, Lisa, 43, 54, 206n13, 212n8, 213n10
Ryan, Betsy Alayne, 67, 215n4

Sacks, Harvey, 1, 52, 75–78, 215n2, 217n24
Saint Odile, 153, 157, 162
Sand, George, 232n3
Saroyan, William, 137
Sartre, Jean-Paul, 151, 156
Saussure, Ferdinand de, 1, 46, 117
Sawyer, R. Keith, 75, 234n9
Schegloff, Emanuel A., 77–78, 215n2
Schlesinger, Arthur, Jr., 149
Schriftgiesser, Karl, 119
Scollon, Ron, 215n9
Scollon, Suzanne B.K., 215n9
Seeley, Evelyn, 94
Severeid, Eric, 149, 225n3
Shakespeare, William, 12, 15, 19, 86–88, 110, 142, 214n11, 218n33, 219n7, 220n9
    As You Like It, 86
    Hamlet, 142
    Macbeth, 86–88, 218n34–35
    Othello, 220n8
Shepherd, Gregory J., 6, 172
Sheridan, Richard, 221n10
Shuler, Sherianne, 205n8
sight and sound of words, 31–4, 45, 47, 176, 152–53, 171
Silverman, David, 75–76, 217n24
Simon, Linda, 15
Simonson, Peter, 4
Sitwell, Edith, 60
Skinner, B.F., 96, 209n16
Smith, Gerrit, 233n4
Smith, Harrison, 134, 224n13
Smollett, Tobias, 19, 111–12, 220n9, 221n10–11
Solomons, Leon Mendez, 32, 209n16
Souhami, Diana, 219n7
Spenser, Edmund, 124
Stalin, Joseph, 152, 195
Stalinist Russia, 226n6, 226n10, 227n15
Stanton, Elizabeth Cady, 233n7

Stein, Gertrude
    adolescence, 15
    death of, 116, 133–34, 224n13
    fame, 119, 126

Stein, Gertrude (*continued*)

Whittier-Ferguson, John, 224n2, 225n4, 226n11
Wilde, Oscar, 169
Wilder, Thornton, 207n6, 226n6
Willamette University, 92
Williams, William Carlos, 3, 219n7
Wilson, Edmund, 60
Winders, James A., 217n20
Wineapple, Brenda, 19
Winsten, Archer, 94–95, 97, 101–2, 228n18
Winston, Elizabeth, 195–96, 232n1, 232n3, 233n7
Winter, Ella, 30, 116–17, 216n15
Wittgenstein, Ludwig, 5, 205n7
World War I, 28, 64, 208n10, 229n24
    doughboys, 65, 172–174
World War II, 7, 10, 13, 27–28, 64, 150, 153–78, 180–84, 186–88
    atomic bomb, 172, 201–2
    black market, 165
    German occupation of France, 155–57, 162, 180–81
    GIs, 170–174
    Jewish Statute of October 1940, arrests and deportations, 163
    maquisard, 150, 163, 224n2, 227n13
    radio broadcasts, 167–68
    refugees, 157, 161–62
    Resistance, French, 150–51, 163, 165–67, 227n12–13
    starvation, fear of, 158–59, 161
    Vichy France, 151, 153, 163, 216n12, 224n2, 225n3, 230n31
Wright, Richard, 16–17, 207n3
Wright, Wilbur and Orville, 100
writing, as technology, 76
writing and speaking, Stein's definitions, 103–4, 106, 114–15

Yaeger, Patricia, 200–1, 234n10–11
Yeats, William Butler, 146
Young, John Wesley, 152, 230n26
Young, Stark, 218n31